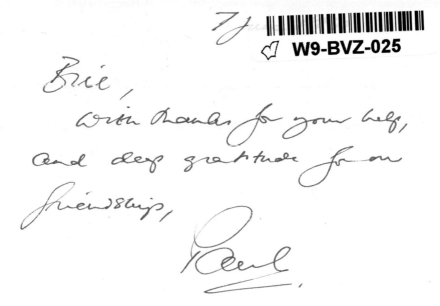

Eric,
    With thanks for your help,
and deep gratitude for our
friendship,

        Paul.

THEOLOGY AND CRITICAL THEORY

Theology
and
Critical
Theory

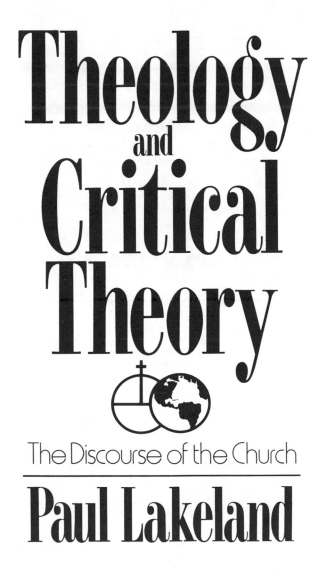

The Discourse of the Church

Paul Lakeland

ABINGDON PRESS
Nashville

THEOLOGY AND CRITICAL THEORY

Library of Congress Cataloging-in-Publication Data

Lakeland, Paul, 1946–
    Theology and critical theory: the discourse of the church / Paul Lakeland.
      p. cm.
    Includes bibliographical references.
    ISBN 0-687-41497-0 (alk. paper)
      1. Theology—Methodology 2. Habermas, Jürgen. 3. Critical theory. 4. Catholic Church—Doctrines. I. Title.
    BR118.L255   1990
230'.01—dc20   89-48886
                                               CIP

For Beth Palmer

PRINTED IN THE UNITED STATES OF AMERICA

CONTENTS

PREFACE

The work which follows here is devoted to the principle that there is only one truth, and that it is not the exclusive possession of religion *or* science. Nor, indeed, is it a matter of dividing up the territory of the human world between them. One need not doubt that scientific understanding will eventually produce a convincing explanation of the origins and functioning of the universe in order to be religious. Nor need one abandon the conviction that in the last analysis the human community must stand silently in awe before the vast, impenetrable, and yet fundamentally benign mystery of the universe, in order to be comfortable with a career in mathematics or theoretical physics. Science and technology are a product of human ingenuity and exist to serve the human community: but perhaps their final and fundamental act of service lies in demonstrating ever more clearly that we are a part of the universe, and not what the universe itself exists to serve.

Religious belief, on the other hand, rests on the unshakable conviction that the universe of which we are truly only a part is in the end the repository of a meaning that goes beyond us and, yes, beyond science and technology too. Science leads to a religion of humility: religion requires a humble science.

In these pages one small part of science and one small question of religion are placed in relationship to each other. The critical social theory of Jürgen Habermas, a sophisticated social scientific instrument that itself is engaged in the question of the relationship of technology and human society, has much to teach about all the institutions of human society. The Roman Catholic Church, one of those institutions, can be understood better and can come to understand itself better through the application of Habermas's critical theory to certain aspects of its functioning. It can also learn from Habermas's analyses of society in its own efforts to consider and prescribe for the social ills of the contemporary world. At the same time, the transcendent frame of reference of religion may offer something to critical social theory which it cannot derive from itself, a sense of the larger mystery in which it is inevitably situated.

The seven chapters of this book discuss various aspects of this relationship of Catholic theology and the Catholic church to critical social theory. A word of warning to the reader: The first two chapters are necessarily somewhat more technical, drier than those that follow. Chapter 1 lays out the historical background to the emergence of the critical theory of the Frankfurt School, itself the immediate intellectual progenitor of Habermas's own system. The argument of the chapter is that the emergence of a true social theory had to await the disappearance of externally and internally imposed restrictions on what could be thought. Only then could social theory become truly reflexive, and thus critical. The second chapter is a discussion of what I and many others consider the most highly developed critical social theory of the present time, that of Jürgen Habermas. The chapter examines crucial aspects of Habermas's critical theory in some detail, not only because of the attractiveness of the theory itself but also because it seems particularly suitable for use within Christian theology and social ethics. The remaining chapters test that belief. Chapter 3 turns to the church, and makes a case for the value of critical social theory in the life of the church in a number of ways, but particularly in its own social teaching. Chapters 4, 5, and 6 are the heart of the book. In chapter 4 the argument is made that the contemporary theology of the church that emerged from the Second Vatican Council (1962–65) envisages the church as, in essence, an ideal exemplar of what Habermas calls the "communicative action community." This kind of community, according to Habermas, follows a particular pattern of communication or "discourse" in which truth is sought through dialogue that respects "the force of the better argument." Chapter 5 examines Catholic understandings of tradition and authority in the light of this theory of discourse, and chapter 6 places the ethical discourse of the church under the same scrutiny. In the final chapter, the place of the church in the postmodern world is discussed: What meaning can salvation have here, and what form does the loving presence of God have to take in a world that is usually at best unimpressed, often repelled, by the claims of Christianity? Some of the material in chapters 2, 3, and 4 is a substantial reworking of articles that have appeared in *The Month, Thought,* and *Cross Currents,* but the remaining chapters are new.

I have tried throughout the book to envisage two potential kinds of readers. It is my hope and expectation that it will appeal first of all to theologians and students of religion, not so much for the profundity of its theological reflection as for the value of placing Catholic theology in dialogue with a modern secular understanding of society. In this respect, although the work obviously envisages the Catholic church as its primary point of reference, it has clear applicability to any religious tradition that is prepared to enter into conversation with the secular world. The second audience who may find the argument interesting are those who are comfortable in the world of critical social theory but who are intrigued about seeing what use could be made of that theory *within* academic theology, that is, without reducing the object of study to a purely secular phenomenon. The first, more theologically educated group will have to forgive much that may seem obvious in commentary on the church, while the latter group will find my discussion of Habermas no doubt superficial or my selection of items for discussion arbitrary. This is the risk that has to be taken in bridge-building. It is my hope that there will be found here an idea or two that either or both groups can press further, whether in agreement or not with my own conclusions. At the very least, I hope that this foray into a "critical social ecclesiology" will not be the last such attempt. I will be absolutely delighted if the suggestions here on the understanding of tradition and discourse can contribute to that *glasnost* and *perestroika* so sorely needed at the present moment by my own cherished Catholic tradition.

In my view, one of the most important issues in this book, emerging most clearly in chapters 5 and 6, is that of the status of the lay theologian. Events over the past decade have convinced me that the age of the lay Catholic theologian may be upon us, not only because of the immense contributions made by feminist theologians in the church, many of whom are laywomen, but also because of the handicap under which the institutional authorities of the Catholic church force its clerical and religious theologians to work. When I left the Society of Jesus some ten years ago, my motives were certainly not entirely clear. With the benefit of hindsight, I can now thank the Jesuits of the English Province for a theological education that can be put to work for the church from a standpoint of independence, which official representatives of the church can currently adopt only at their peril. The theological ideas expressed here are, I believe, fully in accord with the Catholic theological tradition. But I am proud to say that this is unofficial Catholic theology.

It remains only to thank those whose cooperation and advice have made this book no doubt better than it would otherwise have been, even if its final form remains my responsibility, and mine alone. My thanks go first to Davis Perkins and Ulrike Guthrie of Abingdon Press, who have maintained their interest in and enthusiasm for the project along the way. I have also to thank New York University and the Ford Foundation for a semester as Scholar-in-Residence in the fall of 1985, when this project first began to form itself in my mind, and Fairfield University for a summer research stipend in 1987 and a sabbatical leave in the spring semester of 1988, during which the bulk of the writing was done. Those who have read parts of the manuscript and made helpful suggestions are Bill McConville, Christopher Mooney, Beth Palmer, and Bernadette Topel. To my close friend and respected colleague, John Thiel, goes my great gratitude for a careful and critical reading of the entire manuscript, and in particular for innumerable instances of stylistic clarifications and the removal of many infelicities of expression. This book, finally, is dedicated to Beth, my partner in life, who never lets me get away with that sophistry and accommodation that creeps up so easily on those of academic temperament.

Fairfield University
Fairfield, Connecticut
5 December 1988

CHAPTER ONE

THE IDEA OF A CRITICAL THEORY

The term "critical theory" is shorthand for "critical social theory" or "critical theory of society."[1] It refers to a theory of the character of society distinguished by something we can call a "critical" capacity. Another way to put it would be to say that it is a reflective, or perhaps "reflexive," theory of society. Critical theory emerged historically out of "social theory" that was neither critical nor reflexive in the full sense of these terms. Of course, to say that something is neither critical nor reflexive is not to say that it is unintelligent but rather to point to limits placed consciously or unconsciously upon the range or depth of reflection. The emergence of *critical* theory had to await the precise historical circumstances which would free the human reflective capacity from self-imposed or societal restraints.

Nothing could be more distinctive of human beings than their capacity to reflect. This is not to say that all human beings are particularly good at reflecting, or even that they enjoy the effort that it sometimes takes. Nor is it the expression of a belief that reflection is something human beings could or should constantly be doing. A day in the life of any of us will be a mixture of instinctual or learned responses to our everyday environment, skillful manipulation of that same environment to achieve a desired outcome, the constant inflow of emotive reactions to any and every phenomenon we encounter or thought we think, and, if we are fortunate or disciplined enough, at least a few moments of reflection.

Although reflection may be only an intermittent human activity, it is that which makes us human. Think for a moment about taking a drive in the car. Much of what we do as experienced drivers is almost automatic, so much so that in very routine driving, on a highway for example, our minds may drift away from what we are doing and, moments or minutes later, we return to our senses with that cold shiver which tells us that we don't really know how we covered the last mile. If we are driving over an unfamiliar route, we are more conscious of the act of driving, though we are almost certainly not conscious of moving the foot to the brake or the accelerator pedal. And even the most placid and well-adjusted driver will at times experience the onrush of emotion, whether it is a feeling of impatience, aggression, or pleasure. Only rarely, perhaps, will we be moved to analyze *why* we feel this particular pleasure on this one day, and still less often will we give thought to what is going on under the hood of the car which is carrying us forward so smoothly. But it is at these times that we are doing what a well-trained primate could not do.

Although reflection is so central to being human, in its pure form it has no necessary connection to action. In theory, there could be excellent mechanics who drive badly, and there are certainly highly competent drivers who have absolutely no idea of the principles of the internal combustion engine. We all know of the paralysis of the scholar, like the Reverend Mr. Casaubon in George Eliot's *Middlemarch*, for whom reflection was endless, and who in consequence never wrote the book that he had made his life's work. And there are many sad examples in recent history of scholars, whether philosophers, theologians, or historians, whose highly developed reflective skills left them powerless to take courageous actions in their everyday lives. The heroism of a Dietrich Bonhoeffer is, unfortunately, exceptional.

If the connection to praxis is often problematic for reflection, a second and even more important limitation is the effect of historical circumstances upon the range and depth of reflection. This will almost certainly not be wholly or even in part the fault of the individual or society. In all probability, it will be a matter of the depth-structures of the culture conditioning society and the individual never even to consider carrying reflection beyond a certain point. For vast expanses of history, there have simply been no reasons to question whether the earth was flat, or whether the earth was the center of the universe, or whether the table that felt solid really was solid. Empirical observations gave no reason to think otherwise. At other times, the power of religious or secular institutions could impose limitations on reflection. In the days of "faith seeking understanding," almost always understanding was found confirming faith. And when the limits of reflection were breached, by Galileo or Darwin or Einstein, the world divided into those who shouted "Heretic!" and those who countered "Genius!" Or, to put it in terms that we all understand, today's orthodoxy is yesterday's heretical insight.[2]

Although oppressive social or religious powers can impose limitations on action, their power over reflection is less clear. Certainly, they cannot in any crude sense prevent individuals thinking, even thinking critically about the limitations the structures impose. However, the most effective repressive force may be operative at a less conscious level, perhaps occasionally unnoticed even by the powerful institution, when individuals freely limit their own reflection. As anyone who has read Orwell's *1984* knows, the truly successful repression is the one embraced in the name of freedom. This phenomenon—which Max Horkheimer calls the "introjection" of structures of domination—is illustrated quite clearly in Marx's designation of religion as "the opium of the people," a drug laid upon them by the powerful, but one to which they themselves have become addicted.[3]

In tracing the emergence of social theory and of critical theory proper, we have to take account of a number of consciously and unconsciously operative factors deriving from the cultural and historical assumptions of the time, the current paradigms of thought, and the control mechanisms exercised by one or both of the political and religious structures. We shall, in other words, have to pay attention to ideological considerations, and that means establishing the sense or senses in which the word "ideology" will be used here.

So varied are the meanings people attach to the word "ideology" that it is only reluctantly that it is introduced. Fortunately, Raymond Geuss has taken much of the pain out of working with that word, at least in the context of social theory.[4] Geuss distinguishes three ways of using the term: ideology in the descriptive, pejorative, and positive senses.

Ideology in the descriptive sense may be a term to cover all the beliefs held by the members of a particular society, or those beliefs which cohere in some form of world view, or those beliefs consciously held as a program of action for the transformation of the world. This use of the term is descriptive because it makes no judgment of the adequacy of the particular ideology, or of the wisdom of operating with an ideology.

In the pejorative use of the term, "ideology" is some set of beliefs or attitudes that distorts reality, creating a false consciousness. Geuss describes three explanations of false consciousness: maintaining that it is owing to an epistemological error in the ideology, or to legitimizing or masking some social illusion, or to the conscious or unconscious defense of the interests of a particular subgroup in society to the exclusion of the interests of others.

Finally, there is the positive sense of ideology, in which it is seen as an enabling mechanism for the satisfactory cohesion of a culture. Obviously, how an ideology is viewed is a function not of what it does in a particular society but of the assumptions of the interpreter about the social role of ideologies.

Although it is immediately apparent that theories of society could subscribe to any one of the three understandings of ideology, *critical* theory belongs in the second category. Indeed, one of the clearest distinguishing marks of critical theory is its use of "ideology critique" to unmask illusion. Although different thinkers within critical theory prefer the epistemological, functional, or genetic explanation for false consciousness, all see critical theory as a way of overcoming the illusions of a particular society. To the critical theorist, the critique of ideology leads to the unmasking of false consciousness and with it the emancipation of the individual and society from that false consciousness. With the introduction of the idea of emancipation, we are able to turn back to the earlier inquiry into the relation of reflection and praxis.

Reflection, as we said above, has no necessary direct connection to praxis. But if false consciousness or the introjection of structures of repression has served to

create subservience to an ideology that itself circum-
scribes action, then that reflection which operates as an
emancipatory critique of ideology will, once successful,
remove those barriers to action. What does not necessarily follow, however, is that it will provide clear guidelines
for the emancipated action that will presumably succeed
the dispelling of the illusions. So critical reflection on
society is a necessary if not sufficient condition of
emancipated praxis. What else may be required to fire up
the engines of a renewed praxis is an important question
that will concern us later.

THE EMERGENCE OF SOCIAL THEORY

In searching out the historical circumstances that
created the conditions of possibility for a social theory, we
have to look for those phenomena which signified the
removal of intellectual or conceptual restraint. Social
theory becomes a possibility as modernity becomes a
reality, therefore, and it is found in the three great
historical steps of Renaissance, Reformation, and Enlightenment. Each of the three contributes something of
importance to the possibility of a theory of society. But
before commenting on these stages, we need to establish
the context of the medieval Catholic synthesis of faith and
reason.

It would be a mistake to oversimplify the Middle Ages as
a monolithic "age of faith."[5] Studies in language and
grammar, classical philosophy, and the natural sciences
were all part of a genuine intellectual ferment. The
Carolingian renaissance devoted much of its intellectual
energy to the production of a satisfactory text of the Bible,
and a large amount to reading the rediscovered classical
authors. Yet care was taken to maintain a "right relation"

between the two, as Alcuin's famous remark to Charlemagne illustrates very well:

> If many are infected by your aims, a new Athens will be
> created in France, nay, an Athens finer than the old, for
> ours, ennobled by the teachings of Christ, will surpass all the
> wisdom of the Academy. The old had only the disciplines of
> Plato for teacher and yet inspired by the seven liberal arts it
> still shone with splendor; but ours will be endowed besides
> with the sevenfold plenitude of the Holy Ghost and will
> outshine the dignity of secular wisdom.[6]

How much Alcuin and others like him were motivated by
personal conviction, and how much by political considerations, will always be hard to tell. For whatever reason,
however, clearly it was appropriate to compare a Christian
renaissance favorably with the merely pagan wisdom of
the past.

That there was a great deal of philosophical, literary,
and scientific development is beyond dispute, but it had to
be held within the theology and cosmology of the medieval
Christian world view. For centuries after the time of
Alcuin and Charlemagne, the Catholic church remained
in intellectual hegemony over the whole of European
civilization. Even at its most flexible, consequently, the
ideology maintained a strict subordination of the natural
to the supernatural, of reason to revelation. There was no
possible conflict between the two, since God was the author
of revelation and the creator of the natural order. Hence
any apparent conflict between the two had to be owing to a
deficiency in reasoning. Natural law was consistent with
the law of God, since God had written the natural law in
the hearts of human beings, and its lineaments could be
seen in the very fabric of the world.

The high Renaissance demonstrates the inexorability of

the process visible in the time of Alcuin and Charlemagne. On all fronts, economic, social, and political, literary and scientific, experimentation flourished and the church for the most part engaged in damage control. Papal patronage of the arts on a grand scale was as much a reassertion of the primacy of revelation over reason and the unity of truth, as much a gesture of defense against the incursions of the profane, as it was any love of beauty. Of course, it was also a love of beauty, whatever may have been claimed to the contrary, for its own sake. In another realm of public life, from the thirteenth century onward the tremendous expansion in economic life and the growth of what was to become capitalism created other problems for the guardians of the grand synthesis. The preservation of truth and sensible accommodation to what was obviously never going to be the same again involved the church at times in complex intellectual maneuvering, which must have made it very grateful for the existence of the tradition of casuistry.[7]

With the benefit of hindsight, it is obvious that the tensions growing in society through the fifteenth century were going to lead to a great intellectual crisis. In the Reformation and its sequel the Enlightenment, history witnessed what Thomas Kuhn has called a "paradigm shift."[8] Although Kuhn resists the application of his theories in the realm of social science, at least taken metaphorically the term is apt. A series of phenomena and the lives of a number of "world-historical individuals" simply turned the world upside down, never to be the same again. After Martin Luther there was really no going back.

Given that the intellectual currents of the Middle Ages were a function of a religious hegemony, it has to be no surprise that it was a religious thinker who precipitated the crisis that changed everything forever. Though Luther was by no stretch of the imagination a philosopher or a scientist, he was something much more important to history. A successful religious reformer, he led the movement that resulted in the irreversible breakdown of the religio-cultural hegemony of the Catholic church. The collapse of the great synthesis of reason and revelation was not only irreversible, it had also been inevitable, and it detracts nothing from Luther's achievement to point out that had he not been in the right place at the right time, someone else would have emerged as the historical agent, and brought about the same end.

Although Luther himself was contingent to the Reformation, the particular character of his thought as a matter of fact colored the newly developing religious understanding, for better or worse, and through the changes in the religious world view that followed, profoundly affected the social and cultural temper of history. With Luther, history and human achievement within history is given its autonomy, if not from God then certainly from the church. Bypassing the church, the human individual approaches God in the realm of faith, over which the church has no control. Paradoxically, this world becomes at one and the same time irrelevant to the salvation of the individual believer and important in its own right. Reason, now separated from faith, is the operative human capacity in history. With this new vision, the church is made dramatically less important, religion is radically privatized, and the world is freed to be understood on its own terms, and a world view constructed according to the dictates of reason.

If Luther's theological vision was responsible for the origins of secularization,[9] it took the philosophers of the Enlightenment to begin to bring out the full consequences of a world irrelevant to the salvation of the individual believer. In this regard it is interesting to note that it was in

Catholic, absolutist France that the Enlightenment took the most rationalistic and antireligious turn, in Protestant Germany that the new ideas could find comfortable lodging with at least some religious orientations.[10] And, if the watchword of the Enlightenment is "autonomy" when it is not "reason," this should come as no surprise. Protestantism can coexist with secularity more easily than Catholicism, because in the last analysis the world does not matter. The German *Aufklärer* have less need to oppose religion than do the French *philosophes*, because Lutheran Protestantism is less interested in their doings, and some forms of Calvinism are actually quite well-disposed toward them.

With the Enlightenment's proclamation of the autonomy of human reason, external restraints upon human reflection had largely disappeared. The power of the church to insist on natural law and a natural order, to enforce a cosmology and a metaphysic, were already things of the distant past. Where religion remained alive among philosophers, nature was no longer perceived as the work of a creator in which the eye of faith could everywhere discern the divine plan. Instead, nature was an expression of God, a work of God that stood on its own apart from the creator. This world, even perceived as a work of God, was interpreted through reason, the category appropriate to this world and to nature, not through revelation. The rational nature of the human being was the means of access to the truth of things.

The thinkers of the Enlightenment were not so free as they thought, since the removal of external restraint upon reflection really counted for less than the continued presence of internal restraint. Cultural and intellectual presuppositions lying too deep for notice, let alone analysis, established hidden limits to what could be thought. The presuppositions of Enlightenment thought, which remain in many respects today, cluster around two main ideas. First, deriving ultimately from Descartes and flowering in the thought of British empiricism, there was the assumption that there is an unassailable human ego, the subject which thinks, observing an objective reality that is external to it. Second, and in some ways deriving from the first, there was an at first implicit, later explicit, conviction that the empiricist, "scientific" model of understanding is the conceptual paradigm for human knowing, and that those realms of human experience not accessible to such methodology—art, ethics, religion—are at best privatistic luxuries, at worst either sheer sensation or dogmatic irrelevancies. The advent of genuinely *critical* thinking would have to await the realization that hidden restraints on reflection still existed. That insight first emerged in the work of Hegel. However, before we look at Hegel, Marx, and the emergence of a critical theory of society, we have to turn back and consider briefly the implications of the intellectual development outlined above for the character of social theory.

Since in the classical Catholic view reason is always subordinated to revelation, society and the state, if they conform to the natural law, are ordained by God. As Joseph Fuchs put it quite bluntly,

> The State is an absolute institution of the natural law. It would have existed in paradise together with the authority to govern. Man's freedom and equality would not have excluded an organic structure of superiors and subjects. . . . As soon as men began to fall into sinful egoism, the State, family, and institutions could no longer depend on unselfish love, they required of necessity certain means of coercion.[11]

The state, by which is meant the political structure of the community, is here ordained by God. The existence of the

21

state is willed by the individuals who through the exercise of right reason recognize its necessity, though the authority of the state comes from God and is not dependent on the will of the individuals. The role of the state is the government and organization of society, respecting the moral law while leaving to the church the responsibility for the cultivation of morality.

The freedom of the individual to envisage radical change in the underlying understanding of the state is on this view quite circumscribed, and consequently the likelihood of developing a genuine social theory is greatly diminished. Indeed, if it is a tenet of social theory that the individuals in concert make and unmake the state, and a tenet of the classical Catholic view that God wills the existence of the state as an expression of the divine plan for human beings, there seems almost no hope of reconciliation. This is particularly the case if the same social theorists hold to a belief *either* that human "nature" comes down to the possession of a radical freedom exercised through reason, *or* that there is no such thing as human nature, while the classical Catholic view maintains that the practice of human beings and the human community should conform to the laws of human nature as created by God.

Social theory which is not simply a branch of practical theology must therefore await the end of the vision of the state as a quasi-sacramental reality. Once again, it is with the thought of Luther that this break is made. In Luther's vision the state does not become unimportant, but it does fall under the control of autonomous human reason. Although in a sense this limits its importance, or at least its status, in another way the state becomes more significant, since its governance of the secular community becomes more all-embracing. In particular, its role in legislating morality and law increases, compared with the Catholic understanding The Lutheran impulse, if we may call it such, lays the foundations for the modern secular state, for good and ill, by releasing reason from the specifics of revelation, and establishing the realm of history as reason's proper ambit. From this point on, the rational consideration of the rationality and rational functioning of the state and human society (in other words, social theory) becomes a real possibility.

HEGEL

As in so many other respects within the history of ideas, so in the development of critical theory Hegel stands as a bridge and a bulwark between premodern and modern understandings.[12] For our purposes, the most creative distinction Hegel makes within his social theory is between "civil society" and "State." There is also much to be learned from his understanding of the relationships between political life, religious life, and ethical life. Theologically, the richest harvest is to be found in relating his social theory to his notion of Spirit *(Geist)*. But his significance in the development of critical theory resides, more than in any of the above, in the willingness not just to commit himself to the use of reason, or even in his making reason the motor of the dialectic of history, but in his submitting reason itself to critical scrutiny. It is less important, therefore, to examine the details of his social theory than it is to see how his philosophical method advances the cause of reflection.[13] Nevertheless, a brief glance at the details of his mature social theory, the integration of the system, and the theological import of his social and political thought will serve as helpful background to an examination of his idea of reflection.

The key distinction Hegel makes in his social theory is

between "civil society" and "State."[14] Broadly speaking, the former refers to the developed set of economic exchange relationships that characterize the everyday life of the community, the "system of needs," to use Hegel's own phrase. The State, which is the true home of "the ethical life" *(Sittlichkeit)*, is the political expression of the people, the generalized will through which the common good of the nation is sought and through whose institutions it is protected. Civil society is an agglomeration of individuals, the State is constituted by citizens. The political is therefore superior to and independent of the economic.

To see the significance of Hegel's distinction between civil society and state, we have to set it in the larger context of his system. For Hegel human history is that dimension of reality in which Spirit is engaged in a dialectical process through which it will come to its full self-realization. History is the realm of "objective Spirit" in which the rational interchange of "finite spirits" represents the necessary "negative" moment between the mere subjectivity of "subjective Spirit" and the fully developed totality of "absolute Spirit." The key here is "freedom," which for Hegel describes the condition of the exercise of reason, and thus the significance of political life is that it is here, not in the real and imaginary needs of economic interchange and market forces, that true freedom is at home. It is in the State that the nation chooses the good. The State, as Hegel puts it, is "the ethical substance."

Hegel is a real curiosity. He is more concerned perhaps than any previous philosopher with "reason," but his treatment of reason represents an abrupt break with the thinkers of the Enlightenment, particularly with Immanuel Kant. For Kant, the categories of reason order the human access, such as it is, to "reality": For Hegel, the exercise of reason is the way human beings share in the divine life. One can in consequence see Hegel as

24

something of a throwback, at least to the degree that his social theory has a clearly theological dimension. History is the moment of negation within the infinity of Spirit. The Lutheran disjunction between faith and works is thus overcome by this self-professed Luthcran.[15] Hegel's social theory gives theological import to political life.

The peculiarity of Hegel is not only that he is associable in some ways with a pre-Enlightenment synthesis of faith and life, but also that he is the first genuinely modern thinker. This is apparent above all in his first major work, *The Phenomenology of Spirit*, which is a tour de force of internal critique.[16] The subject of the *Phenomenology* is consciousness, its growth from the simplest forms of sense-knowledge to the highest knowledge of the self-knowing of Spirit. As Hegel was well aware, one cannot step outside consciousness to examine consciousness, any more than one can step outside reason in order to examine rationality. The object of study is also the investigative tool. But what Hegel added to this awareness was the realization that human reasoning is a pool of falsity, illusion, and deception, and that to trace the path of reason to the heights of the *Phenomenology* involved a critique of the bases of these illusions. Hegel's *Phenomenology* is thus a critical reflection on experience, devoted to examining the illusions and, in their dismemberment, restoring freedom. With the important proviso that for Hegel "freedom" continues to reside primarily in the use of reason, we can even characterize the Hegelian method as an emancipatory critique of false consciousness.

It is now possible to see more clearly the import of Hegel's mature work, *The Philosophy of Right*.[17] In this book Hegel is looking at the life of the polis, and the true freedom of the citizen within it. He traces the growth of the sense of the self and the exercise of freedom while simultaneously outlining the development of the social and political institutions of a civilized culture. Indeed the two must go together, for the fullness of freedom is its expression in the concrete structure of the State. However, most if not all states are distinguished by their failure to incarnate freedom in the political structures of the nation, thinks Hegel, and this failure is their historical challenge. While there is no doubt that Hegel has a teleological conception of history as the realization of freedom, he has a realist's perception of the struggles that the actualization of freedom entails.

In the final analysis there remains one important restraint upon the exercise of reflection in Hegel's thought. Hegel's teleological vision is one of necessity. There has been much ink spilled on the question of whether Hegel believed the perfect state to have been actualized in history, in Prussia or elsewhere, and it seems likely that he did not so believe. But there is no doubt that he thought the perfect state in principle could be realized. Clearly, if history is the objective moment in the growth of Spirit to full self-consciousness, and Spirit cannot be balked, history must progress toward the consciousness of freedom. This is what the "cunning of reason" is about, this is what it means to declare that "the rational is the actual." Hence even in Hegel's entry into modernity he carries with him the remnants of the past. He does not overcome the last manifestation of false consciousness, the belief in the necessity of the triumph of reason. But it does not take much for some at least of his followers to make the transition.

LEFT-WING HEGELIANISM: FROM HEGEL TO MARX

The story of how Marx "overturned" the Hegelian system is too well known to need detailed repetition here.[18] A member of the group of "young Hegelians" who were to form the "left wing" of Hegelian interpretation, Marx like the others sought to follow the intellectual legacy of Hegel while rejecting his central systematic principle. For Hegel, as we noted above, the importance of history is that it is the milieu in which Spirit is objectified, in a necessary dialectical process through which Spirit will achieve its fullness of self-consciousness as *absolute* Spirit. This occurs in rational human activity, above all in the rational institutions of the State, and in different ways in art, religion, and philosophy. Thus human beings become instrumental to the progress of Spirit, "necessary" only in the sense that objective Spirit is necessary to the dialectic. It was this assertion of the reality of Spirit that left-wing Hegelians conspired to reject.

Although the story of left-wing and right-wing Hegelians is well known, it is a good idea to dwell momentarily on the import of the split for the development of critical theory. Since we have already established the importance of Hegel himself for such a development, neither right-wing nor left-wing interpreters will be entirely without resources for the pursuit of social theory. Anyone who is an heir to the *Phenomenology* stands in the tradition of critical reflection upon the illusions of human consciousness. Of course, the tendency of right-wing Hegelians is to concentrate more upon the later works of Hegel, the *Logic,* the *Philosophy of Right,* and the *Encyclopedia,* where systematic completeness is the supreme virtue. But the more important distinguishing principle is in the interpretation of the idea of necessity, the teleological drive of the Hegelian system.

Neither right-wing nor left-wing Hegelians oppose the principle of necessity. The dialectic of Spirit and the theory of dialectical materialism are equally utopian, even if Marx apparently felt that history had somewhat farther to go than at least Hegel *appears* to think in some of his later

27

works. The early writings of Marx are clearly substantially influenced by Hegel's political philosophy,[19] which is perhaps why so much of the *Philosophy of Right* seems to be an anticipation of Marx. Hegel's depiction of the evils of civil society, for example, is startingly prescient, and his famous inability to incorporate the "rabble of the poor" into his developed philosophy of the State could not provide clearer evidence of the need for a correction to his fundamental hypothesis, a correction to be provided in Marx's development of the notion of the proletariat.[20]

Although Hegel's division of the economic from the political, of civil society from the State, and his assertion of the ethical primacy of the latter, raised the conception of political activity to a height not reached since the demise of his beloved Athens, subsequent history suggests that there was to be no necessary actualization of his vision. His theory also envisaged an aristocratic ideal of political service as the responsibility of the landed, leisured classes, and that notion has gone forever. Nevertheless, the principle of a representative government that owed nothing to economic interests was a valuable one, which in the European welfare states of the mid–twentieth century had a brief flowering—as Wordsworth said of another important moment in history, "Bliss was it in that dawn to be alive, But to be young was very heaven!" Looking back from the end of the century, we can now see more clearly that the phenomenon of welfare capitalism was merely an interlude in a history of the progressive triumph within "bourgeois society" of the economic over the political.

If Hegel seems to have been at fault in his belief in the necessity of Spirit's self-actualization through history, this does not mean that the prize must be handed to Marx. The developed notion of necessity in Marx's "scientific socialism" is one of the inevitable demise of capitalism and the triumph of socialism. The same late-twentieth-century commentator who sees the lacunae in Hegel's political vision may equally discern them in that of Marx. Marxism as a totalizing account of historical forces, a utopian pseudoscientific system, the Marxism of *Das Kapital,* is as discredited as Hegel's bourgeois democracy. Both may continue to appeal for good reasons to different people; neither is a factor in the inevitable march of history. Perhaps this means that history demonstrates no inevitability, except perhaps for the collapse of all totalizing ideologies?

If we seem to have placed Marx on a par with Hegel, at least for the unreliability of their respective utopian politics, we have still to assert Marx's greater importance for the development of genuinely critical theory. In Hegel's system, as we noted above, the notion of necessity presents a final and extremely significant restraint upon critical reflection. Although Marx did himself develop a theory of economic necessity, one which many now believe to have been a blind alley of a particularly unfortunate kind, in essence Marx removes the concept of necessity as a transcendental principle by abolishing the idea of Spirit. To Marx, influenced by Feuerbach here, Hegel's Spirit is what Freud would come to call an "illusion," the product of wishful thinking, an opiate to a historical vision that simply could not contemplate the suggestion that human beings are alone in a history of their own making.

Human history is a record, then, of human struggle for human emancipation, not a means by which Spirit will achieve its full freedom as the in-and-for-itself. The Marxist social theorist, consequently, is not bound by the need to assume the ideology of the "cunning of reason." Indeed, the Marxist social theorist will begin by exposing that and any other such principle of necessity as a foundational illusion of the worst kind. But what is it that frees the Marxist theorist from the ideological face of dialectical materialism?

NEO-MARXISM: THE FRANKFURT SCHOOL

Although it was Karl Marx who defined critical theory as "the self-clarification of the struggles and wishes of the age,"[21] it is with the so-called Frankfurt School that the term "critical social theory" will always be associated. The *Institut für Sozialforschung* was established in Frankfurt in 1923, and in subsequent years devoted itself to the study of an astonishing range of issues, first in Frankfurt, later in exile in the United States, and then again in Frankfurt after the Second World War. Although an enormous number of intellectuals had some association with the Institute, its central members were Max Horkheimer, Theodor Adorno, and Herbert Marcuse. From among a younger generation, the name of Jürgen Habermas is often associated with the Frankfurt School, and he was undoubtedly greatly influenced at least initially by some of its work. But it makes for greater clarity to think of him as engaging in a further corrective of the Marxist tradition that the Frankfurt School was consciously trying to reformulate.

The founding fathers of critical theory were not entirely of one mind, nor did they think and write in 1940 or 1950 as they had in 1930. Taken all in all, however, it is fair to describe them as radical Marxist critics, both in the sense that their critique of society was inspired to a degree by Marxist categories, and in the sense that their writings constitute a drastic revision of Marxist orthodoxy. It has become a commonplace observation today to say that Marxism needs to be more flexible if it is to be useful, that Marx underestimated the power of capitalism, that Marx's writings simply did not envisage a world of today's complexity, and so on. The writers of the Frankfurt School were among the first to come to this conclusion, though it did not lead them away from Marx so much as behind the Marx of state socialism and on to the early "Hegelian" Marx. In particular, it did not divert them from their essential faithfulness to Marx's purpose, the struggle for human emancipation and for the construction of a good and just society.

This is not the place to attempt to do justice to the complexity of the development of the Frankfurt School, and in any case Martin Jay's *Dialectical Imagination* has already performed this service admirably.[22] It is necessary, however, to delineate the main lines of thought distinguishing the work of the Frankfurt School, for two reasons. In the first place, it is here that a developed critical social theory that takes account of principal currents of twentieth-century modernity is initially accessible. Second, it is as an attempt to rub the rough edges off the critical theory of the Frankfurt School that Habermas's early work is best understood, and indeed all his work to date constitutes a more dialectical reading of the same social and cultural phenomena that engaged the attention of Horkheimer, Adorno, and Marcuse.

In order to give some account of the critical theory of the Frankfurt School in a short space, I propose to restrict consideration here to two works, the essay by Max Horkheimer entitled "Traditional and Critical Theory,"[23] and the major later collaboration of Horkheimer and Adorno, *Dialectic of Enlightenment*.[24] Both works focus on what Horkheimer referred to as "the critique of instrumental reason," a phrase he later used for the title of a collection of essays.[25] As we shall see, the way to the heart of critical theory is through its perception of the varieties, importance, and danger of reason.

"Traditional and Critical Theory" was first published in 1937 in the journal of the Frankfurt School, the *Zeitschrift für Sozialforschung*.[26] Horkheimer begins with an account of traditional theory, by which he means empirical, positivist, or scientific theory: "Theory for most researchers is the sum-total of propositions about a subject, the propositions being so linked with each other that a few are basic and the rest derive from these."[27] This understanding of theory as "stored-up knowledge" belongs to mathematics and the sciences, to all philosophical thinking under the influence of Descartes, to all forms of rationalism and even to phenomenology, thinks Horkheimer. Although theory in this sense has an obvious applicability to natural sciences, it has also been extended to "the sciences of man and society" *(Geisteswissenschaften)*, where emphatically it does not belong. The social implications of this traditional idea of theory are significant. It leads the subject to view the world as "a sum-total of facts," which "is there and must be accepted." In reality the individual has been subsumed into the system:

> The seeming self-sufficiency enjoyed by work processes whose course is supposedly determined by the very nature of the object corresponds to the seeming freedom of the economic subject in bourgeois society. The latter believe they are acting according to personal determinations, whereas in fact even in their most complicated calculations they but exemplify the working of an incalculable social mechanism.[28]

Thus the individual is reduced to his or her instrumental functions in the (seemingly) successful manipulation of society. Although it is always thought, says Horkheimer, that tools are the extensions of organs, it may be the case that organs are the extensions of tools.

Critical theory, on the contrary, is "a human activity which has society itself for its object." Those who adopt the critical attitude recognize that at one and the same time this world is their own world and that "it is not their own but the world of capital."[29] Filled with this tension, says Horkheimer, critical theory "is motivated today by the effort really to transcend the tension and to abolish the opposition between the individual's purposefulness, spontaneity, and rationality, and those work-process relationships on which society is built."[30]

In other words, human beings in society are alienated in a number of ways. In the first place, they are seen and see themselves as individuals over against their environment, and consequently are inclined to adopt an instrumental approach to every aspect of their environment, which includes other people. Second, they see their work as the mastery or domination of some division of nature, alongside others who are similarly engaged. Both sets of assumptions are myths fostered by the system of capitalism, through which individuals have been led to believe what the system needs them to believe, namely, that they are first and foremost individuals, secondly in community, and that they are (economically) successful manipulators of technology. In reality, the system has deprived them of their essential humanity.

If the world is the way Horkheimer sees it in this essay, then of course critical theory, while remaining theory, is itself emancipatory, since it unmasks the illusions upon which society has based itself. To return to the terminology of ideology we discussed at the beginning of this chapter, critical theory utilizes a pejorative understanding of ideology, true to its Marxist heritage. The twentieth-century Western world through its capitalist system, with its attendant philosophical theories and scientist assumptions, fostering the illusions of success and freedom, has achieved a frightening level of introjection of the structures of domination. The task for critical theory is nothing less than the overcoming of the Cartesian, scientist dichotomy of the subject and the object.

The later *Dialectic of Enlightenment* demonstrates one or two important shifts in the work of the Frankfurt School. They become less interested in economic, more in cultural and social issues, and, frankly, they become much less optimistic. In "Traditional and Critical Theory," Horkheimer had argued for the necessary connection of critical theory to praxis, without being able to specify quite what that connection should be. In the *Dialectic,* Horkheimer and Adorno have nothing to offer on this score. Theory must lead to praxis, but to what praxis it leads is difficult to say.

As the title of the work suggests, it was with the Enlightenment and its cultural significance that the authors were concerned. They took issue with the entire phenomenon for many of the reasons that flit somewhat less directly through the pages of "Traditional and Critical Theory." For Adorno and Horkheimer, the Enlightenment was not the intellectual liberation from religion and metaphysical false consciousness that the popular imagination believed. Rather than being a disenchantment (Weber's term) or demystification of the world, it was the exchange of one myth for another. The Enlightenment was the origin of the focus on the instrumentalization of reason, the source of what Joe Holland and Peter Henriot refer to as the "mechanistic root-metaphor" of modern society.[31] "God" or "Being" give way to "Science" or (instrumental) "Reason." This new god continued to support anthropocentric views of the human domination of nature previously justified by reference to the book of Genesis. Even Marx, with his insistence on the role of labor, was to that extent to be included within the ranks of Enlightenment thinkers.[32]

In the *Dialectic of Enlightenment*, there is a direct connection established between the Enlightenment's supposed liberation of humankind from the superstitions of religion and metaphysics, through the liberal embracing of the mechanistic root-metaphor of a scientist, technological consumer society, to the worst excesses of totalitarianism. As we noted above, Horkheimer's view of the instrumentality of reason extends beyond the use of objects to the use of individuals. When a radically individualistic vision of human beings is accompanied by the possibility of manipulative, instrumentalized human relationships in a society built upon the metaphor of product and consumer, then the conditions for one individual's exploitation of the mass of individuals are created. And, with the benefit of the hindsight that an extra fifty years of the twentieth century have provided, we might want to extend that set of observations to include the destruction of popular involvement in the political process that seems also to have followed in capitalist societies, particularly in the United States. Subject-object dualism leads to radical individualism, and the individual is helpless when the social fabric has also been eroded. It is not too fanciful, then, to posit a direct line from Luther and Descartes through the Enlightenment to the national security state of advanced Western capitalism. Nor, if we follow Horkheimer and Adorno, is it any more fanciful to see a similar line through Marx to a positivism and dogmatism that end up in the state socialism of Stalin.

It would be wrong to leave the impression that the Frankfurt School produced a solution for the problems of modernity. More correctly, it produced a critical theory. Both as a matter of fact and as an acknowledged principle of its chief exponents, critical theory had much more success as a critique of society than as a program for the reconstruction of human life. The *Dialectic of Enlightenment* is a pessimistic if not a despairing work. Its authors, particular Horkheimer, became even more pessimistic as time went on. They also steadfastly resisted the suggestion that critical theory could provide an outline of the praxis that had to follow, most notoriously at the time of the student protests in Europe in 1968. Critical theory is an intellectual movement, not a revolutionary party. It believed and believes firmly in the primacy of theory over praxis. In the next chapter we shall go in some detail into the modifications introduced into critical theory by the intellectual descendent of the Frankfurt School, Jürgen Habermas, to counteract some of these deficiencies and some of its exaggerations.

THE IDEA OF A CRITICAL THEORY

The progress of intellectual history charted in this chapter may seem peculiar. We began by talking of the progressive removal of restraints that must take place before a social theory is possible, and the further relaxation that is required for that social theory to develop such an extensive practice of reflection that it will become truly critical. We saw that it is with the secularization of the world brought about by the Reformation and the "disenchantment" reinforced by the Enlightenment that the world was made safe for the radical critique practiced by Hegel, Marx, and the members of the Frankfurt School. But we have also discovered that this freedom to engage in critical social theory has been turned back upon those social forces and figures who made it possible in the first place. Critical theory seems to be biting the hands that fed it.

The peculiar ungratefulness of critical social theory teaches two useful lessons. In the first place, whatever the negative effect of Enlightenment thought, it was certainly not an unmixed curse. It clearly had much to teach, and its weaknesses were the shadow side of its strengths. But its truth has to be appropriated dialectically—that is, the moment of negation must also be held fast—if it is not to distort as much as it reveals. Second, critical theory does not set out to undo or judge the past, but to reveal those contemporary illusions and examples of false consciousness that result from an undialectical appropriation of the past. Critical theory is interested not in intellectual history but in the emancipation of the present for the sake of the future.

What, then, are we left with? We seem in critical theory to have an intellectual tool whose claim to usefulness rests in the final analysis on its avoidance of ideology. It seeks to unmask illusion and false consciousness, themselves the legitimate children of ideologies. To the extent that it succeeds in stripping them bare, it must lead to the dissolution of those same phenomena. Thus it opens up space for a purified praxis, a praxis of human emancipation. But because critical theory is a function, a process without content except for the moment of critique, it cannot provide a direction for that praxis. Must it then await a new ideology to give direction to praxis, and if so can it eschew immediate further critique in the name of getting *something* done?

In discussing Habermas, we shall investigate further the claim that critical theory avoids ideology. Such claims are of course always difficult to maintain successfully. Nevertheless, critical theory itself can justifiably be seen as in principle nonideological. The question is whether any human being can maintain a critical theory without feeling constrained to adopt in addition an ideology, so that praxis can occur. The moment of critique and the moment of praxis are different but related, if the individual is not a complete schizophrenic. It may be that in the contemporary world, human communities need both a critical theory and an ideology. If so, there shall have to be a way to escape the solely pejorative understanding of ideology. We shall have to be able to present ideology as an enabling phenomenon, not necessarily the fabricator of illusions. If we can do so, then at least in principle we should be able to envisage the dialectical appropriation of a critical theory and an emancipatory religious ideology.

CHAPTER TWO

THE CRITICAL THEORY OF JÜRGEN HABERMAS

The published works of Jürgen Habermas thus far are by any standards an impressive body of material.[1] They have also given rise to a veritable industry of commentary and explication.[2] Since it is with Habermas's developed (and developing) critical theory that the theology and social situation of the Catholic church will be juxtaposed and intertwined throughout our discussion, we have to face squarely a number of initially discouraging elements.

In the first place, Habermas is one of those thinkers whose published books and articles are always "works in progress." One consequence of this is that interpreters of Habermas are always struggling to keep up with the flow of his works. Prolific as a writer, and one who ranges widely across sociology, philosophy, aesthetics, and political theory, Habermas may be gaining on us. To be sure, just as students of Habermas are beginning to come to terms with his project of dialogue with Anglo-Saxon thinkers such as Peirce, Searle, and Austin, his most recent work is in conversation with French post-structuralism![3]

A second and obviously crucial matter for any attempt to utilize the thought of Habermas in a theological context is his unpromising attitude toward religion. Frankly, if Habermas is going to be helpful in our current project we shall have to engage in a species of intellectual kidnapping, since most of the relatively few references to religion in his works are anything but helpful.[4]

A third and final set of problems clusters around the completed work itself: the inherent complexity of the ideas with which Habermas is working; the breadth of range across so many fields of intellectual endeavor, with which few can be so comfortable as Habermas himself; and finally the terminology and arid style he has either chosen or been cursed with to realize his objectives. With all of these we shall have to contend, but it is worth the effort.

After a brief overview of the intellectual roots of Habermas and the shape of his work to date, we shall concentrate on five central ideas: knowledge-constitutive interests; communicative action theory; discourse ethics; the relation of "system" and "lifeworld"; and Habermas's critique of modernity. These somewhat technical considerations should help introduce Habermas's critical theory as it stands at its present point of development, though there is no reason to think that his pattern of constantly adjusting his ideas is at an end. At that point the ground will be prepared for direct attention to the role of critical theory in general and that of Habermas in particular within the structure and theology of the Catholic church. As we proceed with that discussion, which is the theme of the remainder of this book, the ideas introduced in the present chapter will be addressed in much more detail.

HABERMAS: AN INTELLECTUAL PROFILE

Habermas's lifelong concern has been to devise and perfect a critical theory of society, to promote the perduring value of critical reason in a world that leaves less and less space between totalitarianism and an obsession with technology. His thought belongs to what has been called the "radical Enlightenment," to a trend rather than a movement, a de facto intellectual resistance organization comprising all those varied efforts to preserve some kind of humanism within that climate of late-twentieth-century life that Denis Donoghue has characterized as "the promiscuous cool of postmodernism."

Habermas's intellectual interests from his earliest adult years linked him with those of the Frankfurt School. Born a generation or so later than the leading thinkers of the Frankfurt School, Habermas came of age in Germany in the years after the Second World War and held his first post as an *Assistent* at the Frankfurt School's *Institut für Sozialforschung*. More than to any particular idea or individual, he was drawn to the School's conviction that social theory had to occupy the ground between science and philosophy, to their roots in a humanistic Marxism, and to their belief in linking theoretical work with practically oriented research into a wide range of social issues, which they conducted within the *Institut*. He has remained faithful to these guiding principles.

Despite the clear debt Habermas owes to the leading figures of the Frankfurt School, he is best understood as both a modifying and a corrective influence on what their work had become by the time he joined the *Institut* in the mid 1950s. Leaving aside Herbert Marcuse, whose break with the School was indicated in his not returning to Germany with its other members when the postwar invitation was issued, the Frankfurt School had become deeply pessimistic and had all but abandoned its Marxist roots and convictions. Horkheimer, most of all, showed a clearly discernible shift to the right, and was a visible establishment figure in the Adenauer years in West Germany. The work to which we paid attention in the preceding chapter, *Dialectic of Enlightenment*, expressed a deeply gloomy prognosis for Western civilization, which the authors saw as having capitulated completely to the instrumentalizing forces of capitalism and technology. At the same time, their own critical vision itself provided no hope, because the relationship of theory and praxis had all but collapsed. Theory now was a form of praxis, but a form of praxis that in no way helped to chart a new course for a society tired of the old choices.

Habermas has in his own work attempted to reestablish the connection between theory and praxis, restore a modified but genuine intellectual connection to Marx, and moderate the one-sided critique of technology and instrumental reason. At the same time, he has investigated the possibility of reclaiming something of the Enlightenment commitment to the role of reason, finding himself in consequence often labeled "the last great rationalist." Essentially he has engaged in a sustained attempt to create a theoretical system in which European idealism and utopian thought can conspire with the philosophy of language. Habermas's work, in contrast to that of the Frankfurt School, is positive, "upbeat" and, to a degree, at home in today's world. But it also incorporates a penetrating attack on contemporary "national security" capitalism, which in Habermas's terms represents a wholly negative intrusion of the system into the "lifeworld" (the cultural background) and the "colonization" of the lifeworld by the impersonal forces and mechanisms of economy and security.

KNOWLEDGE-CONSTITUTIVE INTERESTS

The distinctive outline of Habermas's "own" critical theory, independent of the influence of the Frankfurt School, first emerges in his theory of "knowledge-constitutive interests," expounded in *Knowledge and Human Interests*.[5] There are a number of critical issues and a controversy or two surrounding this 1968 publication, as there have been with every subsequent book or article he has written. It is equally certain that Habermas later modified many of the positions taken in this work. Nevertheless this text is the locus for the first "trial version" of what becomes an extensive and idiosyncratic "theory of communicative action."

In *Knowledge and Human Interests* Habermas sets out to show that the critical exercise of reason is emancipatory. To a degree he identifies with the Platonic notion of pure theory, involvement in which *is* emancipation from the interests that accompany lower forms of thinking. To a degree he identifies emancipation as the interest constitutive of critique. Critics of his position have pointed out that there seems to be a dangerous ambiguity latent here, with "reason" used to refer now to reflection on the conditions of rational activity, now to a Marx-inspired ideology critique. It has also been noted that it is by no means automatic or self-evident that reason in either case leads to praxis, which is an unproblematic observation on transcendental reflection but is a much more serious challenge to critical theory's wish to bridge the theory-praxis divide.

Habermas identifies three different forms of knowing: that of the empirical-analytic sciences, that of the historical-hermeneutic sciences, and that of critical social science and philosophy. Each of these ways of knowing is motivated by a particular cognitive "interest," which structures knowledge a priori. Thus, the empirical and analytic sciences demonstrate a "cognitive interest in technical control over objectified processes" (p. 309). The historical-hermeneutical sciences display a "practical-cognitive interest" concerned with "the attainment of possible consensus among actors in the framework of a self-understanding derived from tradition" (p. 310). Finally, critical social science and critical philosophy have an emancipatory interest, seeking out the bases for human autonomy and responsibility, and striving to see through the rationalizations or ideologies of uncritical thought. Each knowledge-constitutive interest has its appropriate social medium: respectively, labor, interaction, and power. Thus the first has to do with the relations between human beings and things to be manipulated, the second to do with relations between human beings and other human beings, who are not to be manipulated as if they were things, and the third to do with release through reflective critique from the hidden constraints operative within the other two.

It would be a mistake to think of Habermas as denigrating the value or achievements of either the empirical-analytic or the historical-hermeneutic forms of knowing. Chapters in *Knowledge and Human Interests* are devoted to evaluations of the importance of each. However, each is prone to a particular distortion, to the corrupting tendencies of, respectively, positivism and historicism. Positivism is the weakness to which science and technology are prone, the reduction of human knowing to the empirical-analytic method. Historicism is a naive or uncritical attitude to human history, in which the meaning of historically conditioned judgments or events is taken to be that given them by the subjects uttering them or involved in them. The empirical sciences must (and increasingly do) recognize the human factor; the historical-hermeneutic sciences must be open to the possibility of the distortions of ideology and false consciousness. Thus, critical theory and critical philosophy are dependent but radical forms of knowing. They have as their objects of scrutiny other forms of knowing, but they have as their constituting interest a concern for freedom, and indeed for the free (that is, undistorted) exercise of human reason, in the realms of labor and human interaction.

Although there is no doubt that human beings do have a grounding cognitive interest in dealing appropriately with things and with other human beings, it is less obvious that we possess an a priori interest in emancipation. It is in arguing for the a priori character of the emancipatory interest that Habermas takes the next step in developing his communicative action theory. He turns to the phenomenon of language, which he says is "the only thing whose nature we can know." He suggests in the appendix to *Knowledge and Human Interests* that autonomy and responsibility are posited in the structure of language, and claims that "our first sentence expresses unequivocally the intention of universal and unconstrained consensus" (p. 314). His point is that all forms of (linguistic) communication, even those which are intended to deceive, presuppose the orientation of communication to the achievement of agreement on one point or another.

Habermas is arguing that if language between human beings is not to be sheer babble, it must be either about what it seems to be about, or about some other (hidden) agenda, which requires for its successful accomplishment the other's automatic assumption that the conversation in progress is about what it seems to be about. In linguistic interaction the individuals assume that there are rules and that all participants are playing by them. That assumption is as necessary to the one who decides to break the rules as to those who abide by them. If everyone breaks the rules, communication is impossible. Consequently, language itself reveals a fundamental orientation to freedom from hidden constraints. It is thus a priori and *par excellence* the medium of emancipatory critique.

THE THEORY OF COMMUNICATIVE ACTION

Beginning with the essay "What Is Universal Pragmatics?"[6] Habermas has increasingly devoted his attention to the elaboration of a theory of "communicative action" required to sustain the claim for emancipation as a knowledge-constitutive interest, in the light of the extensive critical attention to *Knowledge and Human Interests*. His search for methodological tools to substantiate his belief in the inherently emancipatory orientation of communication led him to the speech-act theory of Searle and Austin.[7] From the development of his theory of "universal pragmatics" to the fully fledged vision of communicative reason presented in great detail in *The Theory of Communicative Action*, Habermas modified and developed speech-act theory until it fit his purpose. He was able to leave behind the language of quasi-transcendental knowledge-constitutive interests and base his critical theory on a phenomenological examination of the rules of communication and social action.

Habermas distinguishes between two kinds of social action: that oriented toward success and that oriented toward understanding. Action oriented to success may again be subdivided, into "instrumental action" or technical manipulation of the environment measured by efficiency, and "strategic action," in which individuals or groups seek to accomplish particular ends, and tailor their actions accordingly. Action oriented to achieving understanding, on the other hand, is *only* possible intersubjectively, and its paradigmatic form is found in human communication, the precondition for which we have already seen as an implicit commitment to openness and freedom from constraint or domination.

Action oriented toward achieving understanding or "communicative action" presupposes a notion of an "ideal speech situation."[8] Linguistic interaction does not make sense unless the participants believe in the possibility of genuine consensus. Such consensus is approached when communication proceeds purely by *the force of the better argument*, that is, when nothing external or internal constrains the participants. As Thomas McCarthy puts it, "The structure is free from constraint only when for all participants there is a symmetrical distribution of chances to select and employ speech acts, when there is an effective equality of opportunity for the assumption of dialogue roles."[9] There has to be no false or arbitrary conclusion to discussion, but rather an arrival at unforced consensus. There has to be complete openness and equality among the participants. For Habermas, "These three symmetries represent . . . a linguistic conceptualization for that which we traditionally apprehend as the ideas of truth, freedom, and justice."[10]

Communicative action implies assent to universal validity claims. That is to say, any genuine attempt at communication must assume the presence of *comprehensibility, truth, truthfulness,* and *rightness.* Communication implies that the speaker has chosen a form of language through which understanding can occur, that the proposition contains some "truth" that can be shared, that the speaker intends to communicate, and that the form of communication is "right" for establishing the conditions for an understanding between the two individuals concerned.

Habermas makes two important qualifications. First, although at a minimum this understanding can be purely linguistic, "Its maximal meaning is that between the two [interlocutors] there exists an accord concerning the rightness of an utterance in relation to a mutually recognized normative background."[11] Second, the conditions for such full agreement are not normally the case, and therefore the process of "coming to agreement" will consist of the "discursive redemption" of these validity claims. Thus the "ideal speech situation" in which these four validity claims would be the basis of full agreement is a counterfactual notion, though one which provides the dynamics of "coming to agreement." The orientation of communicative praxis toward genuine consensus, the requirement that the process be open-ended, and the status of the ideal speech situation all reveal a teleological dimension to Habermas's project that, although at points in his work he seems to deny it, is indisputable.

This admittedly technical discussion of Habermas's theory of communicative action bears repetition in terms perhaps somewhat less tied to Habermas's own vocabulary. What Habermas recognizes is that any human community unable to maintain harmony at the deepest level is destined to fall apart. Of course, this deep harmony should not be confused with superficial accord; still less should the presence of disagreement and dispute be taken to indicate the absence of this underlying, trustful equilibrium. The acid test of harmony is the way in which difference of opinion or even more fundamental division is dealt with in the community. Is it suppressed or addressed?

The continuing conversation of any human community about the direction and value of its actions can be referred to as its "communicative action." Communicative action also describes the efforts of any two or more individuals to understand one another and to come to agreement. As a practice, it requires a commitment to openness and truthfulness, and a willingness to give each member of the community or all the partners in a dialogue equal voice, equal respect, and attention. Without these two prerequisites, communicative action is aborted at the outset, and in its place is manipulation and sometimes even deceit, whether deliberate or accidental. When that happens, the action becomes instrumental or strategic rather than communicative. That is to say, something is going on under the surface, there is some hidden agenda, to which the apparent conversation is made instrumental.

The practice of communicative action is of course not always carried out perfectly. In fact, perfect communication is an ideal, something counterfactual, to which everyday attempts at communicative action may approximate, but which they cannot reach this side of utopia or the reign of God. But sincere striving for communicative action does mean that the moment breakdown occurs in the conversation, the moment there is a real or apparent rupture in the search for consensus, the participants will try to deal with the problem. With this recognition we are brought to a consideration of Habermas's idea of discourse.

DISCOURSE ETHICS

"Discourse" is a term we can use for the conversational and even argumentative practice necessary to deal with the breakdown in communicative praxis. This discourse is primarily directed to the clarification of whatever has been the cause of the conversational breakdown, and the consequent restoration of the path of communicative praxis. Within human history, therefore, discourse is an ever-present sign of commitment to the process of communicative praxis.

49

Discourse or argumentation comes into play whenever everyday communication does not correspond to the ideal type represented in the notion of the ideal speech situation. Since as we have seen this ideal speech situation is counterfactual, it is obvious that communicative action will more frequently be in the mode of discourse than in that of consensus. More often than not, the background consensus is imperfect, whether because of misunderstanding or intentional deceit. One or more of the implied validity claims will then come under challenge. The most obvious violation would of course occur in the case of the implied claim to comprehensibility. Moreover, this would also be the easiest violation to overcome, as one of the interlocutors asks the other for clarification on the meaning of terms, and conversation proceeds until comprehension is reestablished. The process of the "discursive redemption" of the third validity claim, that of truthfulness or sincerity, is also relatively straightforward. If I challenge your sincerity, then we can and even must proceed immediately and within the same context to try to establish conditions for a proof or demonstration of that sincere purpose to utter the truth in a right and comprehensible fashion. The remaining two claims, to truth and rightness, can similarly be open to scrutiny, but when questioned the process of argumentation that ensues may be much more far-reaching and complex. If truth-claims or fundamental norms are challenged, and the speakers yet wish to avoid recourse to deceit or force to establish their positions, then some very complex discussions may follow.

Habermas distinguishes between five categories of discourse. The two with which we shall be most occupied are theoretical discourse, which is concerned with truth-claims, and practical discourse, which has as its objective the examination of the rightness of norms of action. But there are also aesthetic criticism, devoted to the "adequacy of standards of value," therapeutic critique, which examines the "truthfulness or sincerity of expressions," and explicative discourse, concerned with the "comprehensibility or well-formedness of symbolic constructs."[12] Of course, the use of the term "argumentation" does not necessarily imply heated discussion. "Argumentation" or discourse only occurs because the participants remain committed to achieving understanding and to avoiding the exercise of force or the use of duplicity. Argumentation, I suppose we could say, is that kind of conversation in which something is at stake. In fact, it is very like the idea of "conversation" outlined by David Tracy in *his* attempt to distinguish the merits of conversation from the narrowness of argumentation:

> Conversation is a game with some hard rules: say only what you mean; say it as accurately as you can; listen to and respect what the other says, however different or other; be willing to correct or defend your opinions if challenged by the conversation partner; be willing to argue if necessary, to confront if demanded, to endure necessary conflict, to change your mind if the evidence suggests it.[13]

"Conversation," understood broadly, is communicative action. "Argumentation" is that moment in conversation which restores the reality of communicative action when one or another validity claim is challenged.[14]

When the validity claim to truth is challenged in theoretical discourse, it is the nature of truth itself that has to be clarified and defended. The investigation of the validity claim to truth properly resides not in discovering whether what I have said is in fact true (by taking a look), but in revealing through discussion the justification for my assertion. Take an example: I might assert that there is intelligent life in the universe beyond our solar system. This might in fact be the case. However, there is no way at this point in human history for me to justify making this assertion. My claim, though in a certain sense possibly true, cannot at the moment be discursively redeemed. The discursive redemption of the validity claim to truth is only to be reached through achieving a *rational* consensus. That is to say, mere consensus cannot make something true, since we could all be wrong. *Justified* consensus constitutes an assertion's truth. In Habermas's own words, "I may ascribe a predicate to an object if and only if every other person who *could* enter in a dialogue with me *would* ascribe the same predicate to the same object. . . . The condition of the truth of statements is the potential agreement of all others."[15] The basis of truth is consensus. But the consensus is itself based on cogency rather than logical necessity. It must be a claim that the community can find justifiable, though it need not be empirically verifiable. We shall return in much more detail to this discussion of the consensus theory of truth in the second part of chapter 5.

In a parallel fashion, when the claim to rightness is questioned, when norms must be discursively redeemed, what is at issue is not whether a given speech-act corresponds to the accepted norms, but whether indeed there is rational agreement on those norms. Practical discourse is then devoted to the establishment of rational consensus on norms. In the case of practical discourse, Habermas prefers to talk about the "universalizability" of norms. It is important to distinguish his position from the abstract universality of formalist ethics, which establishes a hypothetical universalizability (the categorical imperative) in order to justify a highly individualist ethical position. Habermas's discourse model requires the process of what he calls "generalized will formation." That norm is right which is or can be the basis of a rationally motivated agreement among all those potentially affected by it.

Habermas's discourse ethics is clearly distinguishable both from a natural law ethic in which ethical statements are true in the same way that descriptive statements are true, and from the positivist position that they are not true at all. "Reasonable" discussion that shows a respect for "the force of the better argument" can lead to the formation of a rational will that expresses a consensus on norms.[16] As we saw above, the emphasis in "reasonable" discussion is on presenting arguments that convince by their cogency, not by the strict force of logical necessity.

Critical discussion of Habermas's discourse ethics centers on the "universalizability principle," and its similarity or lack thereof to Kantian ethical formalism. The most thorough discussion to date of the problematic nature of Habermas's adoption of a universalist position is to be found in Seyla Benhabib's *Critique, Norm and Utopia*.[17] Although this complex and often brilliant analysis cannot be expounded fully here, Benhabib's conclusions are a convincing reading of Habermas's discourse ethics to which, as far as I know, Habermas has not yet responded. One of her insights into the nature of discourse ethics may be particularly useful to our argument.

In one of his most recent works, Habermas formulates the following definition of the universalizability principle: "The consequences and side-effects which would foreseeably result from the universal subscription to a disputed norm, and as they would affect the satisfaction of the interests of *each* single individual, could be accepted by all *without constraints*."[18] Benhabib's discussion of the universalizability principle leads her to see it as "a maxim-testing procedure for distinguishing universalizable from non-universalizable interests."[19] But what must we understand by the universalizable or "general" interest? She takes up a hint in *Legitimation Crisis* and presses a critical reading of normative discourse as a "moral-transformative process."[20] In other words, in moral discourse the individual will have to allow even his or her own needs to be subject to discursive will-formation. "Through discourses," says Benhabib, "individuals come to realize a certain truth about their needs and interests and change their previously held beliefs about them."[21] Thus discourse ethics has to be seen as "a participatory-democratic process" and not "as one more universalizability theorem in the tradition of neo-Kantian ethics operating with the myth of a general interest transparent to all rational minds."[22] On this view it also becomes a mechanism for the conversion of private or individual morality to genuinely social ethics. The openness of the process of discourse has to mean that the individual may find herself or himself abandoning narrow self-interest for the common good.

Benhabib's reading of Habermas's discourse ethics is consistent with the profoundly social focus of his theory of communicative action. It is substantiated by the connection Habermas strives to make in his theory of social evolution between the capacity of the individual to engage in communicative action and the openness of societies to the "discursive redemption" of implied validity claims. Not all societies have reached the stage at which discourse ethics operates generally, thinks Habermas, any more than all individuals have reached in their personal development the capacity to engage in discourse.

Habermas's principle that modernization is equivalent to increasing rationalization entails a theory of personal, group, and social evolution. The "mature" individual like the well-developed group or society is distinguished by the capacity to engage in the practice of communicative action, and by the possession of an individual or collective moral consciousness adequate to discourse directed to the discursive redemption of validity claims. That is to say, a free society of emancipated individuals will be one in which the force of the better argument prevails in dispute, and thus by implication one in which all have in principle equal voice in discourse. For Habermas the skills to take part in the necessary "discursive will-formation" belong only to those who have achieved what Lawrence Kohlberg calls "post-conventional morality,"[23] and to societies whose social evolution has developed to a parallel point.

In his most recent work on communicative action and discourse ethics, Habermas has a distinctly moral purpose. The complex explication of the forms of speech-act directed toward achieving success (strategic action) and those directed toward achieving understanding (communicative action) itself demonstrates the author's belief that the truly human action is one that rises above the purely instrumental or the simply deceitful to a conscious recognition that it too is not free of an agenda, but that that agenda is in fact the assertion of human freedom and responsibility. In other words, the study of speech-acts uncovers the emancipatory interest embedded in the fabric of normal everyday conversation. Through his apparently arid attention to universal pragmatics, Habermas raises the assertion of the emancipatory interest of humankind above the level of mere wish fulfillment.

To make and keep the human community free from systematically distorted communication, as well as from mere deceit, is a project of profound sociopolitical significance whose ramifications easily spill over into realms of economics, education, bioethics, and more. It is also a project in defense of the human spirit, and as such it has a *prima facie* compatibility with the aims of religion. What is not clear is how or even whether an ethic of communicative praxis could find a place for those dimensions of religion which go beyond the support religious groups offer to human emancipation through their defense of, for example, human rights. The question of this and other potential values of discourse ethics in clarifying the moral discourse of the church must await chapter 6.

LIFEWORLD AND SYSTEM

In the second volume of his *Theory of Communicative Action*,[24] Habermas develops these ideas at much greater length, drawing the idea of communicative action into relation with his critique of the narrow instrumentality of late capitalism (which was initially treated at some length in *Legitimation Crisis*[25]). The communicative rationality of the lifeworld must accompany the instrumental rationality of the system if human autonomy and responsibility are to be preserved for the future. His argument is essentially the humanistic one, that in a time in which means-ends rationality and the assumptions of systems theories threaten to overwhelm and even instrumentalize the human subject and the human community, freedom and responsibility are strengthened in the awareness that these values lie beneath human communication. Thus, systems, technology, and the sciences are in the last analysis instrumental to the achievement of human consensus based upon achieving understanding.

Habermas's notion of the lifeworld is not straightforward. The lifeworld is the social and cultural background of the community and hence of the individual. It is everything that pertains to a society and that lies implicitly behind all acts of communication. Just as we saw that communicative praxis is the distinctively human form of interpersonal behavior, so the lifeworld is both base and background to communicative praxis. "In a certain sense," says Habermas, "the lifeworld to which participants in communication belong is always present, but only in such a way that it forms the background for an actual scene."[26] The lifeworld is "a reservoir of taken-for-granteds, of unshaken convictions that participants in communication draw upon in cooperative process of interpretation."[27]

Any element in the lifeworld can be thematized and brought forward for scrutiny, but all that is tacit, implicit, and unthematized stands in the background of the thematization of any particular element. We cannot be conscious of the whole of the lifeworld in our communicative praxis, though of course we can be conscious of this or that element in it at a particular time, and we can be conscious that there is an implicit lifeworld behind our communicative praxis. What is more, because lifeworlds and linguistic worldviews are internally connected, "language and cultural tradition take on a certain transcendental status in relation to everything that can become an element of a situation."[28] In fact,

> Communicative actors can no more take up an extramundane position in relation to their lifeworld than they can in relation to language as the medium for the processes of reaching understanding through which their lifeworld maintains itself. In drawing upon a cultural tradition, they also continue it.[29]

Preferring the "lay" or everyday concept of the lifeworld as "the totality of sociocultural facts," Habermas asks how this lifeworld is maintained.[30] He believes that communicative action performs three important maintaining roles for the lifeworld: the development of mutual understanding, the fostering of social integration and solidarity, and socialization as the formation of personal identities. The structural components corresponding to these are culture, society, and person.

Habermas next focuses more closely on society and the role of communicative praxis in social integration. This is the realm of "legitimately ordered interpersonal relations,"[31] brought about through "coordination of actions via intersubjectively recognized validity claims."[32] Modern society, says Habermas, is distinguished by the differentiation of the structural components of the lifeworld (culture, society, person) as they emerge from the authority of the sacred that backed the "impenetrable, basic, normative consensus" that distinguished earlier societies. As this occurs, the lifeworld falls increasingly under the influence of "consensus formation that rests *in the end* on the authority of the better argument."[33] This rosy picture of the steadily increasing role of consensus and communicative praxis in modern societies is an ideal form, of course. Modern societies are in fact distinguished by crises in reproduction processes in general and in social integration in particular. The anomie that results, conjectures Habermas, may be explained as the effect of system differentiation on the lifeworld.

When we look at our own society or community from the inside, we focus naturally on social integration, on the role of consensus, cooperation, and communication. But we are mistaken if we think that the formation and structuring of society is entirely by way of what is visible to us within our own society. There are also "functional interconnections" that we do not intend and that "are usually not even perceived within the horizon of everyday practice." This is the realm of system integration, in which society is affected by "the non-normative steering of individual decisions not subjectively coordinated."[34] That is to say, society is not only a human organism, it is also to a degree a self-regulating system, and to the degree that this is true society may escape the control of communicative action.

Habermas's terminology is arcane and difficult even for the practiced theoretical sociologist, but behind the complexity of the language the description of modern society he presents is relatively simple. Society is composed both of the human community and of systems. The former operates (ideally) according to norms, consensus formation, and discourse. Its orientation is to understanding. Although still related to the realms of culture and personality, it has become more and more differentiated from them as modern societies have come to base themselves on reason rather than on the sacred. The systems dimension of society relates to effective structural elements that are independent of this process of normative discourse and consensus formation. Among the examples Habermas gives for capitalist society are money, power, and the market. A successful society will hold lifeworld and system in a unity in which the lifeworld will have priority, in the sense that systems must in the last analysis be explicable within the lifeworld, even if they operate in society independent of communicative action.

But modern capitalist societies are for Habermas examples of pathological distortions of this necessary equilibrium. In capitalist societies, systems integration is always in danger of getting out of control, and threatening to instrumentalize the lifeworld, reversing what Habermas believes to be their right relationship. Money, power, and the market become the facts of life, before which culture, consensus formation, and even personality must bend. Above all, perhaps, Habermas is speaking to the pervasive feeling in developed capitalist societies that much is beyond the control of individuals or of community action, and that certain realities—money or the market, for example—are simply givens for which communicative praxis has no option but to make space. Genuinely human interrelationships, the sphere of communicative action, is then progressively diminished, being forced to live in the space left by the unhinging of systems integration from social integration. Habermas is unusual in wanting a place for both lifeworld and system within society, but in the right relationship. We shall conclude this chapter with a discussion of how he develops his explanation of the pathological forms of this relationship into a critique of modernity.

THE CRITIQUE OF MODERNITY

Habermas believes that "while discourse ethics has a utopian content it does not *sketch out* a utopia."[35] In other words, ethical universalism of this form is devoted to the establishment and maintenance of norms expressing generalizable interests, but because it is universalist in character its actual content is only the norms governing action contexts. The utopian vision must lie in the resources of the lifeworld, it would seem, and though these can be retrieved from their normally implicit status they cannot become the content of discourse ethics.

In his more recent works, as Seyla Benhabib has pointed out, Habermas uses his ethical theory more and more as a critical tool in his examination of modernity: "Clearly, since the *Legitimation Crisis,* Habermas intends discourse or communicative ethics to be . . . a critical test for uncovering non-generalizable interests rather than for generating a universal one."[36]

Benhabib is concerned that such use of communicative ethics might amount to saying that if only people would look into their hearts they would see that their true needs coincide with those of everyone else. She wishes to distinguish Habermas's position from such a Rousseauian "myth of a self-transparent collectivity,"[37] and prefers a second interpretation: "That through discourses individuals come to realize a certain truth about their needs and interests and change their previously held beliefs about them."[38] On this understanding, she says, "Discourses would have to be viewed as *moral-transformative* processes."[39] Communicative ethics "is not one more thought experiment in universalizability but an ethics of practical transformation through participation."[40] Key to understanding this is a response to the question, Who are involved in discourses? Benhabib answers:

> In principle, of course, all beings capable of speech are entitled to participate in discourses, but particular discourses take place among those concerned, affected by, and interested in the implementation and establishment of particular norms. Discourse ethics does not simulate a thought experiment for all beings capable of speech, and establish what norms they ought to accept as binding. It requires that controversies over the validity of contested norms be settled through an argumentative process in which the *consensus of all concerned* decides upon the legitimacy of the controversial norm.[41]

The identification of those nongeneralizable interests passed off as generalizable and the excavation of "suppressed generalizable interests" constitute two possible uses of discourse ethics in the critique of society.

Habermas himself maintains that an ideology critique appropriate to the critical theory of society must begin with the model of "the suppression of generalizable interests." Having, in *Legitimation Crisis*, distinguished between the discursive approach to generalizable interests and the process of compromise formation necessary to society when nongeneralizable interests are at issue, he makes the claim that "in traditional and liberal-capitalist societies, it is rather the *ideological form* of justification, which either asserts or counterfactually supposes a generalizability of interests, that is dominant." Such societies legitimate themselves, he continues, through "interpretations . . . narrative presentations or (for example in natural law) systematized explanations and chains of arguments."[42] Such a system avoids the need to be explicit about validity claims or to test them; such ideologies systematically limit communication.

The procedure for ideology critique requires a search for suppressed generalizable interests, that is, norms that would be in the interests of all but which the system does not allow to surface. It is necessary to compare the actual norms of a society and those which would exist if discourse were free. To that end Habermas frames the following question:

> How would the members of a social system, at a given stage in the development of productive forces, have collectively and bindingly interpreted their needs (and which norms would they have accepted as justified) if they could and would have decided on organization of social intercourse through discursive will-formation, with adequate knowledge of the limiting conditions and functional imperatives of their society?[43]

Utilizing some of the insights of Claus Offe,[44] Habermas suggests four "empirical indicators of suppressed interests":

> (1) The existence of an observed discrepancy between legal norms and actual legal practices; (2) codified rules which systematically exclude claims from the political agenda (claims which thus express suppressed interests); (3) the existence of a discrepancy between claims that are made and the level at which they are politically allowed

satisfaction; and (4) comparative evidence, drawn from different political systems, which indicates, *ceteris paribus*, which possibilities are actualized when putatively repressive structures are absent or removed.[45]

Habermas believes that through discourses utilizing such indicators it might be possible "to prove that practical questions can be treated discursively and that it is *possible* for social-scientific analysis to take the relation of norm systems to truth methodically into consideration."[46] However, he is not so sure that it is actually the case that the formation of motivation in modern societies does in fact remain tied to norms that require justification. It may be, he thinks, that norm systems have become divorced from truth.

In both lifeworld and system, there arise what Habermas calls "relief mechanisms," that is, "communication media that either condense or replace mutual understanding in language." The reader will recall that the lifeworld is the arena of actions oriented toward understanding, the system is that of action oriented toward success. The former is appropriate to communicative action, the latter to instrumental and strategic action. In the lifeworld, communicative action is condensed through the role of "prestige," which Habermas glosses as "cognitive, expressive and moral-practical virtues of action oriented to validity claims." In the system it is replaced by "influence." Prestige is related to personal attributes, influence to "disposition over resources."[47] But these "relief mechanisms" themselves become "generalized media," distinguished from one another through their basis in empirical or rational motivation:

Media such as money and power attach to empirically motivated ties, while generalized forms of communication such as professional reputation or "value commitment" (i.e., moral-practical leadership) rest on specific kinds of trust that are supposedly rationally motivated.[48]

Habermas's point is that a lifeworld under pressure needs to find ways to foreshorten the process of achieving consensus through communicative action, and that it can do this by relying on leadership that in the last instance depends on and respects consensus formation, or by adopting "steering media" that "uncouple" interaction from the lifeworld. In the first case, though the community might take certain matters on trust in the beginning, in the end consensus remains "dependent on the actions of responsible actors." In the second, "delinguistified media of communication such as money and power connect up interactions in space and time into more and more complex networks that no one has to comprehend or be responsible for."[49] Hence, the steering mechanisms of money and power generate norm-free and value-free networks from which the "shared cultural knowledge, valid norms and accountable motivations" of the lifeworld are simply excluded.[50] System integration is uncoupled from social integration.

The uncoupling of system and lifeworld does not of itself, thinks Habermas, create the dependency of one upon the other. Money and power as steering mechanisms could direct influence from the lifeworld to the system, or vice-versa. As a matter of fact, however, it is Habermas's belief that in contemporary capitalist society the steering mechanisms have worked to impose the domination of the system on the lifeworld. In the development of modern society, the distinction between the sacred and the secular made it possible for system integration to claim the secular as its appropriate realm, but as the sacred has been progressively diminished and replaced by communicative reason (sometimes he refers to this as "rationalization," sometimes as "linguistification"), the role of the system is increasingly revealed as one of the "colonization" of the lifeworld. Without the convenience of the sacred-secular distinction, the structural violence of norm-free system integration has nowhere to hide, as it were. Thus modern society becomes at one and the same time the place where the colonization of the lifeworld by the system is most rampant, and the place where, through the transparency that comes into society as a result of the "linguistification of the sacred," struggle against this movement is possible.

In the concluding chapter of *The Theory of Communicative Action,* Habermas offers a series of conjectures about the areas in which disturbances in the lifeworld have occurred as a result of its colonization by the steering mechanisms of the system. He discusses forms of integration in postliberal societies, problems of family socialization and ego development, mass media and mass culture, and the possibility of protest movements. Since one of the most frequently voiced criticisms of Habermas is that his emphasis on procedural rationality and procedural ethics has nothing to offer substantively, and since he himself has to a degree admitted that his theory of communicative action cannot comment on the specifics internal to this or that lifeworld (it has a utopian content but "cannot sketch out a utopia"), it seems appropriate to look in more detail at one or two of his apparently more substantive comments.

The modern world for Habermas is in the era of postliberal societies, which take one of two forms, both of which have emerged from bourgeois capitalist society. In one, organized capitalism leads to welfare-state mass democracy, which, under the pressure of economic crisis, can sometimes "be maintained for a time only in the political form of authoritarian or fascist orders." Bureaucratic socialism follows a similar path to "a political order of dictatorship by state parties."[51] In both cases there is a bifurcation of the private (lifeworld) and public (system) spheres. But "systemic disequilibria" have to be managed, and one way of managing them is to transfer their effects from the system to the lifeworld, thus producing "pathologies." Since the context of our discussion is that of an advanced capitalist society, I shall concentrate on Habermas's treatment of this kind of society, though parallel problems arise in bureaucratic socialist states.

Developed capitalism oscillates, thinks Habermas, between a belief in the self-healing powers of the market and intervention by the state. Such disequilibrium can become a crisis "when the performances of economy and state remain manifestly below an established level of aspiration and harm the symbolic reproduction of the lifeworld by calling forth conflicts and reactions of resistance there."[52] Such steering crises are dealt with through transferring the problem to the lifeworld, principally through the family structure, thus creating pathologies in the lifeworld: "Culture and personality come under attack for the sake of warding off crises and stabilizing society." Alienation and "the unsettling of collective identity" are the price paid in the lifeworld when the problem actually lies in questions of legitimation and motivation within the system.[53]

Although Habermas does not go into specific examples of lifeworld pathologies occasioned by systemic crises, it is clear that what he is offering is an explanation of why modernity is distinguished by a sharp division between private and public life, why private life tends to be viewed as the realm of affect, ethic, religion, art, and philosophy, and why the "private" individual feels increasingly helpless before the reified forces of the economy (money) or the state (power). It is worth stressing once again that Habermas does not believe that the division into lifeworld and system is itself pathological. On the contrary, it is one of necessary stages in society's development. However, since it is the lifeworld that is the realm of communicative rationality, and communicative rationality is the appropriate form of human interchange, the lifeworld must be the place where even the system is ultimately grounded. Systems and steering mechanisms are necessary to modern society, but the decision about what are the appropriate perimeters within which the system must work is one that has to remain in the hands of the human community. At the same time, the fact that the steering mechanisms of money and power do not in themselves depend on linguisticality increases the likelihood that they can become rogue elements in society, and ultimately threaten the integrity of the lifeworld itself.

It is hard to come up with concrete examples of lifeworld pathologies that would be generally recognized, but since Habermas offers no clues himself, it has to be attempted. Examples must lie in the direction of the effects upon the family of capitalist society's inherent tension between free-market forces and state intervention. Thus, an obvious candidate for exemplary status would be the well-publicized policy of the first-term Reagan administration of using unemployment to cure inflation. Here a problem within the system was handled by transferring the problem to the lifeworld, where it had immediate and devastating effect on any number of American families. A second possibility might be the failure of successive United States administrations to address the issue of acid rain or environmental hazards in general. The power of the interests emerging from the economic system to prevent steps being taken to preserve the quality of human life and the remainder of nonrenewable resources is all too successful. Even more obvious, the failure of government to place adequate controls on the tobacco industry, and the transfer of the problems there to the lifeworld in the form of claims that basic human freedoms are at stake, is a cynical example of an induced lifeworld pathology.

Because the scale of crises and pathologies is so immense, thinks Habermas, the character of protest has changed from the days of class conflict. No longer is protest focused on demanding from the political system what the political system is itself supposed to provide; rather, "The new problems have to do with quality of life, equal rights, individual self-realization, participation and human rights."[54] In late capitalist societies a whole plethora of varied and often small and single-issue groups seek to defend the world and the human community from the depredations of the unchecked system. These groups are united in their "critique of growth," and *almost* all are primarily defensive in character. The only exception to this in Habermas's view is the feminist movement, which has an alternative hermeneutic and a comprehensive alternative vision of society to offer: "The struggle against patriarchal oppression and for the redemption of a promise that has long been anchored in the acknowledged universalistic foundations of morality and law gives feminism the impetus of an offensive movement."[55]

The defensive groups are either bourgeois groups focused on the defense of class interests—for example, groups to oppose tax reform; or they are groups in effect involved in "resistance to tendencies toward a colonization of the lifeworld"—such as, for example, groups opposing nuclear energy, pollution, deprivation of privacy, and so on. Most sinister of all, anxiety runs through society about risks that people do not even know about:

> The anxieties function as catalysts for a feeling of being overwhelmed in view of the possible consequences of

processes for which we are morally accountable—since we do set them in motion technically and politically—and yet for which we can no longer take moral responsibility—since their scale has put them beyond our control.[56]

We all know such feelings: for example, our dependence on an international economic system which even as we benefit is inducing pathologies in the lifeworld of other cultures, disrupting cultural patterns, destroying family life, indirectly causing increases in crime and poor health.

We should be aware, if we are of Habermas's mind, that we cannot look to the system to solve the problems of the system. The system maintains itself and is entirely non-normative in character. We can only look to the exercise of human rationality in and through the communication community to fight back against human loss of control over the system. Whether the fight will be a success or a failure is an open question. Habermas's argument would suggest that a first step is to begin to resist mightily the forces that privatize art, philosophy, ethics, and even religion, and to promote a vigorous communication community dedicated to a public ethic that will win back control for the lifeworld of the system that is, inevitably, a good servant but a very bad ruler.

In this struggle the churches may play a crucial role, but to do so effectively they will have to recognize their own character as communities of communicative action oriented to consensus and understanding.

CHAPTER THREE

THE VALUE OF CRITICAL THEORY FOR CATHOLIC THEOLOGY

Thus far, religion has been paid little attention in this consideration of critical theory. But we are now ready to face the matter squarely: What is the significance of critical theory for contemporary Christian theology in general, and that of the Catholic tradition in particular? The position I want to maintain in this chapter and then fill out in detail in the remainder of the work is that Habermas's critical theory is an immensely valuable theological resource. The initial step in this argument, and the one to be attempted here, is a demonstration that in the most noticeable way, in its own dialogue with modernity, the Catholic tradition's position is lacking something that Habermas's critical theory could provide. To do this, we first have to outline the problematic elements in the generally constructive dialogue with the world that goes by the name of Catholic Social Teaching (CST).[1] Second, we have to consider how the *lacunae* (critical theorists are fond of the term "aporias") in CST can be corrected through the application of Habermas's critical theory. Third, a relatively brief excursus must show in general terms the importance of social theory as a "mediator" of theology.

This will prepare the way in subsequent chapters for the construction in outline of what I shall call a critical theology, and I shall pay particular attention to two "moments" in that theology, a critical ecclesiology and a critical social ethics.

PROBLEMATIC ELEMENTS IN CATHOLIC SOCIAL TEACHING

The Catholic church, for better or worse, is a political force. Its words and actions often have an impact that goes far beyond its own members to trouble or inspire other Christians, to challenge or comfort governments and political parties, to inspire heroic efforts for the improvement of our world and, at times, to confound outside observers. In recent decades, in fact since the Second Vatican Council (1962–65), the church has had a much higher public profile, partly because of the very teaching of the Council, and in part through the charismatic impact of two popes, John XXIII (1958–63) and John Paul II (elected in 1978).

The wider world is most directly addressed by that body of documents which has come to be called Catholic Social Teaching. In these writings, popes since Leo XIII in the late nineteenth century have engaged the Catholic tradition with the great social currents of the times. Thus it is fair to identify Catholic Social Teaching as the Catholic church's "dialogue with modernity."[2] In the first place, of course, popes are heard within the church, but particularly over the last twenty-five years they have increasingly come to be heard, if not necessarily heeded, even by governments that profess a constitutional atheism, and not only by those for whom the need to ensure re-election dictates at least the appearance of respectful attention.

The principles of Catholic Social Teaching are unlikely to be publicly rejected by many, and CST is undoubtedly a frequent source of hope and heartening even to outsiders. Nevertheless, it has its limitations.

Principal among the problematic elements of Catholic Social Teaching are the following four phenomena: an often-noted openness to varied and even conflicting interpretations; an apparent lack of consistency between the content of the teaching and the praxis of the church; the absence of a modern theory of society; and the tendency to have recourse to religious language and theological concepts that have not been subjected to critical scrutiny. The first of these I shall treat rather briefly. The remaining three charges will be considered in more detail.

a. *Conflict of Interpretations*

The problem of varied interpretation can be illustrated quite succinctly by a look at judgments on the character of Catholic Social Teaching expressed by Donal Dorr, Michael Novak, and Gregory Baum.[3] Dorr's 1984 book, *Option for the Poor*,[4] comes closest to a serious critique of CST. It discerns in CST a steady development of an option for the poor, a gain in momentum with John XXIII, and the achievement of its best expression to date in John Paul II's 1982 letter, *On Human Work*.[5] The high regard Dorr has for this letter is echoed by Gregory Baum in his commentary on it.[6] To Baum, "The economic system proposed by *Laborem Exercens* is a form of socialism," but "one in which the subject character of society is safeguarded."[7] Although Michael Novak perhaps surprisingly takes no exception to Baum's views, he presents Catholic Social Teaching as favoring a "democratic capitalist" rather than a socialist society, and hence as essentially consistent with American society's particular mix of political system, economic patterns, and cultural values.[8]

The differences between Novak and Dorr are many. Dorr praises Paul VI's *Populorum Progressio*, though he finds its critique of neocolonialism to be perhaps too lenient.[9] Novak, in stark contrast, thinks Pope Paul "interrupts the steady realism which flows from John XXIII to John Paul II today," and sounds a "note of doom" and defeatism.[10] Dorr finds John Paul II to have distanced himself from capitalism; Novak believes that behind the inaccurate observations on capitalism that mar *On Human Work* the Pope stands in the tradition of John Stuart Mill and, if he were better informed about American society, would find that "his concerns about the ordering of private property to the common good are already observed in a multitude of institutional ways."[11] Baum, as we have already noted, maintains a much more leftward-leaning view of the Pope's letter, and gets surprising support from Carlo Marzani, a lifelong Communist and atheist, in his article, "The Vatican as a Left Ally?"[12]

It is of course possible that the variety of interpretations of papal social teaching, of which the paragraphs above are but a small sample, could be a reflection of the hidden agendas of the commentators rather than attributable to ambiguity in the minds of the popes. To a degree, I am sure that this is true. However, other factors are also at work. In the first place, Catholic Social Teaching is not monolithic and, though popes do not explicitly contradict one another, they are as subject to the development of doctrine and moral teaching as anyone else. Thus, Leo XIII's commitment to a classist social order and Pius XI's leaning to a corporatist state have been left behind, as perhaps has the overly sanguine liberalism of John XXIII and even Paul VI. John Paul II seems to have a far more evenhanded view of the respective weaknesses of both capitalism and socialist systems, even while his autocratic attitudes seem to many to have undone much of the good work of opening up the church begun by his recent predecessors. Second, official church documents seem often to bear the marks of different hands, even when they come ostensibly from a single individual. Vatican II's principal document on the church, for example, is notoriously self-contradictory in places.[13] Third, the level of abstraction of the documents means that they often fail to address issues with any degree of specificity, and their frequently unfortunate tone makes them difficult to hear with any equanimity.

b. *The Issue of Consistency*

The consistency issue raises the question of motivations. There do on the face of it seem to be problems with an institution whose teaching proclaims the rights of the oppressed in the social, economic, and political realms but whose internal practice restricts the rights of its own members in ecclesial affairs. The human rights teaching of Catholic Social Teaching is sublime. The church's behavior toward women, homosexuals, expriests, "meddlesome" theologians, nuns who speak up for open discussion of abortion, and divorced and remarried Catholics is far short even of what common human decency would suggest. The question of consistency thus leads to the question of sincerity.

Among recent commentators on the issue of consistency, Peter Hebblethwaite locates the problem in the strategic agenda of John Paul II.[14] Hebblethwaite is less concerned with the content of Catholic Social Teaching than with the reemergence of the concept—after John XXIII, Vatican II, and especially Paul VI seemed to have consigned it to oblivion. Paul VI had written that "in view of the varied situations in the world, it is difficult to give one teaching to cover them all or to offer a solution which has universal value."[15] John Paul's reassertion of the idea of Catholic Social Teaching, Hebblethwaite thinks, is not "doing battle for a mere word" but "can be seen as an attempt to assert that the Church, the popes and the Gospel . . . have always had something to say on social questions."[16] Moreover, most of the uses of the term have been reserve for the Polish and Latin American arenas. In the former, CST was used to defend *Solidarity* and put the Soviet Union in its place. In the latter, it was to provide the Pope some ground on which to express his serious reservations about liberation theology.

The Brazilian Franciscan Leonardo Boff has been even more critical.[17] For this liberation theologian, "The gap between ecclesial theory and praxis in terms of human rights" needs a structural explanation since "the majority of those in authority in the church are men of good faith, clear conscience, [and] impeccable personal character."[18] As part of his thorough and substantially accurate analysis of power structures in the Catholic church Boff refers to CST's consistent condemnation of violent revolution. He believes that the church is not faithful to its views when the regime in question is inimical to it, as in the Mexican revolution or during the Spanish Civil War. "Whatever the interpretation," Boff comments, "first in one direction and then in another, it always points to the same effort: to strengthen the survival of the institution so that the Gospel may be made present in the world."[19] For Boff, then, there is nothing cynical about the lack of consistency. Rather, the laudable concern for the proclamation of the gospel and the consequent commitment to preserving the power of the institution relativize the wisdom of the teaching on human rights.

There is, however, another and more significant explanation for the apparent inconsistency between the principles of social teaching and ecclesial practice, located in the paradigm of teaching prevalent in the Catholic tradition. Although this paradigm could be described under a number of sophisticated categories, at its root it amounts to a belief that there are some who teach and there are some who are taught. Anyone who has ever sat in a classroom knows that there are moments in the learning process when that has to be true, when sheer expertise or control over a body of information must be attended to. But as a view of the process of education as a whole it is woefully inadequate. Any teacher of any quality will tell you that students sometime teach and teachers occasionally learn. Any student knows that the teacher who comes into the classroom simply to impart knowledge, convey information, or blind with his or her own wisdom may be the least demanding but also among the least educative.

The most glaring example of the gap between theory and practice lies in the field of human rights. Successive papal encyclicals since *Pacem in Terris* have hammered home the message that the Christian vision's creational theology demands recognition of the fundamental equality of all people, and hence their rights to bodily integrity, freedom of speech and religion, and even (more recently) to employment. Yet the church has not always paid attention to the notion of human rights, and if it is a clear implication of John Paul's creational theology that all human beings are fundamentally equal, then lack of attention to those rights was presumably at least erroneous, if not actually culpable. Moreover, at present the church's treatment of large sections of its own membership seems on the face of it to belie the sincerity of the commitment.

Because the paradigm of teaching in Catholic Social

Teaching is that "there are some who teach and there are some who are taught," it is possible to see the message of liberation and the practice of oppression as demonstrating a curious kind of consistency. Common to the logic of social reform demanded in CST and the logic of internal repression is a pattern of aprioristic and prescriptive thinking. Neither in social teaching nor in internal structural reform does a genuine listening to the lessons of extraecclesial wisdom ever occur.

Throughout history, the church has had a less than admirable record on defense of the poor against a hostile status quo. *On Human Work* makes the long overdue identification of the church with the working poor without a pause for breath, without recognition of the nonidentity of church and poor for many centuries. The truth is that the church in general and the present Pope in particular have learned something that they did not always know, or at the very least been reminded of something they had forgotten, namely, that the gospel requires this kind of identification. But the lessons of history are not admitted and the church's debts to others go unrecognized, whether it owes what it owes to Marx's critique of religion or liberation theology's "preferential option for the poor."

The same attitudes govern a body of teaching that can borrow from Marxist analysis or liberation theology without attribution, that has learned from what is extra-ecclesial but would never admit it, and a form of ecclesial practice in which open discussion of vital issues is deemed not only unnecessary but even hazardous. Obviously, on this view, the more insightful and out-standing the public teaching, the further reinforced is the institution's conviction that it has nothing to learn and that internal dissent, dispute, and discussion can only serve to muddy the clear waters of CST. Loyal opposition must then be interpreted as a deeper if unintentional treachery.

The tragedy of this inability to accept humbly the discrepancies between truth and history, theory and practice, is that the theological resources that would support such a recognition do in fact exist within the tradition. Twenty and more years ago *Gaudium et Spes* recognized the need for the church to learn from the world,[20] and Leonardo Boff devotes a whole chapter to the requirement that the "teaching church" also be a "learning church."[21] However, there is a theological argument which is stronger than either the Vatican document or Boff's appeal. The logic of the "eschatological reservation" means that the tension between present performance and future expectation, between existential and ideal, is at the heart of the Christian theology.

The apostle Paul constantly stresses the nonidentity of the Christian community with the kingdom of God. The church which is in travail here in history eagerly awaits the coming of God's reign. Here and now it is freed proleptically from bondage to sin, death, and the law, yet it must also deal with just these realities. It is *already* the community of the redeemed, but *not yet* fully so. The community strives to live in the present according to the values which, it has been led to hope, lie in their fullness in God's kingdom, but Paul's letters to the Corinthians show only too clearly how great the nonidentity between theory and practice really can be.

c. *The Absence of Social Theory*

The third phenomenon worthy of comment is Catholic Social Teaching's lack of a developed contemporary analysis of society. Of course, church teaching makes observations about society, often shrewdly, but apparently either in ignorance or in unwillingness to utilize secular social theory. This is a surprising omission in a documentary tradition that has at its heart the conciliar document *Gaudium et Spes*, otherwise called the "Pastoral Constitution on the Church in the Modern World." But it is less a matter for marvel if we recall that social ethics in the Catholic tradition is impelled by a belief that the conduct of Christians in their daily lives is directly related to and influential upon the state of their saving relationship with God. Although such a belief gives religious significance to ethical conduct, it leads to a concomitant devaluation of the status of worldly reality. Because the moral life is a religious reality, the world cannot be autonomous and its importance is thus relativized to the religious vision. A premodern theology of the world, such as Catholic Social Teaching still possesses, does not necessarily lack perception about the significance of this or that historical phenomenon, but because it is ideologically predisposed to see the world as a part of the divine plan from the standpoint of an "economy of salvation" articulated in narrowly religious terms, no energy is devoted to an intrahistorical understanding of human society. When human sciences have insights to offer that are not part of the privileged vision of Revelation, as happened in earlier times in the cases of Galileo and Darwin, they cannot easily be incorporated into the religious world view. Still less can the attempt at an overall social theory that leaves no gaps for salvation history be reconciled, apparently, with the ideology of Catholicism.[22]

The consequence of the absence of a social theory is that although Catholic Social Teaching is often right, it is frequently very difficult to see why it is right. Its critique is acute but unsystematic, its proposals often insightful, frequently humane, but invariably ad hoc. As an example of what I mean, I propose looking more closely at the analysis of work in John Paul's 1981 letter, *On Human Work*. Although the letter is excellent in many respects, the unsatisfactory nature of the analysis of work results from the absence of social theory. That same absence is owing to a premature recourse to the categories of revelation, and thus will lead neatly into the fourth phenomenon we have to consider. In *On Human Work* the term "work" is made to do far too much. The opening paragraph illustrates the problem:

And work means any activity by man, whether manual or intellectual, whatever its nature or circumstances; it means any human activity that can and must be recognized as work, in the midst of all the many activities of which man is capable and to which he is predisposed by his very nature, by virtue of humanity itself.

The Pope is of course aware of the dialectical reality of work, that it is somehow closely related to the possibility of human dignity, and yet "contains the unceasing measure of toil and suffering" that is its shadow side. However, in essence all forms of work are perceived to have the same essential relation to the human subject. The subjective dimension of work—its role in human fulfillment—takes precedence over other considerations:

In fact, in the final analysis it is always man who is the purpose of the work, whatever work it is that is done by man—even if the common scale of values rates it as the merest "service," as the most monotonous, even the most alienating work.[23]

Clearly, this means that wherever work is taken up, which in fact makes the worker an instrument of capital or of the productive process, it is unethical and unchristian. However, all too frequently the worker is not free to seek other, less alienating work elsewhere. In other situations certain forms of work are looked down upon by society, but "someone has to do them." In both such situations and in others imaginable it seems reasonable to ask what it means to talk of the relationship between work and human dignity. Work, despite all it should be, is very often the principal means by which the dignity of an individual is affronted.

It is quite easy to envisage circumstances in which the individual who chose not to work would be acting more in accord with human dignity than the one who chose to accept the objectively alienating or unjust working environment. The nonworker does not seem to fit the Pope's categories, however. How is such a person engaging in "co-creation" if work is the principal means of being so occupied? Of course there are many reasons why a person might be coerced or oppressed into dehumanizing work, and there would be no question of moral guilt. But if the work itself is not just possibly dehumanizing (as, for example, in many very routine occupations) or tedious and of little social respectability, but actually objectively immoral, how could the subject be expressing his or her human dignity or obedience to the divine command to "subdue" the earth by engaging in such work? Many people are locked into work in chemical warfare technology, or occupied making nuclear weapons. They are often not truly free to change their work situation, at least not overnight. But is their work co-creative?

There are several things that could be done to strengthen the Pope's analysis of what is clearly a substantial contemporary problem. The first would be to subject the term "work" to an analysis that would subdivide it in such a way that some work would meet the criteria for co-creation, and some would not. This, incidentally, would introduce a more dynamic element into the analysis than it possesses in *On Human Work*. The second would be to replace the term with another more all-embracing term, of which "work" might be a subdivision. The idea of praxis developed in liberation theology or in Hannah Arendt's *The Human Condition*,[24] or Habermas's notion of communicative action are obvious possibilities. In either case it would become apparent that the connection between human dignity and work is neither so clear nor so unproblematic as John Paul suggests.

The more deep-seated weakness of the analysis in this letter is one that it shares to a greater or lesser degree with the whole corpus of Catholic Social Teaching. The possibility of setting the discussion in the context of a true social theory is aborted by premature or even preemptive recourse to scriptural evidence. In the particular case under consideration, John Paul connects the centrality of work in human life from the outset with the Genesis command to "subdue the earth and have dominion over it." Although he makes quite explicit his awareness of the "archaic way of manifesting thought" to which Genesis is sometimes subject, nevertheless these texts "express the fundamental truths about man."

> Man is the image of God partly through the mandate received from his creator to subdue, to dominate, the earth. In carrying out this mandate, man, every human being, reflects the very action of the creator of the universe.[25]

Interpretation of history through reading off the words of scripture is open to being ideological distortion if it is not accompanied by a reverse moment in which historical reality scrutinizes scripture for signs of its own bias. Hence, although it is quite possible to define the command to "subdue" the earth in a way that excludes its despoliation, both the ordinary meaning of the terms "subdue" and "dominate" and the almost unvarying practice of the Christian world for two thousand years make it impossible to accept this particular text with anything approaching equanimity. Christian "civilization" is unfortunately a conspicuous and consistent example of the almost complete inability to take God's command in Genesis as anything other than license to exploit the finite resources of the world. But this is obscured here in the proclamation of a religious truth to which history is supposed to conform.

The recourse to scripture is one example of an unsatisfactory notion of truth at work in *Laborem Exercens*. The Pope uses idealist presuppositions curiously at odds with his own training in phenomenology, so that the limited examples of work that truly do express human dignity, or of subjugation of the earth that respects its created nature, are "true" because they conform to an aprioristically established truth, and the myriad examples of the frustration of this abstract truth are explained as failures to express it. A modified materialist epistemology in which truth is a term reserved for some (but not all) phenomena which possess actual historical existence would be one way out of this deductive impasse. The truth and the error of history would then not be relative to the injunction of Genesis but to something discovered within history. The best candidate for this "something," as we saw in chapter 2, is the emancipatory interest that grounds action and discourse.

d. *The Limitations of Scripture*

Although it is quite possible to interpret the workings of the institutional church as infected by an ideology in which the dominant class systematically distorts communication in order to maintain its power and privileges, a more insightful way to explain the "irrationality" of Catholic Social Teaching is provided by Habermas's account of mythical and modern world views. Mythical thought can be as logical as modern, says Habermas, but it restricts rationality to certain spheres of life. The mythical mind cannot separate nature and culture or, to express this in terms of the modern variant, language and world. Language is taken to be identical with what language intends. An explanation of the world is the truth, and a naive dogmatism results:

> Thus a linguistically constituted world-view can be identi-
> fied with the world order itself to such an extent that it
> cannot be perceived *as* an interpretation of the world that is
> subject to error and open to criticism. In this respect the
> confusion of nature and culture takes on the significance of
> a reification of world-view. . . . As a result the concept of
> world is dogmatically invested with a specific content that is
> withdrawn from rational discussion and thus from criti-
> cism.[26]

Although I am not at all convinced that Habermas has correctly perceived the contemporary advances of theology away from the mythical position toward what he would call a modern stance, I am convinced that the world view expressed in Catholic Social Teaching, for all that teaching's individual insights and occasional sophistication, is understood to be beyond discussion or criticism.

An examination of the "theology of the world" presented in John Paul's late 1987 encyclical letter, *The Social Concern of the Church,* will serve to illustrate both the strengths of the tradition and the underlying systematic problems involved in premature or inappropriate recourse to scripture.[27] Intended to coincide (more or less) with the twentieth anniversary of the publication of Paul VI's *On the Development of Peoples,* the letter proceeds even more than previous papal encyclicals in respectful dialogue with the earlier document.

In 1967 Paul VI sounded a warning note about some understandings of the idea of development. For two decades the planners of the First World had been extending an idea of development to "under-developed" or "less-developed" or "developing" societies intended to industrialize and hence "modernize" and often even "democratize" these same nations. Leaving aside the thorny problems of motivation, there were two principal drawbacks to this program. First, the assumption was that an economic model of development, if not everything that development might mean, was certainly where the process should begin, and was the necessary condition for development in other sectors of society (which usually meant primarily the emergence of Western-style liberal democracy). Second, the model of development utilized was ideological and deductive, assuming an identity between development and GNP, and assuming that any nation could find its place on one sliding scale of development according to its collective wealth. These limitations meant that, in the first place, there was little or no attention to other possible dimensions of genuine development, and second, that scant consideration was given to how the wealth generated by industrialization, for example, affected the standard of living of the population as a whole. Many Marxist economists saw this process as the institutionalization of dependency rather than real development. In *The Development of Peoples* Paul VI did not take up the Marxist critique, but responded to these problems by calling for a notion of "integral development," development that would affect the whole person and every person.

The same issue of development is also John Paul's central concern. The *treatment* of the idea of development in Paul VI's letter is what John Paul sees as its genuine originality. Times have changed since 1967, however, and John Paul enumerates several important differences between today and that more optimistic age. The gap between rich and poor continues to widen. Both capitalism and state socialism can now more clearly be seen frequently to lead to the alienation of the worker. The growing problem of housing and homelessness is highlighting as never before the limitations of the capacity for genuine development even within the richer nations of the world. The international debt crisis intensifies the problems of poor nations while simultaneously revealing the increasing interdependence of "developed" and "developing" worlds.

The most important of John Paul's observations on today's world, and the one which has raised some eyebrows in the Catholic community in the United States in particular, is his isolation of geopolitics as "a striking fact about the political picture since World War II, a fact which has considerable impact on the forward movement of the development of peoples." Geopolitical thinking effectively instrumentalizes the needs of the poor nations to the strategic concerns of the world powers and power blocks. The developing countries "become cogs on a gigantic wheel." The problems of disparity and relationship between North and South are intensified if not wholly created by the ideological bickering of East and West.

In his discussion of geopolitics, John Paul shows no favoritism between East and West. He poses the question that arises with remarkable evenhandedness:

> This is one of the reasons why the church's social doctrine adopts a critical attitude toward both liberal capitalism and Marxist collectivism, for from the point of view of development the question naturally arises: In what way and

to what extent are these two systems capable of changes and updating such as to favor or promote a true and integral development of individuals and peoples in modern society?[28]

The limitations of the papal perspective begin to appear in his response to the question he has posed. Change in relations of power is clearly necessary if genuine justice and hence peace are to be possible. Some commentators, presented with this issue, would undoubtedly turn to revolutionary movements as the best chance for change. The Pope, on the contrary, singles out the need for conversion, in the sense of a moral awakening that would inspire the will to change relations of power. Thus he condemns isolationist impulses among the great powers. Although his analysis is penetrating, considerable obscurity surrounds the conclusions. Where will the nations find that moral will?

If we can see development as the act of "respectful dominion" over the world, then, in the Pope's words, "the notion of development is not only 'lay' or 'profane,' but is also seen to be, while having a socioeconomic dimension of its own, the modern expression of an essential dimension of man's vocation."[29] Authentic development, in other words, is what many a theologian, if not yet a pope, might call the political imperative of the gospel. When the spirituality of assimilation or of "following Christ" is given expression in the language of political reality, it becomes "development."

In Christian terms, consequently, it is possible to look at the present socioeconomic and political reality of the world and read it as failure to follow out God's mandate to Adam and Eve, while seeing the church as "an expert in humanity" which preaches out of a biblical context whose vision has to be articulated in the structures of society. The circumstances of human historical failure are processed through the scriptural message, as it were, to produce a renewed commitment to an essentially historical struggle for realization of justice and peace. The role that scripture plays in Christian social ethics, then, corresponds to the role of ideology or utopian vision in any secular teleology.

Development in the thought of John Paul is all a part of the divine plan, and it is at this point that some serious questions have to be raised. The Pope's theology of history is consistently optimistic, but it is difficult to see the historical license that would make this more than a vain hope. "The story of the human race described by Sacred Scripture," says John Paul, "is, even after the fall into sin, a story of constant achievements which, although always called into question and threatened by sin, are nonetheless repeated, increased and extended in response to the divine vocation given from the beginning to man and to woman and inscribed in the image which they received."[30] What is missing, as the Pope goes on to elaborate his vision of hope in an "unlimited progress" based in God's free decision "to make man a sharer of his glory in Jesus Christ risen from the dead," is what we might call a theological meditation on the human race's newfound capacity for complete self-annihilation.

A contemporary Christian theology of the world must face squarely the theological implications of potential human self-destruction. Christian social ethics and a theology of history have no choice any longer but to take into account that "progress" has apparently given the human race the capacity to confound the "divine plan." The possible responses to the idea of nuclear holocaust are clear. We could argue that since God's plan cannot be confounded in the end, it must be impossible for the human race to destroy itself. We could, on the contrary, maintain that God may intend the end of the world to come in a nuclear catastrophe. Both responses would be motivated more by a conviction of the human need to preserve a naive understanding of the divine plan than by any use of common sense or theological acumen. The remaining possibility is more radical, but has the advantage of letting God be God and human beings be what they are. An incarnational theology must take seriously the extent to which, in God's self-emptying, the "economy of salvation" is placed in human hands. One manifestation of such a theological approach would be the ability to accept the possibility that authentic development, though God's charge to the human race, is not guaranteed fulfillment. Moving in a somewhat different direction, the idea of a "divine plan" could be saved at the cost of anthropocentricity. There is no reason, simply from looking at the cosmos, to conclude that it is *about* the human race and its destiny. Because, for whatever reason, the Pope chooses rather to reiterate a premodern theology of history, the sharp realism of much of the rest of the letter is unfortunately blunted.

I have gone into some detail here because it is necessary to establish clearly two points. In the first place, the teaching of John Paul II on the subject of development is sensitive and, if it is heard, important to the world. It advances the views of his predecessors, and it shows the Pope recognizing some of the limitations of his own use of the language of "dominion" in his letter *On Human Work.* Second, however, it moves from relatively sober empirical observation to relatively sanguine expectations. It does this by seeing the stark realities of the socioeconomic and political situation of the modern world in the light of a dehistoricized and depoliticized eschatological hope, which of its nature will mediate optimistic attitudes however gloomy things seem. "However bad things look, fight on for justice" is an honorable attitude. The problem is that it preempts the less romantic but no less necessary stage of facing up to the question, Just how bad are things? What is missing, what is preempted by the turn to scripture, in Catholic Social Teaching is the "moment" or mediation of social theory.

THE VALUE OF CRITICAL THEORY
FOR CATHOLIC SOCIAL TEACHING

In the first part of this chapter, I identified four problematic elements in Catholic Social Teaching: openness to conflicting interpretations; lack of a healthy theory-praxis relationship; the absence of a modern theory of society; and insufficiently critical recourse to religious language and theological concepts. Now I would like to comment in a preliminary fashion on the ways in which Habermasian critical social theory can help overcome these weaknesses.

a. *Conflict of Interpretations*

There is an obvious sense in which openness to a variety of interpretations is a sign of health rather than the opposite. In the modern world theology has striven to emerge from absolute or universal approaches, with their tendency to adopt purely deductive methodologies. Instead, political and liberation theologies in particular have emphasized the importance of the precise political, economic, and cultural setting and have proclaimed the value of constructing local theologies.[31] Feminist exegetical methodologies have come to quite strikingly untraditional conclusions about the scriptures and the nature of the early church.[32] Moreover, though these new approaches to the Christian tradition emerging in the second half of the twentieth century have presented serious challenges to the received wisdom, they have also added genuine depth and richness, and in at least the case of liberation theology have already permanently modified the tradition by which they were initially perceived simply as threatening.

There are, on the other hand, respects in which openness to differing interpretations represents a real weakness. The gospel and Christian tradition exhibit an openness deriving from a "surplus of meaning," which not only permits but also actively stimulates a plurality of interpretations. This is what makes development possible. But moral teaching does not work by the same rules, at least not when it is more than the enunciation of the most general principles. A pope who can proclaim "the sanctity of human life" in language of great beauty, and say no more than that, may well be promoting serious ethical reflection in the universal church upon how such an inviolable principle must take expression within this or that particular culture in this or that historical epoch. Even a pope who goes beyond that level of generality to enunciate precise judgments on licit and illicit means of birth control, judgments that moreover derive from a particular historically circumscribed vision of "natural law," cannot be accused of lack of clarity (though his teaching may be unwelcome or anachronistic). But when the Roman pontiff can write a letter on the centrality of work in the human experience, as John Paul II did in 1981, which one commentator can praise as "socialism" and another as supportive of "democratic capitalism," then even allowing for the special interests of the respective commentators, something is awry. And when the United States Catholic bishops published their letter "The Challenge of Peace," there must have been some ambiguity or lack of clarity, if not ill will, if both hawks and doves could claim it for themselves.

It is perhaps possible that lack of complete clarity and consequent openness to conflicting interpretations cannot wholly be avoided even by the supreme magisterium, and more likely that complete clarity is not always a virtue. However, in such circumstances there is a concomitant need for a process by which differences can be aired and movement toward clarity and consensus can emerge. It is at this point that the teaching model in the Catholic church is seriously deficient. Whether this is a product of a system that serves to preserve relations of power and oppression, whether it is a matter of a view of the laity that is simply obsolescent, or whether indeed all are held captive in an outmoded church structure is a matter of opinion. But that, for whatever reason, mature and well-informed adult members of the church who are not bishops, and many who are, play no active role in the formulation of ethical or theological thought, is a fact beyond dispute and a scandal of growing proportions.

Habermas's theory of communicative action is an attempt to understand the nature of speech-acts oriented toward understanding. It assumes that what is under discussion will exclude attempts to manipulate individuals and groups, intentionally or not, and will also exclude group instrumental action designed to simplify the smooth running of society. Communicative action, then, is what distinguishes distinctively human communication, in which larger or smaller groups engage in a process, as equal partners, oriented to consensus formation. Clearly, before we can go any farther, we have to agree that it is this kind of action with which we are concerned in any discussion of the formation of ethical teaching.

It is my contention that ethical teaching has to be viewed under the rubric of communicative action precisely because the entire life of the church must be so envisaged. We shall go into this issue in considerable detail in the next chapter. For the moment we must content ourselves with pointing out that the Catholic tradition in Christianity emphasizes the free consent of the individual to the gift of God's saving grace on the one hand, and on the other enunciates a philosophical anthropology in which the human being is an individual-in-community.[33] Moreover, the tradition understands these twin principles of human dignity and community responsibility to underpin its entire social ethics. The imperative follows from the indicative. Because Catholic theology sees not only the church but also the whole human community as in some sense the free people of God, the Catholic tradition *must* organize its own community around this same conception.

In consequence, Habermas's theory of communicative action furnishes Catholic ecclesiology with an updated account of human communication that would, if employed, enable the theology of the church to move from the indicative to the imperative mood. As we shall see in the next chapter, it would in no way contradict the fundamental ecclesial vision of the Second Vatican Council. On the contrary, it offers a mode of expression to the Catholic theology of the church that brings it more easily into the general conversation of humankind, and it contains a logic that presses that ecclesiology to a thorough consideration of its own internal problems of consistency.

b. *The Theory-Praxis Relationship*

The question of consistency raised by examining the conflict of interpretations brings the discussion to the theory-praxis relationship. In establishing consistency, where shall the priority rest? Shall it be with the principles of Catholic Social Teaching or with the ecclesiological vision of the Second Vatican Council on the one hand, or with the internal and external social praxis of the church on the other? We can clarify this question of priority by briefly examining Matthew Lamb's recent attempt to address the theory-praxis question.

Lamb suggests five competing models of the theory-praxis relationship in today's Christian theology.[34] There is a "primacy of theory" model[35] and, at the opposite extreme, a primacy of praxis model.[36] The third model is a Barthian dismissal of the theory-praxis relationship "for identifying Christianity with either classical or modern cultural matrices" and the substitution of "the *decision* of Christian faith-love responding to the Word of God."[37] A fourth type of reflection, characteristic of thinkers like Bultmann, Tillich, the Niebuhrs, Rahner, Pannenberg, and Tracy, says Lamb, is one that envisages a dialectical relationship between Christianity and the categories of theory-praxis.[38] Their correlation is primarily theoretical, and thus they differ from the fifth and final model. Unlike the undialectical first model, these thinkers "insist that the *aim* or goal of theory is praxis," but in the fifth model, that of "critical praxis correlations," praxis "is not only the goal but also the foundation of theory."[39] Within this group Lamb lists Lonergan and Metz, contemporary feminist theology, and the theologies of liberation. What they have in common "is a realization that the practical and theoretical issues facing academies, churches, and societies can only be met in an ongoing critical collaboration mediating the cries of the victims to those interested in transforming the structures of world and church."[40]

For our purposes, as for Lamb's, the crucial point is the distinction between the fourth and fifth models. Lamb locates the differences not only in the primacy of praxis over theory, but also, and growing out of the primacy of praxis, in a context that is both interdisciplinary and critical. The practice of theology must emerge from "authentic religious, moral, intellectual, psychic, and social forms of praxis."[41] Such authentic praxis renders it impossible any longer to practice theology in a vacuum, or to see the present as a simple development out of the past, or to allow academy, church, or society to remain unconverted. To depart from Lamb's terminology, and borrow from Thomas Kuhn's, the "critical praxis correlation" model represents a "paradigm shift" in the self-understanding of the theological enterprise, comparable and in some ways related to the shift that the development of quantum theory or relativity theory marked in the natural sciences.[42] In Marshall Berman's telling adoption from Karl Marx, modernity is characterized by the prevalent feeling that "all that is solid melts into air," and from this universal experience theology and theologians are not immune.[43]

"Critical praxis correlation" leads to a theology that is most deeply embedded in historicality. By nature, theology and the theologian are products of particular social and historical milieus, and late twentieth-century political theologies and theologians are supremely historically self-conscious. The tools to be used in the practice of theology are human experience, with which the whole panoply of human knowledge must be brought into creative contact, and the specific texts and documents of the religious tradition, which can themselves be appropriated today only when they are viewed through the lens of modern historical consciousness. The theologian as interpreter is also a product of particular historical forces, and must as far as possible try to be aware of if not exactly free from the presuppositions of the historical moment. He or she cannot practice theology today without *critically* appropriating his or her own subjectivity.

Theology that claims to take history and historicality so seriously stands in need of a unifying matrix that avoids the pitfalls of deductive thought and the apriorism of metaphysical systems. For this reason critical theory, particularly in the Habermasian form, is extremely valuable. As we have already had occasion to note at several points, the mature form of the Habermasian vision begins from an analysis of the implications of peculiarly human speech-acts, in other words, from ordinary human conversation that celebrates the wish to communicate and the drive to understand. Without this point of focus in what is the fundamental exercise of emancipatory praxis, Habermas would offer nothing more than another smart theory. With the interest in emancipation, he provides in critical theory the best current mediating vision for theology. This will be discussed further in the third and final section of this chapter.

c. *A Theory of Modernity*

We saw earlier in this chapter that even the good insights of much of Catholic Social Teaching suffer from that tradition's lack of a consistent vision of modernity into which discrete insights could be fitted. I would like to suggest that without such a theory of modernity, genuine late-twentieth-century theology is impossible. A theory of modernity is not merely an important preliminary to theology: It is a part of theology itself. It is a primary component of a "theology of the world."[44] The best theology must be thoroughly at home in the world, and the good theologian must bestride the humanities and social and natural sciences as no other member of the academy. The world is, after all, the place of revelation.

One theory of modernity that may prove particularly suggestive for theology is that of Jürgen Habermas. Implicit in all his more recent work, it is directly presented in the second volume of *A Theory of Communicative Action* and in *The Philosophical Discourse of Modernity*.[45] The former text takes a more social-scientific approach to the comprehension of the modern world, while the latter addresses the same subject in the language of philosophy. The first was discussed in chapter 2; the second will be examined in detail in chapter 7. Here it will suffice to explain briefly why Habermas's theory of modernity seems to suit it to religious purposes.

The fundamental attractiveness of Habermas's theory of modernity to a religious temper must lie in his theory's essentially humanistic bent. There is a kind of neo-Marxist anthropological vision at work in which the overriding concern is for the continuing health of the human community. At the same time, his vision is suffused with the realization that only in cooperation and dialogue with one another does the human community have a future, and only then if its members can be persuaded to accept the equation of true self-interest with the common interest. Just such understandings lie behind his concern for the integrity of the lifeworld and his alarm at the destructiveness of instrumental reason when applied to the human dimension. Similar thinking explains his regret, spelled out in *The Philosophical Discourse of Modernity,* for the wrong turnings that modern philosophy has taken, especially through the influence of Nietzsche, into "subject-centered" rather than intersubjective or communicative reason.

The peculiar value of Habermas's theory of modernity for theology is perhaps that he has rescued (post)modernity from the grip of one or another variant of nihilism, be it Derridean, Foucaultesque, or Orwellian. Postmodernity may be the fulfillment of modernity, rather than the overturning of it. It may, on the other hand, be a label for the times, or a demonstration that the times do not know how to label themselves. Truth to tell, there is no such thing as postmodernism, only postmodernisms, and

Habermas's proposal for a return to communicative rationality represents a therapeutic alternative to the various strands of nihilism that must appeal to those who seek to maintain a religious account of even postmodern reality.[46] We shall return to this set of issues in more detail in the final chapter.

d. *The Critical Appropriation of the Tradition*

The consistent failings of Catholic Social Teaching, as we have had occasion to note earlier in this chapter, have been the premature invocation of conversion and the premature recourse to the biblical vision. Social teaching here reflects a problem in theology itself, which amounts to an uncritical or premodern attitude to the tradition of the church. In the context of social teaching, these ill-timed steps have the effect of aborting a genuinely critical social theory, which will move social teaching beyond the insightful enumeration of the pathological factors at work in modernity to an explanation of their sources in power relations and to an explanation in historical and material terms of where the struggle for emancipation is located. There is a dialectical relationship between personal conversion and structural change. Revolution, if the term refers to a transformation of political structures alone, cannot succeed in creating the new human being. But conversion without a political vision is prone to squander its goodwill in directionless, ad hoc philanthropy. The magisterium is understandably chary of alignment with one political option or another, but it is naive to believe that the conversion of historical beings will be devoid of a political dimension.

Scripture and the developed set of reflections on scripture that constitute the theological tradition are of course a primary component of today's theology. However, they require mediation just as much as the theologian's experience of the modern world or the self-understanding of the theologian does. As historical documents and moments the meaning of which depends at least partly on their context, they cannot be appropriated without being critically appropriated. Once again, the choice in the (post)modern world among methodologically sophisticated mediums lies between the intellectual traditions represented by Derrida, Foucault, and Habermas. Theology would as surely commit suicide by its choice of Derrida or Foucault as it would degenerate into senescence by a fearful retention of a precritical outlook. The irony is that the Marxist tradition, after all, may be the savior of theology.

CRITICAL SOCIAL THEORY AS
THEOLOGICAL MEDIATION

Theology, as a process of religious reflection, is of its nature a second-order activity. Theology, of course, does not emerge directly from experience: Rather, individual or group reflection leads to the formulation of theology. The act of reflection utilizes, consciously or unconsciously, some interpretive framework, some methodology, and it is this "hermeneutical" moment to which the term "mediation" refers. Clearly, therefore, the choice of mediation is crucial to the kind of theology that will emerge, since the mediation exercises a hermeneutical function. The mediation is the interpretation, the hermeneutic that prepares raw experience for the theological moment. And, of course, the mediation is always already present in experience, for without principles of interpretation the experience would not be recognizable as an experience *of* something.

The mediation of experience that produces theology is often, to use Habermas's term, either an unquestioned component of the lifeworld, or may be deemed to be an unquestionable component of the lifeworld. If it is not critically scrutinized, it will be *either* unthematized *or* ideological, *or* both. An unthematized mediation might be the naive scriptural positivism of fundamentalism. A thematized ideological mediation could be found in the Catholic tradition's early-twentieth-century insistence on Thomist theological and philosophical method, or in that institutional understanding of the Catholic theologian's role as justifying from scripture and tradition the theological positions of the *magisterium*.

Reflection on the process of practicing theology, as opposed to the reflection on experience that constitutes theology, must be devoted to making explicit the implicit form of mediation, uncovering its strengths and flaws, modifying it if necessary, and then returning it to use. *This* kind of investigation is primarily critical, and the critique of ideology will be one important component. But is critical theory an appropriate instrument not merely in the investigation of how theology has been done, but also in the reflection on the sources (experience, scripture, tradition) that *is* the act of practicing theology?

Liberation theologians were among the first in the Catholic tradition to call for the systematic use of social sciences in theology. For liberation theology, reflection on praxis, that is, on action to transform society, in the light of scripture, is theology. Social science methodologies are important for serious analysis of the milieu within which experience occurs, and within which theology is practiced. Liberation theologians concluded that social science method should therefore replace philosophy as the ruling methodological paradigm. They perceived philosophy as too theoretical, as too interested in understanding the world and insufficiently devoted to changing it. Social sciences, on the contrary, were able to provide hard data and thus prepare the way for informed reflection and programs for change. To be sure, it is true that some philosophy is mere theory and some social science does provide hard data; however, the simple juxtaposition hides more than it reveals. Social science methodology is just as much a product of hidden theoretical and ideological assumptions about reality, even and perhaps especially when it is of the positivistic, scientistic, "value-free" variety that seems most successful in the accumulation of data. On the other hand, as we have already seen in chapter 1, even the idealist philosophy of a Hegel claims to be a critical reflection on experience, and with at least some justification.

The corrective to too neat a contrast between philosophy and social science lies in the adoption of a critical theory of society in which are united an epistemological and a pragmatic dimension. Habermas's critical theory develops its analysis and critique of contemporary society out of a philosophical analysis of the universal human phenomenon of speech-acts. It thus unites theory and praxis, not in the usual way of delineating a vision of the world and adding a program of practical proposals consistent with the theoretical vision, but rather by outlining the social consequences of the implicit commitment to undistorted communication without which *any* human community would not be worthy of the name.

Critical theory as theological mediation will focus primarily on the tension between open and distorted communication, on truth, truthfulness, and sincerity, on instrumental, strategic, and communicative action, on the illocutionary force of utterances and the perlocutionary purposes to which they can be put, and on the emancipatory impulse at the heart of human communication. "Critical theology" will be a purified form of theology, in which the language of scripture and tradition and the articulation of experience will have had stripped away all that disguises the centrality of the Christian claim that "the truth will make you free."

Theology does not become "critical" simply by adding a social theory or adopting the methods of ideology critique. Critical theology allows the entire theological enterprise to be informed by critical theory, and it is of course the weight of the argument of this whole book that that is best done by adopting critical theory as developed by Jürgen Habermas. Clearly, other forms of critical theology could emerge through utilizing some other model of critical theory. However, the attractiveness of Habermas should by now be apparent. No other form of critical theory is so comprehensive, not even that of orthodox Marxism. In Habermas's model of critical theory, there come together epistemology, linguistics, sociology, political theory, ethics and, increasingly, aesthetics.

Critical theology, like other contemporary theological models, will emerge in the relationships between text, world, and interpreter. Each component of theological reflection will require investigation from the perspective of a critical hermeneutics and must be subjected to the canons of procedural rationality. Each must have discovered within itself its own fundamental orientation to emancipation. The ensuing theology must be at home in a critically appropriated modernity, must be an expression of the lifeworld of twentieth-century Christianity, must conform to the canons of procedural rationality, and must proclaim a message of emancipation, *within* the social, economic, political, and cultural conditions of (post)modernity. This is a tall order, but anything less will be either outdated, irrelevant, incoherent, or oppressive.

CHAPTER FOUR

THE CHURCH: COMMUNITY OF COMMUNICATIVE ACTION

Over the centuries there has been a consistent and periodically justifiable conviction among non-Catholic Christians that the Catholic tradition makes too much of the church. The historic creeds of Christianity place faith *in* the one, holy, catholic, and apostolic church well down the list of propositions to be affirmed, yet too often Catholics have seemed to put the church first. If not as important as God, the church was after all the one place where salvation could be found, the place in which faith in God through Christ could be encountered. In this seriously faulty but typically Catholic misconception, the institution was only too ready to cooperate, substituting for the Protestant misconception of reliance on the scriptural principle its own "house of authority."[1] Thus was fostered that attitude to membership of the church as the condition *sine qua non* for salvation which must be named ecclesial fundamentalism.

Catholic ecclesiolatry notwithstanding, there is one excellent reason why a Christian theology of today should begin by focusing on the reality of the church. The single greatest weakness of contemporary Christian theology from any tradition, and in particular of the spirituality and homiletics of Christianity, is its tendency to be disembodied. The supposed divorce between religion and life, the frequently heard charge of the irrelevance of religion, and the confusion surrounding the relationship of belief and conduct are all symptoms of this theological disembodiment. All three in their different ways point to the problematic character of the theory-praxis relationship in today's Christian thought.

Because authentic theology must be embodied, it is necessary to start with the church. Theology begins with the reflection of the individual-in-community upon experience in the light of the scriptures and traditions of revelation. Although raw experience, if there is such a thing, is not churchly, its appropriation by the Christian take place communally. The interpretive community that provides the individual with the hermeneutic categories to appropriate experience as matter for theological reflection is the faith-community of the church. Thus, the church is always the interpretive arena of faithful reflection on experience. Indeed, perhaps this is what the church most centrally is, when all else that seems grander is said and done.

From another angle, the church is also made up of individuals living out their lives in the world, as the latest generations in a reality that has a history made up of other individuals doing precisely the same. The church, then, is not an idea but a fact. Ecclesiology, as theological reflection on the church, has to be reflection on the fact of the praxis of the believing community, not reflection on this or that idea of the church. The validation of ecclesiology is to be found in the praxis of the believing community. Disembodied theology would find the validation of the praxis of the believing community in the idea of the church.[2]

In this chapter we shall be seeking an embodied theology of the church, and looking for the assistance that this task can receive from the critical theory of Jürgen Habermas. The focus of discussion will be partly on the work of Habermas on the characteristics of a community whose action is "oriented towards understanding." We shall also be taking a close look at the ecclesiology of the Second Vatican Council (1962–65), and I will suggest that the theological breakthrough represented there was an initial step along a path whose later stages seem indicated by the ideas of Habermas. In the final section of the chapter I shall pay attention to some current ecclesial thought and practice that qualify as hopeful signs of embodied ecclesiology in the Catholic tradition.

ACTION THEORY AND ECCLESIOLOGY

In chapter 2 we first encountered the distinction Habermas makes between action oriented toward success and action oriented toward understanding. We saw that the former can be subdivided into instrumental and strategic action, and that the latter is what Habermas believes to be distinctively human action. Action oriented toward understanding, or communicative action, is the only form of action in which two or more human beings meet as equal partners in open dialogue oriented toward consensus. Communicative action is the only action consistent with the implicit commitment to emancipation present in every speech-act.

Habermas's theory of action is worked out in a critical dialogue with that of Max Weber.[3] His overall problem with Weber's theory is that his concept of social action is restricted to "purposive-rational action," that is, to action with a means-ends orientation rather than one of consensus. Habermas's own model modifies Weber's not only to distinguish between the orientations of action to success or understanding, but also to differentiate between a nonsocial and a social action *situation*. Instrumental action is nonsocial success-oriented action, while strategic action is social action oriented to success. There is no action appropriately categorized as nonsocial action oriented toward understanding, since such action requires at least two human participants treating each other as humans. Finally, social action oriented toward understanding, that is, the type of action in which human beings treat one another as human beings, is "communicative action."

The distinction between action oriented toward success and that oriented toward understanding is not of itself adequate to the complexity of human societies. Habermas goes on to investigate more closely the character of linguistically mediated interaction, leaving behind the nonsocial realm of instrumental action. He distinguishes between four types of action, the first of which is the strategic action we have already mentioned, but then subdivides action oriented to achieving understanding into "conversation," "normatively regulated action," and "dramaturgical action."[4] Strategic action itself, we should add, is divisible into open and concealed strategic action, and the latter into conscious deception or manipulation, and unconscious deception, or "systematically distorted communication."[5]

The Christian church is a human community, or a family of communities, depending on how one views either the relations between different traditions or the dynamic of universal and local church. It should therefore be possible to relate Habermas's distinctions between "pure types of linguistically mediated interactions" to the phenomenon of the church. Because we seek an embodied theology, we shall need, like Habermas, to attend to concreteness. I shall therefore restrict myself to examining the Catholic tradition and shall try as far as possible to provide actual historical examples of the pure types.

Strategic action is a category about which it ought to be relatively easy to lay down some guidelines. For example, *any* human community that tries to respect the humanity of its members, and the church at least claims to be prominent among this group, will reject all forms of manipulation and strive to purify its own praxis to root out systematically distorted communication. Of course, rejecting conscious manipulation is far easier than uprooting systematically distorted communication, precisely because the latter is unconscious. The process of becoming conscious of that which is unconsciously present is what we have referred to already as the exercise of critical reflection.

A critical theory of society, with its orientation to the use of critical reflection in the service of emancipation, is clearly an option for a society bent on eradicating its own systematically distorted communication. Like any therapeutic mechanism, however, its efficacy depends on a willingness on the part of the subject to recognize in at least some initial way the need for healing. Here we encounter one of the problematic ways in which the church is *not* like other apparently similar human groupings. Because the church sees itself as divinely mandated to be the community of faith that proclaims the gospel, and believes itself to be imbued with the spirit, there is a resistance to the recognition of the failings of merely natural human societies. The church might easily be able to admit the occasional presence in its history of deliberate distortions and manipulations, since its members are only human. Thus it might recognize excesses in the conduct of crusades, purges, or inquisitions. But it would be quite another matter to recognize that it could be victimized by a variety of unconscious deception, since that weakness would go to the roots of the whole society, rather than be placed on the shoulders of sinful individuals.

We might look for the evidence of systematically distorted communication at any of the many levels of complexity at which the church exists. It could conceivably be found in the ways in which fear or hatred or misinformation might lead one member of the church to browbeat another on a matter of church practice, or in the discussion of important moral issues. It might also be present in the unconscious clericalism that can operate at the parochial or diocesan level. It could equally well emerge in the teaching of the magisterium. No one of these is immune from unconsciously concealed deception, because none of them, not even the last, is entirely immune from the human condition. At this last and highest level, of course, problems created by the theology of authority come into play. The relation between authoritative teaching and the infallible magisterium has been a subject of much debate, but no one has yet suggested that the pastor's bulletin or the way in which the pastor conducts parish council meetings is exempt from the possibility of error!

The best examples of systematically distorted communication are those found at every level of ecclesial complexity, and I can think of none better than the present sexism of the church. It is painfully clear to those with any kind of critical-historical perspective that the Catholic church at the present day is a thoroughly sexist institution. It is equally clear that at the most complex levels of the church, in its official teaching, this sexism is not motivated so much by a conscious determination to suppress the rights of women, but is more a product of the inability of church leaders to think in a seriously critical fashion about the roots of the position of women in culture and society. Exactly why church leaders are so ideologically hidebound is a complex question that would require a book in itself. That they are so is apparent to almost all but themselves.

The charge of sexism would of course be denied by church leaders, and with it the accusation that they are unconsciously victimized by the historical and social forces that have shaped the ideology of the powerful in the church. Following upon Habermas's schema, however, they would seem to me to have to admit that if they are not guilty of concealed strategic action, then the whole of their teaching, good and not so good, falls into the category of open strategic action. Although such strategy is oriented toward success, its openness has to mean that it is not necessarily a transgression of human freedom. Open strategic action, for example, occurs whenever a recognizable group agrees on a strategy for common action. To call it strategic action means only that it possesses an objective other than that of truth, rightness, or truthfulness, namely, that of "effectiveness." What they cannot argue and would not want to say is that church teaching is an example of action oriented toward understanding, for if they did this, then they would have to recognize the logic of communicative action theory. They would have to give all members of the church an equal role in the discourse, would have to be open to the "discursive redemption of validity claims," and would have to accept the permanently open-ended status of the struggle for consensus, this side of the ideal-speech situation to be found in the reign of God. None of this is easy if some traditional understanding of authority is to be retained.

To exemplify open strategic action, I would like to consider the phenomenon of evangelization. The idea of "spreading the Good News" is fundamental to, though variously understood by, the whole range of Christian traditions. Moreover, in different ways it is considered to be the responsibility of all members of the church, whether in direct preaching or by means of the more universal and arguably more effective force of example. Evangelization is an act of the whole church, agreed upon by the whole to be important to the whole. It is taken to be important because it is believed to be the church's mission, given it by God in Christ, and powered by the life of the Spirit of God at work in the whole community. Without the emphasis on evangelization, the church would not be faithful to its mission, and thus would not be the church. Clearly, therefore, evangelization is a paradigmatic example of "action oriented toward success," if being the church God intended is taken to be being successful. But if success is measured by conformity to the divine intent, then being clear about what God's mission for the church is will be a necessary step in being able to distinguish between appropriate and inappropriate strategic action.

In order to clarify what I am saying here, we need to return to Habermas's distinctions between strategic action and the three types of action oriented toward understanding, namely, conversation, normatively regulated action, and dramaturgical action. These three forms of communicative action encompass the range of linguistically mediated interactions of the group by which it seeks an understanding of the truth of its representations of states of affairs, the rightness of the norms which govern interpersonal relations, and the truthfulness of the expressions by which it represents itself. Under the constraints of the logic of the ideal speech situation, this continuing process must be free and equal, at work with a consensus model of truth, and constantly open to revising its ever-provisional conclusions. Appropriate strategic action oriented to success and claiming effectiveness must measure its success in terms of the efficacy of the actions as reflective of a body oriented to truth, truthfulness, and rightness. The question of appropriateness becomes one of determining what strategic action respects the character of a community oriented to understanding.

These reflections have led us to the point where we can suggest a way to distinguish between open and unconsciously deceptive strategic action. We have seen that Habermas argues that the action distinctive to human intercommunication is a communicative praxis that respects the freedom and equality of all participants in a consensus-driven dialogue. We have also seen that some strategic action is appropriate, if it is based on the consensus of the whole body about the appropriate action of the whole to safeguard its self-understanding. Thus evangelization is appropriate strategic action for the church, since the possession of the "Good News" leads to a desire to share it with others. Most important, we have seen that strategic action must respect the communicative character of the human group or society. Thus, concealed strategic action, whether conscious or unconscious, is driven by a vision of success that refuses to accept the constraints of discourse. Something intervenes to somehow instrumentalize what should be an open process of communication directed toward understanding.

If we accept that human community is truly about communicative praxis, and that strategic action must respect that character if it is to be the strategic action of the whole community, then the next issue we must consider is whether and in what sense the church can be said to be such a human community. In confronting the issue of whether the church can and should understand itself as a community of communicative praxis, we have to take a look at the ecclesiology found in the documents of the

Second Vatican Council, and in particular at the emergence of new directions in that vision of the church, rather than at those reiterations of traditional formulae that inevitably found their way into what were after all compromise documents. As George Lindbeck wrote shortly after the Council ended, "The new, we have noted, is mixed with the old, but it is the new which is likely to shape the future."[6]

THE ECCLESIOLOGY OF VATICAN II

There is no question that the principal focus of the Second Vatican Council was on the church.[7] Two of its three principal documents (the third was on divine revelation) dealt explicitly with ecclesiological issues. These two, *The Dogmatic Constitution on the Church (Lumen Gentium)* and *The Pastoral Constitution on the Church in the Modern World (Gaudium et Spes)*, were also the longest documents and occasioned the most lengthy debate in Council sessions. The final texts of both are faithful to the past but break much new ground.

The bishops inherited a theology of the church and attempted to bring it up to date, to revise its expression in order to make it more accessible to twentieth-century minds, and also to amplify and correct some problematic elements. In particular, they wrote against the background of what had been said ninety years before at the First Vatican Council, and it is quite justifiable to see Vatican II as consciously completing the work of that unfinished body. Vatican I's preliminary *schema* for a document on the church that was never completed oversimplified the problems of historical reconstruction and overemphasized the institutional element in the church:

We teach and declare: The Church has all the marks of a true Society. Christ did not leave this society undefined and without a set form. Rather, he himself gave it its existence, and his will determined the form of its existence, and gave it its constitution. The Church is not part nor member of any other society and is not mingled in any other way with any other society. It is so perfect in itself that it is distinct from all human societies and stands far above them.[8]

A further passage from the *schema* illustrates just how much the church's earlier thought was out of temper with the times in which Vatican II occurred:

But the Church of Christ is not a community of equals in which all the faithful have the same rights. It is a society of unequals, not only because among the faithful some are clerics and some are laymen, but particularly because there is in the Church the power from God whereby to some it is given to sanctify, teach, and govern, and to others not.[9]

It is my belief that the language of critical theory can be used to shed some light on the ecclesiological shift that Vatican II represented. The legacy of history to the Council fathers in 1962 was of an understanding of the church as essentially an institution charged with a strategic mission. As a "perfect society" it of course already possessed the truth, and its mission to express that truth (which it already possessed in its fullness) made it a community oriented to success. The church of recent centuries, we could say with Habermas, was engaged in *strategic* rather than *communicative* praxis. A militant body by its own admission, it existed to ensure the salvation of its members, and to draw as many nonmembers as possible into the fold. Anyone with faith might join in by becoming a member of the community; those who would not do so could not share the success. The suggestion that anyone outside the community might have something to contribute to the education and even correction of the community was repudiated as rapidly as the thought that the church itself could ever need to undergo radical internal change was suppressed.

The vision of the church as a strategic institution charged with the implementation of a divine plan that did not require the communicative praxis of the whole community was not dead by 1962. This is very evident in the draft schema of the document on the church drawn up for the bishops by the heavily bureaucratic Vatican organization originally assigned the task.[10] The chapter headings of that *schema* are illuminating, particularly when juxtaposed with the chapter headings of the final text of the documents, both for an understanding of the prevailing mentality of the curial bureaucracy and the Council fathers, and for the underlying theological vision.

SCHEMA	DOCUMENT
1. The nature of the church militant.	1. The mystery of the church.
2. The members of the church and the necessity of the church for salvation.	2. On the people of God.
3. The episcopate as the highest grade of the sacrament of orders: the priesthood.	3. On the hierarchical structure of the church, in particular on the episcopate.
4. Residential bishops.	4. The laity.
5. The states of evangelical perfection.	5. The universal call to holiness in the church.

6. The laity.

7. The teaching office of the church

8. Authority and obedience in the church.

9. Relationships between church and state and religious tolerance.

10. The necessity of proclaiming the gospel to all peoples.

11. Ecumenism.

6. Religious.

7. The eschatological nature of the pilgrim church.

8. The Blessed Virgin.

A number of the discrepancies between the two sets of chapter headings are accidental. For example, the presence in the document of chapter 8 on the Blessed Virgin represents the inclusion of a subject some Council bishops had believed ought to have a chapter of its own, and which had appeared in an appendix to the *schema* in any case. Similarly, the deletion of the *schema*'s chapter 11 was in order to devote an entire document to that subject, and to a degree the same can be said of chapters 9 and 10. These rearrangements reflect the recognition that the *schema* itself was more of a list of important topics than any framework that possessed its own principles of construction.

Other changes are however quite significant, both variations in the order of chapters and the adoption of different words to describe the same reality. In the first category, one can see in the document less of the pyramidal model present in the *schema*. After a general chapter in both on the nature of the church, the document chooses the term "people of God," of great significance about which we shall have more to say later, but which

115

certainly emphasizes the fundamental equality before God of all believers. Then, the laity precedes and the religious follows a chapter on the "universal call to holiness," instead of the *schema*'s doggedly hierarchical ordering of bishops, then priests, then religious men and women, then laypeople. However, it is in the changes and omissions in language that the greatest contrasts are revealed. The curial determination to protect their own status as members of the episcopacy by offering the backhanded compliment of a chapter on "residential bishops," as if bishops who lived in their dioceses were a subspecies of bishop rather than essentially what a bishop is, was denied, and the chapter abandoned. The term "states of evangelical perfection" was removed in order to avoid the suggestion that nonreligious were somehow in an imperfect state of life. The use of the idea of the "church militant" was taken out, and the notion of "mystery" replaced it. Chapters on the magisterium and on authority and obedience were removed. In their place appeared the key chapter on the church as a "pilgrim" people, progressing across the face of history *toward* the fullness of truth. All in all, the document presented a more biblical and a more humble profile than had the *schema*.

It is obviously not possible to base wide-ranging claims for a new ecclesial vision on a comparison of chapter headings. Although I cannot leave such a confident claim about the self-understanding of the church of Vatican II as a mere assertion, there is no space to present a comprehensive justification of that claim.[11] What I propose instead is to comment briefly on a few aspects of the ecclesiology of Vatican II, namely: the image of "People of God"; the notion of a pilgrim church; the question of the necessity of the church for salvation; and the relationship of the church and the "secular" world. Moreover, I am aware that my selection of themes could be paralleled by a selection that would produce a quite different, more traditional ecclesiology. Such is the peril of reading consensus documents. In defense of my reading, I want to maintain, along with George Lindbeck, that the significance of the Council is largely to be found in its new emphases, not in its reiteration of the convictions of the past. Although no one can plausibly deny, for example, that the church is and always will be an institution with the necessary visible structures of an institution, the Council clearly moved away from that excessive attention to the institutional and the visible that had marked the ecclesiology of the preceding few centuries.

In making the following brief comments on the ecclesiology of Vatican II, I am of course aware that in the twenty years and more that have intervened since the documents were published and the Council ended, there have been other developments. On the one hand, theologians (like Johann Baptist Metz and Leonardo Boff) have sought to expand upon the bare bones of the documents, and in some places, notably in Latin America, church structures have come to reflect at least some of what the Council fathers apparently had in mind. On the other hand, voices in Vatican curial departments and some of the more conservative episcopal conferences have sought in recent years to tone down some of the key ideas of *Lumen Gentium* and *Gaudium et Spes*.[12] The ostensible explanation for curial intervention is the wish to counter a one-sided reading of the Vatican documents, particularly the interpretation of the notion of People of God as licensing a form of "people's church" to run alongside or even instead of the traditional institutional church. Although this may have occurred here and there, and was *not* what the Council meant by "people of God," the reaction has been an overreaction. It is one example, to use the words of Joseph Komonchak, of "the not uncommon pattern of taking a criticized notion in the worst possible sense while counterposing to this deformation a laboratory-pure sense of the notion one prefers."[13]

Although it is necessary to avoid distortions of the Council documents, it is equally important to realize that what they say, they say, and that nothing of comparable theological authority on the nature of the church has since been written. *Lumen Gentium* is built around the notion of the People of God, and while this deeply scriptural image is of course not intended to obliterate the reality of the church as an institution, it is certainly the intention of the Council to place *all* other images and metaphors for the church in the context of the ruling image of People of God, including that of the Mystical Body beloved of early twentieth-century Catholic theology.

The first chapter of *Lumen Gentium* sets the emergence of the church in the context of the whole economy of salvation, and recognizes the fruitfulness of the many scriptural images and metaphors for the church, both from the Hebrew Bible and the New Testament. It is also modest about the church; it is Christ, not the church, who is the "light to the nations." Chapter 2 is entirely devoted to the image of the People of God, the reality of which is expressive of God's will not to make people "holy and save them merely as individuals," but to bring them together "as one people" (par. 9). Moreover, this image governs the other sections of the documents. Thus, the establishment of ministries in the church is "for the nurturing and constant growth of the People of God" (par. 18). Chapter 7 makes clear that this people is a "pilgrim" people, which "will attain its full perfection only in the glory of heaven" (par. 48).

There is no better brief study of the theological significance of Vatican II than that by the Lutheran theologian George Lindbeck, mentioned above. Lindbeck identifies four theological implications of the emphasis on the church as the pilgrim People of God: an end to a clerical model of the church; a vision of the church as "an historically and sociologically concrete community subject in one dimension of its being to the same laws of change as any other society";[14] a recognition that the church is constantly in need of renewal and "semper reformanda"; and "the people of God is viewed much more than formerly as only one of the instruments of God's saving activity."[15] This last implication itself involves, says Lindbeck, the enunciation of four principles that themselves represent the abandonment of four traditional monopolistic claims: "neither the church nor 'religiousness' itself is the sole avenue to God"; "Christianity has no monopoly on true religiousness"; "the church disclaims a monopoly on Christianity, even of truly ecclesial Christianity"; and finally that there should be no clerical monopoly on the gifts of the Spirit.[16]

Lindbeck's excellent summary touches on all four of the points that I proposed to comment on myself. The idea of the People of God is thoroughly biblical and profoundly historical. It is communitarian rather than institutional, though clearly it does not exclude a necessary institutional element, at least in the treatment the Council gives it. The historical dimension leads the bishops to express the reality of the church eschatologically, as foreshadowing a perfection reserved for its fullness to a realm beyond history, though there is no doubt that this is accompanied by a typically Catholic wish to seek a partial realization of the kingdom in structures of social justice. Although the church itself as the sacrament of the grace of Christ is necessary to the salvation of the world, say the bishops in paragraph 14 of *Lumen Gentium*, the necessity of membership in the church for salvation is not affirmed, since the grace of Christ is somehow universally available. Finally, the mission of the church to the world is not a mission of a perfect church to a sinful world, but of a pilgrim church whose task is to be a fuller sacrament of the grace of Christ to a world in which that grace is already present. Although the church has its own perspective, its own wisdom, and its own practical suggestions to offer to a world in need, the vision of the Council is of a church that sees itself as a partner with the world beyond the church in spreading love and justice, a partner moreover that is open to learning from extra-ecclesial wisdom.[17]

In summary, it seems fair to say that the church of the documents of Vatican II is eschatological, ecumenical, and open to the world. It is a pilgrim church, moving uncertainly though in hope across the face of history, seeking to discern the will of God in the signs of the times, ready to learn from the world, and recognizing the essential solidarity of the ecclesial community not only with all other Christian bodies but also with all sincere seekers after truth. No longer is the church seen as the community of the elect, working to increase its numbers and expand its boundaries, but now as the community charged with a mission to serve the world by placing its resources at the service of all forms of human emancipation. The church's relation to the fullness of truth is no longer a powerful grasp upon an inheritance from the past, but more a hope in the gift of the future.

THE COMMUNICATIVE PRAXIS
OF THE PEOPLE OF GOD

It remains to ask whether all of this is sufficient to establish the claim that the church of Vatican II sees itself as a community oriented toward understanding. Certainly as far as the documents are concerned, the case is not difficult to make. That the church believes itself to be the home of truth is not in itself a barrier, provided that it recognizes (a) that it does not yet possess or understand that truth fully, and (b) that others may also possess the truth, even a truth that the church itself has not yet appropriated. Both are clearly present in *Lumen Gentium* and *Gaudium et Spes*. On the other hand, the actual practice of the church in the years since the documents appeared has not always or even frequently reflected the vision of Vatican II. A comparison of the documents of the Council with subsequent church practice has to raise the question of the sincerity of church leadership.

The Second Vatican Council presented a clear picture of the church. The communicative praxis at least of Catholic bishops produced reasonable consensus on a vision of ecclesial life. Finding the reality of that church, if it indeed exists, will mean looking for an ecclesial community that operates according to the principles of communicative action. Creating that church, where it does not yet exist, will mean engaging in open strategic action that does not distort the essentially communicative character of the community, but that engages the already existent church in a discourse oriented to truth, rightness, and sincerity. In both cases, curiously enough, this communicative praxis will have to come into conflict with that imperfect praxis that created the Council documents in the first place.

The Council was rightly concerned to overcome the clericalism of the church, but it was itself an exercise in clericalism. Obviously, communicative praxis can occur within even quite small groups, where the members of the group seek consensus on what concerns them and them alone. But just as the Council in its notion of People of God opened itself to engaging in public dialogue with the secular world as an equal partner, so the same notion implied, as their practice denied, the necessary involvement of all the members of the People of God as full and equal partners in the continuing communicative praxis that is the internal life of the church. This has profound implications for both the theological development and the ethical praxis of the church. It also challenges long-held traditional beliefs about the role of authority in the church. We can clarify some of these issues by investigating three ecclesial directions: the current phenomenon of "base Christian communities," the "emergent church" of Johann Baptist Metz, and feminism's "women-church."

ECCLESIAL COMMUNITIES

Today's wisdom perhaps, and today's consciousness certainly, adheres to a belief in "equal rights."[18] But whatever else the bishops of the Second Vatican Council intended, it was not the abolition of traditional leadership structures. Chapter 3 of *Lumen Gentium* certainly stresses the element of service in ministry, but it is entitled "On the Hierarchical Structure of the Church and in Particular on the Episcopate." Because they are pastors and the Pope is the Supreme Pastor, the bishops found themselves unable or unwilling to avoid extending the metaphor to the "flock" and the "sheep." And their service is cast in comprehensively traditional terminology:

> Bishops, therefore, with their helpers, the priests and deacons, have taken up the service of the community, presiding in place of God over the flock, whose shepherds they are, as teachers for doctrine, priests for sacred worship, and ministers for governing.[19]

If we remain at the level of the documents, we are faced with a simple impasse. The ecclesiology of the People of God and the ecclesiology of the Institution are not easily assimilated to one another.[20]

To move forward from this point it will be necessary to try a more inductive approach. Instead of abiding by the documents, a look at the changes that have actually occurred in the church in some parts of the world will furnish us with possible examples of the ecclesial structure that might be a logical consequence of the teaching of *Lumen Gentium*. We could, for example, examine the way in which the United States Catholic bishops have modified the method of producing teaching documents to provide for much greater involvement of the whole Catholic community in the discernment process.[21] As significant a development as that is, however, there are other more radical steps that are more instructive at the present time. In looking at some of these, it would be good to keep two questions in mind. What notion of church underlies this particular ecclesial venture? And what is the concept of leadership and authority with which it works?

a. *Base Christian Communities*

The phenomenon of base Christian communities has probably received more attention than any other recent development in the Catholic tradition.[22] Not all of this publicity, by any means, has been positive. As one of the fundamental building blocks of the theology of liberation, base Christian communities have been targets of ill-considered attacks based on misconceptions or malice, and the subject of unjustifiably hyperbolic praise. Truly, though, whatever one's estimate of liberation theology, it is more a product of base Christian communities than are the communities an offshoot of the theology. Theology, as

Gustavo Gutiérrez never tires of saying, "comes after." It might be helpful, therefore, to look at the phenomenon of base communities aside from consideration of the theology for which it has been so responsible.

Grassroots ecclesial communities emerged in Latin America in the 1950s and 60s for a variety of reasons: shortage of priests; the consequent large numbers and huge geographical area of "parishes"; the development of primary groups in church-sponsored educational developments, particularly radio schools; response to unsystematic but often overwhelming oppression, frequently of a local rather than national character. These reasons do not all have a directly religious character. In fact, the majority are primarily social, though given the character of the societies in which they emerged, the stimulus for their development was most often from some sector of the church. From the beginning, then, the socioeconomic and even political interests of the people were an important dimension of grassroots activism. In fact, in the beginning, it was social and economic concern that was crucial.

The catalyst that led to the more systematic development of base Christian communities was the Latin American Bishops' Conference held at Medellin in 1968.[23] It is right to see this conference, at least in intention, as the attempt of the bishops present to relate the teaching of Vatican II, which had ended only three years earlier, to the specific situation of the Latin American church. There are different assessments of the wisdom of the bishops' uncompromising stance in favor of the poor, for justice, for an end to violence and structures of violence, and against the capitalist international economic system. No one would deny, I believe, that Medellin was remarkable for the way in which these particular documents were translated into structural reforms in the life of the Latin American church.

Two concerns above all explain the emergence of base Christian communities in such numbers in the years following the conference. The first was the bishops' determination that the whole church would confront the problem of the poverty of the Latin American people. They carefully distinguished between three kinds of poverty: abject penury, "spiritual poverty," and "poverty for the sake of the gospel."[24] The first of these they soundly and roundly denounced as opposed to the spirit of the gospel, and as something the church should mobilize all its forces to help overcome. The second they praised as the traditional Christian virtue of detachment from material things, but hinted that that was no reason to promote the virtue of being poor in the first sense, and no excuse for the self-satisfaction of the wealthy. Finally, "evangelical poverty" was explained as demanded of the institutional church, particularly a church that exists in the midst of enormous poverty, and they unequivocally committed the personnel of the church to actual, practical identification with the poor, including living in their midst and living poorly.

Though, of course, not all bishops, priests, and religious heeded this call, it is fair to say that there was a reasonable measure of success in getting the institutional church down off the mountain of affluence, in some countries more than in others. The points of this move significant for the development of base Christian communities were two. In the first place, the church's new active identification with the poor and their problems gave dignity and centrality to the poor in the life of the church. Second, the closeness of contact between laity and clergy led the latter to an increasing clarity about the limitedness of their own vision and the way in which they could and should learn from the perspective and the wisdom of the poor.

The second contribution that Medellin made to the

development of base Christian communities is to be found in the document on justice. The bishops pointed out that one of the chief causes of the culture of poverty and the cycle of oppression was the absence in most Latin American societies of opportunities for the poor to have some role in shaping their own circumstances. The poor everywhere are objects, that is, victims, of history, rather than subjects, making their own history. Less oppressive societies provide genuine opportunities for involvement through one or another form of "mediating structure." The individual who joins a mediating structure thus takes at least some responsibility for some dimension of his or her world. Through the association, individuals can act collectively and have a greater impact.

A mediating structure is any organization larger than the individual and smaller than the state. The family, for example, is a social structure that at its best provides its members with an initial opportunity to take responsibility and act in collaboration with others with similar interests. Student associations, labor unions, political parties, and professional organizations are all forms of mediating structures. Unlike the family, however, most such structures are suspect where not banned in more oppressive societies, and in 1968 the political profile of Latin America was worse even than it is today.

Medellin promoted the formation of any and every kind of mediating structure, and promised the support of the church for all initiatives to raise the poor from objects to subjects of their history. As its own particular contribution, it encouraged the growth of grassroots Christian groups, or base Christian communities. Although it is very difficult to give any precise idea of the numbers of such communities at the present time, and although they are more prominent in some countries than in others, best estimates suggest a figure of about 85,000 communities for the church in Brazil, where it is universally agreed that they are most firmly established, and which is in any case by far the largest Latin American country.[25] Not surprisingly, unless one is under the erroneous impression that the base communities are a breakaway or alternative structure, they seem to flourish best where they have a sympathetic or protective institutional church. The one exception to this, which will require a comment below, is in Nicaragua.

A base Christian community is not a very sophisticated phenomenon.[26] Most typically, it consists of a small group of poor and poorly educated people from the same small rural village or the same part of some large urban shantytown. Their leader emerges from among them, and in some places is known as a "delegate of the word." Most often the delegate has received some minimal training, at least in scripture studies. This title of delegate of the word neatly shows the responsibility of leadership in the base communities, namely, to lead the community in communal reflection on a passage of the scripture oriented to hearing its practical message for their lives in their particular community. The methodology clearly follows a simple "see, judge, act" schema. What seems to make the difference is the context of poverty and oppression in which the base communities largely exist, which leads naturally to an emphasis on the gospel as liberating, or even as authenticating a liberating social praxis.

Base Christian communities are obviously organized on a dialogical and consensual model with which Jürgen Habermas would be quite familiar. Their leaders may bring a certain specialized knowledge or wisdom to the clarification of the scripture on which they are to reflect, but have no authority in community discernment and decision making. The communities attempt to understand the message of the scripture and its relation to their life situation (theoretical reason, the validity claim to truth). They are oriented toward the formulation of practical proposals for action (practical reason, the validity claim to rightness). Their communal, egalitarian, and open structure clearly conforms to their vision of a world beyond oppression (sincerity, the validity claim to truthfulness). Finally, the strategic actions emerging from their consensus-oriented deliberations are intended to be expressions of the commitment to social, economic, and political liberation that the liberating power of the gospel has inspired in them.

The question remains of how such base communities view the universal church, and the consequences for the whole church of their acceptance as a legitimate development. In fact, the present Pope has expressed considerable appreciation for the phenomenon of base communities, though more for their attention to the poor and to injustice outside the church, than for their model of ecclesiality. Moreover, he has been at equally great pains to insist that their tendency to use language of a "people's church" or "church of the poor," as if this were some rival to the traditional church, or even a replacement for it, is quite out of place. Although at its best, as we have seen, the base community is not at odds with the hierarchy and the traditional parochial structure, it is difficult to see how the ecclesiality of the base community cannot have serious theological repercussions for the notion of ministry.

Leonardo Boff in his *Ecclesiogenesis: The Base Communities Reinvent the Church* is quite clear about the momentous character of the emergence of base communities:

> We are not dealing with the expansion of an existing ecclesiastical system, rotating on a sacramental, clerical axis, but with the emergence of another form of being church, rotating on the axis of the word and the laity. We may well

anticipate that, from this movement, of which the universal church is becoming aware, a new type of institutional presence of Christianity in the world may now come into being.[27]

However, Boff believes in the coexistence of this church with the institutional church, seeing such coexistence as the latest form of the differentiation of institutional and charismatic elements found in some more traditional theological perspectives. At the same time it is evident that he believes that the base community will lead the institution to a recovery of its authenticity:

> The basic [sic] community constitutes . . . a bountiful wellspring of renewal for the tissues of the body ecclesial, and a call and a demand for the evangelical authenticity of ecclesial institutions, so that they may come more closely to approximate the utopian community ideal.[28]

Boff's principal justification for his view of base communities rests on a realism about the tension in human groups between the "organizational impersonal" and "intimate personal." The emphasis on community helps preserve the instrumental character of structures and promote "the humanization of the human being." Community is easier in small groups, says Boff, but even there it is not achieved by the execution of common tasks:

> What constitutes a human group as a community is the effort to create and maintain community involvement as an ideal, as a spirit ever to be re-created and renewed by overcoming routine and refusing to yield to the spirit of institutionalization and "rut."[29]

The problem with which all this leaves us is the recurring question about leadership, now expressible perhaps with more clarity: What is the relationship between ministry in the community and leadership of the society?

b. Metz's "Emergent Church"

In a book whose very existence is a testimony to the changed role of First and Third World churches, the German political theologian Johann Baptist Metz discusses how basic community emerges in the church.[30] Although Metz's focus is on the First World church of Europe, his inspiration comes largely from the lessons he believes the Third World church is now teaching its traditional mentor.[31]

The ground for Metz's proposals is that of the bourgeois church of the Western world, a very different proposition from the church of the poor and oppressed in Latin America. The bourgeois church has left behind the old paternalistic church, but Christianity has come very close in the Western world to being transformed into bourgeois religion, that is, into a tame creation of bourgeois society, a "services church which no longer offers people real consolation, and which for that very reason we have to fight with every means in our power."[32] Moreover, the bourgeois services church is not a mature church, because it is not one that recognizes that the responsibility for the condition of the church lies with the people. It continues to demonstrate, says Metz, that it has assimilated the old paternalistic church by the way in which it believes that change requires change in the leaders. On the contrary, no true revolution comes from above. What is needed, he believes, is a "post-bourgeois initiative-taking church," which neither rejects the tradition and the leaders of the church, nor wastes its time waiting for change to come from above.

Axiomatic in Metz's vision of the world, as in the social theory of Habermas, is that we are approaching the end of the bourgeois society. We are facing a new barbarism in which the economic and political forces that have compelled the increasing isolation of the bourgeois, the increasing fragmentation of society, and the increasing instrumentalization of the individual to larger and more "scientific" forces could finally triumph. To prevent this, the human race must find grounds for a new solidarity in which these forces can effectively be resisted.[33] Under the inspiration of the example of base communities in Latin America, the churches of the bourgeois world can be effective in this struggle for humanity.

Metz's proposal sees a convergence between the institutional universal church and the base community church. Speaking from his own German vantage point, he recognizes that the "power of the conservative imagination" at work among the German bishops enables them to see the lack of values in bourgeois society. Almost a decade after the publication of his work, the German bishops are if anything more conservative, but there are more hopeful signs now than then of an awakening in the Vatican to the inappropriateness of conservative political solutions and the helplessness of liberal panaceas. Thus what Metz hoped for on the part of the bishops, a "critique of society," has in fact begun to emerge in the writings of the present Pope. So far in Europe and North America there have been fewer signs of the formation of a base community church.

Metz's model, more directly under the influence of the critical theory of his native Germany than the Latin American prototype, is equally wedded to a dialogical, consensual form of church community. Indeed, his picture of the bourgeois services church corresponds quite clearly to the societal distortion of ecclesiality that Boff so roundly condemns. In his insistence that revolution never comes from above, Metz may not be giving sufficient credit to Medellin, although even that was a response to grassroots movement, but in regard to the complacent, bourgeois, First World churches, he is probably correct. What Metz does not provide is any program for such change. How do conversion and maturity arise in a time of plenty and a culture of affluence? A few well-motivated cells of Christians do not a grassroots revolution make. The apocalyptic tenor of our world, which is probably what Metz would appeal to as the likely catalyst, seems to be something that the well-cushioned find it only too easy to ignore.

I would like to suggest that the catalyst may lie in a direction singularly absent from all of Metz's writings, and that is in the feminist challenge to the bourgeois church. At its best, feminist thought is a critique of patriarchal Western society located in a solidarity that knows no boundaries of race, class, or culture. It also has the remarkable capacity to get under the skin of the Western bourgeois world.[34]

c. Women-Church

Whatever else one chooses to say about it, the feminist critique of patriarchy is the most thorough challenge to apparently fundamental tenets and practices of the Catholic tradition. The radical character of the critique is only to be expected, given the totality of the suppression of women in the history of the world in general, of the Western world in particular, and in our case in the tarnished example of Catholic Christianity. An obvious defense of the church's historical weakness in this regard is that it cannot be expected to have done anything other than be a reflection of the historical and cultural currents which gave birth to it and through which it of necessity expresses itself. This defense, of course, is an inadequate fig leaf. The full measure of its responsibility for patriarchy in its own midst, and for the way in which its cultural and religious weight could only further encourage patriarchy in society as a whole, lies in the fact that the example of its founder and the genius of the gospel rests largely in demonstrating how *not* to become victim to the prejudices and presuppositions of this or any other time. The contemptuous tone of those who would criticize Jesus for allowing the "public sinner" to wash his feet, or the lust to stone the "woman taken in adultery," is countered by a Jesus who clearly treated women as equals. The Christian church has in this regard not caught up with the example of its founder.[35]

Rosemary Radford Ruether's *Women-Church* is as its title suggests concerned with the theory and practice of "alternative" feminist ecclesial communities.[36] Although it is set against the general background of Christian feminism, it has most direct relevance to the situation of feminists within the Roman Catholic church, since although almost all traditional Christian denominations are sexist to a degree, in the Catholic tradition this sexism is formalized in the teaching, structure, and practice of the church. Thus it is Roman Catholic women who feel most acutely the conflict between their religious sensibilities, their continued sense of identity as Catholic Christians, and the way in which their church at all levels fails to recognize them as full and equal members.

Ruether argues that critique and social analysis are not sufficiently nourishing for Christian feminists, and that "intentional communities of faith and worship" are needed:

> One needs communities of nurture to guide one through death to the old symbolic order of patriarchy to rebirth into a new community of being and living. One needs not only to engage in rational theoretical discourse about this journey; one also needs deep symbols and symbolic actions to guide and interpret the actual experience of the journey from sexism to liberated humanity.[37]

It is just such reasoning that leads Habermas to single out feminism from other contemporary protest movements, for its emancipatory potential as opposed to the others' mere potential for "resistance and withdrawal."[38] The first step in creating these communities, says Ruether, is one of gathering women together "to articulate their own experience and communicate it with each other." This obviously requires an at least temporary separation from men, even from men who feel and to a degree are sympathetic, since "women need separate spaces and all-female gatherings to form the critical culture that can give them an autonomous ground from which to critique patriarchy."[39] But this is not an "ideology of separation" and the ultimate objective of "women-church" is to become "church."

The ecclesiology of women-church, given that women-church is the "exodus from patriarchy," requires "the dismantling of clericalism," since clericalism is "the separation of ministry from mutual interaction with community and its transformation into hierarchically ordered castes of clergy and laity."[40] Clericalism is "the expropriation of ministry, sacramental life, and theological education from the people," and not only women-church but also all base Christian communities "are engaged in a revolutionary act of reappropriating to the people what has been falsely expropriated from us":

We are reclaiming sacramental life as the symbol of our own entry into and mutual empowerment within the redemptive life, the authentic human life or original blessing upon which we stand naturally when freed from alienating powers. Theological education and teaching are our own reflections on the meaning of reclaiming our authentic life from distortion. Ministry is the active praxis of our authentic life and the building of alternative bases of expression from which to challenge the systems of evil.[41]

Surprisingly, enough, Ruether is not an advocate for dismantling the institutional church. Her vision of ecclesial community is one of dialogue, equality, consensus, ministry to one another, and sacramental life. It is one not of the absence of leadership, but of the exercise of leadership without power. This does not mean the eradication of the institution, rather the recognition that it is not "the cause of grace and the means of dispensing the Spirit," but "the occasion and context where these may take place. . . . The church has created a false faith in the spiritual efficacy of material acts," and "claims to control the mediation of the Spirit."[42] What needs to be rejected is not institutionalization, since the community would be fooling itself if it thought it could live without historical structures. On the contrary, "What must be rejected is . . . the myth that some particular form of historical institution is the only legitimate one and has been dominically and/or apostolically founded. The church, in all its historical expressions, must accept its historical relativity."[43]

Ruether's argument for an institutional church that sees itself as the occasion and backdrop of spirit-filled community, rather than that spirit-filled community itself, seems to me not to be so dramatically radical as it may at first sight appear. It depends upon making the historical case that, contrary to traditional church teaching, Jesus did not intend the foundation of a church distinct from the Jewish tradition, and that he certainly did not envisage any of the particular details of the structure of any of the Christian churches. Given that there is no canonically sanctified church structure, Ruether's view also requires the somewhat more difficult step of justifying the vision of community implied in women-church as a legitimate development of tradition. Of course, an impasse with officialdom would rapidly be reached when the evidently patriarchal tradition was subjected to a feminist critique.

There is little doubt that Habermas would recognize his consensus community in the vision of women-church articulated in Ruether's work. Its open dialogical structure, its affirmation of the radical equality of all its participants, the applying of ideology critique and historical methodology to the creation of a theory of modernity that is oriented to emancipation, all conform to the model of communicative action. Ruether's critique of clericalism and the patriarchy of the institution could be repeated in the language of "systematically distorted communication" and "action oriented toward success." Moreover, there may even be something instructive for the Habermasian position in women-church, articulating as it does a sensitivity to issues of women's oppression that Habermas's social analysis is intended to incorporate though is sometimes not adequate to express.[44] On the other hand, Habermas may have something to offer women-church, namely, the theoretical encouragement to remain open to conversation with groups that do not share its vision, since this universality is the only attitude consistent with communicative action.

To summarize the argument of this chapter, I began by describing the communicative action community in Habermas's vision as the community specific to human interrelations. Although strategic action has its place as the action *of* human beings, it is inappropriate as action *upon* human beings. I then moved on to suggest that the ecclesiology of People of God enunciated by the bishops of Vatican II implied a shift away from a success-driven "society" toward a "community" motivated by truth, truthfulness, and sincerity. Although the institution as a whole and the teaching authority of the church in particular have not yet been able to recognize the full implications of this ecclesiology, and some of those who have have tried to turn back the clock, there are "signs of hope." There are movements within the church which have acted upon the ecclesiology of People of God, even if this is not in all cases the way in which they would describe themselves. These newly developing forms of ecclesia all see a place for the institution, though admittedly the institution that women-church would recognize would be quite, quite different. Nevertheless, although they may seem to be fringe groups, and may even not be recognized by the institution as authentic expressions of Catholic Christianity, to my mind they remain within the pale, because they seek nothing more than open, understanding-oriented dialogue with all those who will accept the conditions for communicative action. Such a claim obviously raises the question of the degree to which the institutional Catholic church can tolerate communicative action. Consequently, in the next two chapters we turn to examining the important issues of dialogue, discourse, and dissent in the Catholic church.

CHAPTER FIVE

TRADITION, THEOLOGY, AND DISCOURSE

Our discussion of the church as communication community has revealed a significant problem we must now address. Although the equality of all the baptized before God is proclaimed in the scriptures and affirmed by the church, the church itself does not take this to mean that everyone is endowed with the capacity or charism to speak with authority on the scriptures or doctrines of the church, nor that everyone in principle has the right to do so. Yet, according to Habermas, for any community to be a communication community—and thus to be a properly human association—it must affirm the equality of all in the process of forming and maintaining consensus. To say the least, this leaves us with a sizable hurdle to overcome if Habermas is to be useful in this intra-ecclesial dialogue. For the church, apparently, the equality of all pertains to the suprahuman reality of the community. Equality in the church is an equality before God, not an equality within the historical church. Precisely as the church is a this-worldly institution, equality gives way to hierarchy.

The idea of a hierarchy could perhaps be reconciled with the Habermasian communication community if it were seen as a functional leadership agreed on by all as a mechanism for preserving the community as a consensus community. But this is not the understanding of hierarchy with which we are faced. The bishops of Vatican II, even as they stressed service, saw themselves as "teachers for doctrine" and "ministers for governing."[1] The bishops collectively or the Pope as their head retain to themselves both the role of teaching doctrine and the related role of preserving the authentic tradition of the church. Although priests and some theologians, as we shall see, can mediate between magisterium and people, in the last analysis no one but the bishops teaches with a divinely mandated authority. Thus, the consensus theory of truth that is fundamental to the Habermasian vision seems to be violated through and through. Is this, then, where critical theory and the church must part company?

That the bishops have a monopoly on teaching with authority does not of itself mean that they and they alone have insight into the content of the gospel. All the baptized have some share in the work of evangelization. We can reasonably ask, therefore, what the relationship is between episcopal teaching authority and non-episcopal insight into the gospel. One obvious way to investigate this, though by no means the only one, is to raise the question of the theological status of the theologian, and most especially of the lay theologian, male or female. Given the understanding of the priesthood and diaconate as a kind of sharing in the fullness of orders possessed only by the bishop, it is not difficult to accommodate the notion of the priest-theologian as assisting the bishop in achieving the necessary clarity upon which to base teaching. Indeed this or something like this seems to have been the ecclesial understanding of the role of the theologian for the greater part of the history of the church.[2] The idea of a lay theologian, however, is not so familiar.

The Vatican Council, in this as in so many other matters, laid groundwork for an understanding of lay ministry that could recognize the role of lay theologians. Chapter 4 of *Lumen Gentium,* on the laity, is a considerable advance on previous understandings. The bishops must recognize the ministries and charisms of the laity, who are specifically characterized by their "secular nature" and who, "by their very vocation, seek the kingdom of God by engaging in temporal affairs and by ordering them according to the plan of God." The laity are engaged "in each and all of the secular professions and occupations" and they "work for the sanctification of the world from within as a leaven."[3] But they are "all called to sanctity and have received an equal privilege of faith."[4] The lay apostolate "is a participation in the salvific mission of the Church itself" and "the laity can also be called in various ways to a more direct form of cooperation in the apostolate of the Hierarchy."[5] The laity have a share in the work of evangelization and "must learn the deepest meaning and the value of all creation, as well as its role in the harmonious praise of God."[6] The bishops would be well advised to pay attention to the advice of the laity: "Aided by the experience of the laity," the bishops "can more clearly and more incisively come to decisions regarding both spiritual and temporal matters."[7]

Vatican II's "Decree on the Apostolate of Lay People" goes somewhat farther than *Lumen Gentium.*[8] In particular it gives clear support to the role of the laity at least in the dissemination of the teaching of the church, and does not restrict the lay apostolate to teaching by force of example:

The Council earnestly exhorts the laity to take a more active part, each according to his talents and knowledge and in fidelity to the mind of the church, in the explanation and defense of Christian principles and in the correct application of them to the problems of our times.[9]

Because there are those who will play such a role, training of the laity must incorporate not only "an integral human education" and spiritual formation, but also "solid grounding in doctrine is required: in theology, ethics and philosophy at least, proportioned to the age, condition and abilities of each one."[10] Finally, allowing for the apparently inevitable sexism of official language, it is notable that nowhere either in *Lumen Gentium*'s chapter on the laity or in the decree on the laity is there any attempt to distinguish between those forms of the lay apostolate more appropriate to men and those that belong more properly to women. Refreshingly, the document envisages no difference.

It is clearly possible to make an argument from the documents of Vatican II for a role for the lay theologian, and even for the involvement of all members of the church, insofar as their talents, inclinations, and training permit, in disseminating the teaching of the church. At the same time, the model of the work of evangelization presented by the Council is that of the bishops as the authentic teachers of doctrine and preservers of authentic tradition, and the priests and deacons, and to some degree the laity, as disseminators of that doctrine as far as their situations permit. Thus, the role of the theologian, lay or otherwise, is at best to enlighten the magisterium with the fruits of his or her study and insight. In the proclamation of the gospel, as the Council sees it, the authoritative positions of the magisterium must be faithfully reflected.

Our task in this chapter is to articulate an understanding of authority, particularly in the teaching of doctrine and the maintenance of the tradition, which is not in simple conflict with the "freedom of the children of God," or with their share in the one priesthood of Christ, and which does not simply postpone this fundamental equality to some eschatological realm. Although it is already obvious that this issue poses a threat to a Habermasian ecclesiology, the issue is crucial in its own right, if the day is fast passing when the church as a whole will tolerate the divorce of authority from expertise, and passively accept the words of a magisterium on matters of which the bishops have no direct experience or the preaching of a clergy whose training is often sadly and clearly lacking. Conversely, the problem for church leadership is to accept Vatican II's advice to heed the laity, even in matters of theological scholarship, while not completely diluting the particular charism of authoritative teaching.

To address this set of problems we shall need to take three steps. In the first part of the chapter, I want to consider the interrelationships of teaching, authority, and tradition, and the aporias with which they leave the church. I shall then outline Habermas's views on speech-acts and on the character of theoretical discourse and its attendant "validity claim to truth," which is of course the validity claim appropriate to doctrinal formulations and discussions. This Habermasian vision will prepare the way for the final section of the chapter in which I shall present an interpretation of authority and tradition in Habermasian categories that preserves the role of the magisterium at the same time as it recognizes that the struggle for theological insight into the gospel is the work of the whole church.

TRADITION, AUTHORITY, AND THE MAGISTERIUM

"Tradition" is a particularly important category in Catholic thought, since the Catholic church posits an extrascriptural "oral" tradition preserved in the community of the church through the centuries, as well as an authoritative institutional interpretation of scripture. At its best, moreover, tradition is a dynamic concept that can comfortably accept the historicality of theology. One of the more interesting archbishops of recent times, the late and beloved former Archbishop of Bombay, Thomas Roberts, has frequently been credited with the illuminating epigram: "Tradition is the living faith of the dead, traditionalism is the dead faith of the living." This formula nicely encapsulates both the value and the danger of recourse to tradition. If tradition is taken to be a process, then it cannot ever stand still, like Newman's river image for the development of doctrine. But if tradition is reified, then it becomes a burden upon the back of the church, one that grows heavier with time.

One of the principal roles of the magisterium is to protect the tradition, sometimes seen as a treasure house, sometimes as a record of the mind of the church over the centuries, and sometimes—though rarely—as the continuing process of historically bound reflection on the gospel, which every new generation inherits, and, as T. S. Eliot said of the literary tradition, which every new thinker somehow modifies. In the church, however, like some ecclesial *Academie Francaise,* the magisterium sometimes seems to stand watchdog over the authenticity of the tradition, conceived very statically as a body of truths, conformity to which constitutes orthodoxy and challenge, grounds for censure.

The term "house of authority" as developed by Edward Farley in his phenomenological ecclesiology, *Ecclesial Reflection,* is relevant to the discussion at this point.[11] "House of authority" refers to the legacy of the theological method of classical Christianity, in its Catholic, Orthodox, and Protestant forms. The fundamental presuppositions of the house of authority are the notion of salvation history and the "principle of identity," which Farley defines as "an identity between what God wills to communicate and what is brought to language in the interpretative act of a human individual or community."[12] The locations of identity are scripture, dogma, and, in the Catholic tradition at least, the "ecclesiastical institution." The problematic aspect of all this is not that institutionalization occurred, since it "is an inevitable accomplishment of any social movement which endures over time," but "the role the institution plays in the classical criteriology":

> What made that role distinctive was the church's extension of the principle and middle axioms of identity to itself and its own institutionalized structure. That being the case, the church itself becomes a third location of divine communication and of divine-human identity.[13]

In consequence, the church "became part of the theological given" and had to "be attended to as normative. . . . With scripture and dogma the church too is an authority."[14]

Farley's interpretation of the church as the peculiarly Catholic form of the "house of authority" describes an institution whose understanding of tradition is a reified one. This becomes clear in his discussion of the role of theology in the "classical criteriology." The classical criteriology is a "way of authority." Unlike the natural, social, and "human" sciences, where authority is a function of expertise, in the classical criteriology authority is vested in the *principium* of revelation, indeed in specific texts. Citation is the theological genre and "theology seems to be knowledge without inquiry."[15] There is "little second-order reflection on theology,"[16] and the truth-question exists only as dogmatics (which utilizes the deposit of revelation to build "a house of dogma") and as apologetics (which investigates the relation between received "true" doctrines and universal rationality). Theology becomes a matter of grasping internal or external coherence:

> The agenda which the authority sets is to interpret and apply, not to assess. The authority can generate different hermeneutical activities: strict exegesis, homily, allegorical interpretation, moral application. What it cannot abide is assessment as to its validity or truth.[17]

Farley's account of the classical criteriology in the house of authority enables us to see the battle lines very clearly. He points out quite correctly that, constructed on either Protestant or Catholic lines, the house of authority is an attempt to situate religious truth and certainty beyond the depredations of history. The implications of Farley's position are that neither scripture itself nor dogma nor church can be insulated in this way. The Catholic church, for one, would certainly disagree, putting its faith in the divine institution of the church, the deposit of revelation over which it is required to stand guard, the inspiration of scripture, and the Spirit-guaranteed infallibility of the magisterium. This is a simple confrontation in which the nature of revelation is the crux of the matter. For the classical criteriology, revelation is truly a "deposit," which the magisterium guards and expounds, and which theologians may cautiously interpret.

There is some support for Farley's assessment of the role of theology in the classical criteriology and a step beyond it in John Thiel's study of classical and romantic paradigms of authority.[18] Thiel locates the late-medieval understanding of theological responsibility—his "classical paradigm"—in "the identification of the individual's theological labors with the tradition of authorities and thus the forsaking of any claim to originality or individual authority."[19] Thiel goes on to show that a notion of individual authority began to emerge in the Reformation but became prominent only later when the churches turned to Romanticism for a defense against Enlightenment rationalism. This "Romantic paradigm of theological responsibility" built upon an evolutionary model of truth, thus conceiving revelation as process: "The theologian was no longer seen as mimetically *representing* an objective revelation but as imaginatively *constructing* the immediate, though historical, experience of salvation."[20] Doctrine now develops in the interplay of orthodox and heterodox elements, the former past and stable, the latter present and enlivening, "these together constituting the integrity of Christian tradition."[21]

If the house of authority persists unchanged in the Catholic tradition, then it would seem that the Romantic paradigm of theological responsibility would receive little recognition from the magisterium. This would be particularly true given the necessary recognition in the Romantic paradigm of an individual theological "talent" or "charism" and the occasional and unfortunate accompaniment of a "heroic" self-understanding on the part of the theologian. Yet Thiel shows that the documents of the Second Vatican Council made room for the Romantic paradigm with their recognition of the "development of doctrine" and the new attention to the "sense of the faithful." With some hiccups, admittedly, the Romantic paradigm of theological responsibility seems to have achieved a measure of acceptance in official pronouncements since the Council, though "the magisterium's actions in theological disputes during the past two decades often exhibit suspicion toward the paradigm as a whole."[22]

Thiel's assessment of the present state of things between magisterium and theologians is that while the latter may occasionally be guilty of a certain narcissistic over-evaluation of their own importance, the former are too inclined to interpret even legitimate criticism along such lines. To overcome such standoffs, of course, requires nothing more nor less than the recognition on all sides that different individuals with different gifts serve the church in different ways, that, as Thiel puts it, "the teaching authority of the magisterium is defined by the responsibility of proclamation, the teaching authority of theologians by the responsibility of research and study."[23] While Thiel is probably correct here, though the question of to whom the theologians' teaching is directed is left open, it is clear that the possibilities for the exercise of power and control remain with the authority of the magisterium. The authority of the theologians is that of experts, and their authority is as good as their theology. But the authority of the proclaimers is more difficult to locate, and is apparently independent of their theological expertise.

To return to Thiel's distinction between the authority of proclamation and the authority of research and study, *my* problem is with the issue of where the authority lies for deciding what will be proclaimed. The theologian does not just engage in research and study. He or she also exercises judgment about the apparent results of this study: Is this so? does this in fact clarify this or that point? The theologian is also working within the perimeter of service to the church, not simply to the magisterium, and is engaged in theological activity in order to assist in the clarification of the gospel to be proclaimed in the here and now. In the assessment of the theologian's contribution to the understanding of the gospel, the magisterium seems to engage in a similar process of theological judgment, but now evaluating the argument of the theologian. Is this so? Does this help to clarify the gospel? Are we then to say that the charism of the magisterium involves their being better theologians than the theologians, or perhaps that the theologians should leave the truth-question to the magisterium? Something like this latter solution is what Farley would consider to be the solution advocated in the house of authority.

If we look at the magisterium's pronouncements since Vatican II with an eye not so much to their recognition of the role of the theologian in study and research, but more to their understanding of how and by whom judgments are made about the value of the theologians' endeavors, then it is apparent that less change has taken place than we might want to believe. Clearly, so long as it remains true that the magisterium decides which theologians are approved, and which are suspect, there is no question about where the authority lies. But the deeper question is of the evidence taken into account for making such judgments, whether about the orthodoxy of a particular thinker or the value of his or her insights. After all, the question is a theological question. The issue to be decided is not whether Hans Küng is insolent or whether Charles Curran is too independent for his own good, but whether their theological insight is sound. The soundness of the theology can only be assessed through serious study that respects the historically developing character of the understanding of revelation, and cannot be ascertained simply by juxtaposing new insights to reified gems plucked from the process of the past. But once again we are in a circle: Is the magisterium simply gifted with better theological insight than nonmagisterial theologians? Or is there supposed to be some extra charism of judgment that is the possession of the magisterium?

One of the more hopeful and helpful documents of recent years on the relation of theologians and the magisterium was produced by the International Theological Commission, itself a kind of halfway body between the two.[24] This official body of selected Catholic theologians has gone into something of an eclipse in the more repressive climate of recent years, but in 1975 it was vigorous and creative. The twelve theses in its 1975 statement discussed three related issues: the elements in common in the ministry of theologians and of the magisterium, the differences, and the best way to promote a less confrontational relationship between them. Their commonality lies in their role in defending, teaching, and explaining the word of God; in their being bound to the scripture, tradition, the "sensus fidei," and to a missionary purpose; and in their collegial spirit. Their differences are in their functions, the form of their authority, the way they are connected to the church, and the character of the freedom appropriate to each. The promotion of fruitful dialogue requires understanding and fairness, and in particular the avoidance of preemptive power plays on the part of the magisterium and the recourse to publicity on the part of the theologian.

If there is anything problematic in this exposition, it will surely be found in the section on differences. Yet, on the whole, it is remarkably evenhanded. That the magisterium and the theologians have different functions is not problematic, though the characterization of the differentiation may remind us of Farley's dogmatic-apologetic divide for theologians within the classical criteriology. Thus, while the magisterium's task is "authoritatively to defend the Catholic integrity and unity of faith and morals," the theologians have two roles, to examine revelation and tradition anew so that theology can "lend its aid to make the magisterium in its turn the enduring light and norm of the church,"[25] and to "lend their aid to the task of spreading, clarifying, confirming and defending the truth which the magisterium authoritatively propounds."[26]

Theses six and seven, on the form of authority and the connection to the church, stand at the heart of the issue. The authority of the magisterium comes from sacramental ordination and is "formal." That of the theologians derives from their "scientific qualifications," but because theology is the science of faith and can only be practiced, in the view of the Commission, in the environment of a "living experience and practice of the faith,"

> the authority that belongs to theology in the Church is not merely profane and scientific, but is a genuinely ecclesial authority, inserted into the order of authorities that derive from the word of God and are confirmed by canonical mission.

On the matter of connection to the church, both magisterium and theologians work "in and for the Church." As an institutional element, the magisterium "can only exist in the Church." Insofar as they are competent, all the baptized can practice theology, though only the baptized, since "even when it is not exercised in virtue of an explicit 'canonical mission,' theology can only be done in a living communion with the faith of the Church."[27]

Clearly, there is much here of considerable value, though I have one serious reservation. Certainly, the role of the theologian is recognized as integral to the church and indeed as possessing a kind of "ecclesial authority." More remarkably, the idea of a lay theologian is at least countenanced, and the complementarity of the roles of the magisterium and the theologians is fully apparent. But the discussion of the "canonical mission" gives pause for thought. A canonical mission is effectively a license given to (and sometimes withdrawn from) a theologian whereby he or she can teach Catholic theology. It is this license that

Hans Küng and Charles Curran lost, that Leonardo Boff and Edward Schillebeeckx may have come close to losing. But there are many Catholic theologians (in the United States, certainly the majority) who hold no such canonical mission. They teach in Catholic colleges and universities, and in non-Catholic institutions of learning, both public and private. What of their status and responsibility? No doubt they qualify as theologians because "even when it is not exercised in virtue of a canonical mission," theology is possible. But the commentary on the thesis in which this statement occurs is cause for some disquiet: "But even when the science of theology is pursued, not as an official exercise, but as personal research, it remains linked with the Church, for theology, as the science of faith, can only be carried out truly in the living context of the Church's faith."[28]

It seems that we are being told that there are two grades of theologians. There are those whose possession of a canonical mission makes their work "an official exercise" and those who merely conduct "personal research." But on inspection both groups are engaged in the same activity. Of course, to the Vatican (and presumably the Theological Commission) this is not controversial, since it is their belief that all those teaching theology in Catholic institutions of higher education have or should have a canonical mission, and it is the teaching, not the research, which is the official exercise. But as a matter of fact the overwhelming majority of Catholic theologians in the United States do not have such a mission, probably do not want one, and in many cases could not get one, if they are women or expriests.

I want to stress the curious fact about these two grades of theologian, the official teacher and the unofficial "personal researcher," that both are most likely engaged in precisely the same activity. Moreover, though proof would be difficult, it is at least possible that some in the latter category are better theologians than some in the former. Still further, the former are no better insulated than the latter from the possibility of error, though their official position may place them under closer scrutiny. Again, many in both categories, perhaps all, share in the living faith of the church. So what is the difference? Presumably that the former teach with authority, the latter either do not teach or teach without authority? But the authority of a canonical mission that comes from the magisterium and is extended for the most part only to ordained men teaching in seminaries and pontifical universities is clearly authority unrelated, except accidentally, to expertise or wisdom. It is authority that belongs with the classical criteriology.

This investigation has not provided us thus far with a sound basis for the mutual but differentiated responsibilities of magisterium and nonmagisterium in reflection on the faith of the community. The relationship between defending the tradition and exploring it is not clear, if only because the capacity to do theological research and to judge the fruits of that research, unless the judgment is simply its juxtaposition to a reified tradition, are too similar. How the magisterium is to defend tradition now defined as process is not something Catholicism has yet acquired the language to express, even if it can find room for the idea. Finally, there is no clarity about just what it is that allows a differentiation between the theological activity of a Roman-trained seminary professor and an active Catholic, lay lesbian feminist "theologian" with a doctorate from, say, the University of Chicago Divinity School. The notion of "canonical mission" only highlights the problem.

The remainder of this chapter addresses the issue of authority and tradition in light of the search for truth as consensus in the Habermasian communication community.

The foregoing chapter suggested that the emergent ecclesiological reality of the Catholic church is clarified by the application of the notion of the consensus community. I want to go on now to show that the role of discourse in the communication community is similarly enlightening, and that it offers an alternative to the house of authority.

THEORETICAL DISCOURSE: THE VALIDITY CLAIM TO TRUTH

Communicative action, the reader will recall, is human interaction directed toward achieving understanding. It is either based on consensus or moving toward a consensus. It proceeds according to a pattern of the "discursive redemption of validity claims." That is to say, the communicative action is constantly hovering on the verge of suspension, a suspension that must occur whenever the progress of understanding, the movement toward consensus, requires the defense of some claim to truth, comprehensibility, sincerity, or rightness. This is, of course, nothing more than a phenomenological account of any unconstrained conversation. An open, frank discussion between two or more individuals not intending the domination or conversion of the other, but the mutual search for truth or rightness, is just such communicative action. To repeat what we have now said a number of times, what makes this different and significant in the case of Habermas is that it is in this structure of human interaction that he locates human autonomy and the struggle for emancipation, as well as the uncovering of truth.

It is in Habermas's theory of truth that we will find the greatest assistance with the range of problems discussed in the first part of this chapter. The "consensus theory of truth" to which Habermas subscribes is treated in a number of his works, most recently in the first volume of the *Theory of Communicative Action*.[29] The context in which the consensus theory of truth most clearly is the discussion of the speech-act theories of Austin and Searle, which Habermas take up because he shares their conviction that the purely semantic approach to language is erroneous. It is language in use that must be investigated. Thus, says Habermas, "Reaching understanding is the inherent telos of human speech," and "we can explain the concept of reaching understanding only if we specify what it means to use sentences with a communicative intent."[30] The first step is to establish that speech is fundamentally (in the sense of originally) about the establishment of understanding. In a world driven largely by persuasion and misinformation, this may be as difficult a task as it is important.

Habermas adopts the distinction invented by Austin between "locution," "illocution," and "perlocution." A locutionary act is a simple statement of a state of affairs, for example, that "today is Monday." The illocutionary act is whatever is "performed" in the locutionary act, that is, what tells the listener the kind of sentence being said—a simple statement, or a command or a promise, and so on. Most often, the illocutionary force of the statement is implicit in the context or the tone of voice, but Habermas is insistent that it is always present, if only implicitly. The perlocutionary act is the act through which an effect is produced on the hearer. This last is the realm of possible distortion, since it is here that strategic considerations may have come into play, though there are trivial perlocutionary acts too—unintended effects. The intentional perlocutionary act deliberately manipulates the hearer: The most blatant example would be the locutionary act "today is Monday" uttered as a simple statement or even an implied illocutionary promise, when in fact it was any day but Monday. Perlocutions, as Habermas defines them, are "a special class of strategic interactions in which illocutions are employed as means in teleological contexts of action."[31] They are thus concealed strategic actions which depend for their success on the hearer perceiving the locution and the illocution and taking them to be genuine communication, and not perceiving the perlocution that is the real aim of the actually feigned communication.

It is with the illocutionary act that the consensus theory of truth comes to the fore. We touched on this in chapter 2, but it is now necessary to take a closer look. Although a purely semantic approach to language might ask questions about the meaning of a simple locution, speech-act theory is more concerned with the illocutionary component, because it is in the illocution that understanding and therefore truth resides. There is no locution without illocution in speech-act theory. Consider the simple if witty Wildean proposition, "A cynic [is] a man who knows the price of everything and the value of nothing." Or the less witty, "There are too many books in this house." Or the more portentous, "And on the third day Jesus rose from the dead." Each or all of these can only be understood by means of an appreciation of the illocutionary force of the utterance. In the first case, it will obviously make a difference if the context is that of the hearer of Oscar Wilde's first enunciation of the epigram or that of the host of a T.V. game show. In the second, the speaker may be lamenting that he or she can no longer find anything, or informing a homeowner that if he or she buys one more book the floor will collapse. In the third case, the speaker may be telling the story of an ancient myth or affirming a fundamental and sacred principle of his or her faith. Understanding and truth are linked to the illocutionary force of the utterance.

155

Given the context of communication,

> A speech-act may be called "acceptable" if it satisfies the conditions that are necessary in order that the hearer be allowed to take a "yes" position on the claim raised by the speaker. . . . A hearer understands the meaning of an utterance when . . . he knows those *essential conditions* under which he could be motivated by a speaker to take an affirmative position.[32]

Reaching understanding means that "at least two speaking and acting subjects understand a linguistic expression in the same way." This agreement occurs simultaneously at three levels, that of rightness in respect to the given context, that of truth, and that of sincerity or truthfulness.[33] There follow directly from these the three "limit-cases" of communicative action: conversation, normatively regulated action, and "dramaturgical" action.[34]

Although we shall not be concerned with dramaturgical action in this book, and our discussion of normatively regulated action will have to await the next chapter, the case of conversation, which conforms to the validity claim to truth, is central to the discussion of the development of doctrine, theology, and the notion of teaching with authority in such a developmental context. Truth as consensus involves something like the universalizability of understanding:

> I may ascribe a predicate to an object if and only if every other person who could enter into a dialogue with me *would* ascribe the same predicate to the same object. In order to distinguish true from false statements, I make reference to the judgment of others—in fact to the judgment of all others with whom I could ever hold a dialogue (among whom I counterfactually include all the dialogue partners I could find if my life history were coextensive with the

history of mankind). The condition of the truth of expressions is the potential agreement of all others.[35]

This understanding of truth is clearly communicative. It requires in principle the agreement of all possible others and cannot be "subjective," since the truth-judgment resides in the validity of the grounds upon which I assert that a particular state of affairs is in fact so. In other words, the truth resides not in the locution's "correspondence" to the state of affairs it represents, but in the validity of the grounds for the assertion that the state of affairs is so. To return to an example we touched on in chapter 2, I can assert if I wish that there is intelligent life elsewhere in the universe, but while in the absence of any method for ascertaining the validity of this assertion others can join me in an equally subjective *certitude*, the question of truth does not arise.

If indeed it is the case that theological reflection takes place in the conversation of the communication community upon the founding texts which define it, then all this can be governed by Habermas's axiom that "the condition of the truth of statements is the potential agreement of all others." However, while an orientation to agreement and a basically dialogical, consensual model for interaction is noncontroversial for the discussions of the theological academy and perhaps even for the ecclesial community as a whole, to the magisterium *truth* seems only to enter the discussion at the point at which consensus is no longer deemed appropriate. Theologians and even ordinary Christians may research and teach and publish, may discuss the merits of this or that interpretation of doctrine, all in a relatively free atmosphere, but the judgment that some theological item is true rests in the last analysis with the magisterium, which alone decides truth questions for the church.

It may at first sight seem as if the root of our problem here is a conflict over theories of truth. Perhaps the magisterium works with a simple correspondence theory of truth and bases its judgments on the adequacy of the newly developed insight to the deposit of revelation understood in a reified manner? And perhaps those who are unhappy with this approach are really seeking a model of truth by consensus that would leave Christian doctrine and tradition at the mercy of the vagaries of the present moment and the emotional waywardness of the Christian masses? If this were so, then obviously it would be preferable to follow a well-intentioned and learned, if autocratic, magisterium rather than submit to "one person, one vote" on the definition of the Trinity.

However, the dispute is not so cut and dried as a correspondence-consensus confrontation. For one thing, although a consensus theory of truth requires equal voice and equal dignity for all the participants in the communication community, it does not abandon, in fact it emphasizes, the authority of expertise and the weight of evidence. The consensus achieved is not *mere* consensus, but consensus arrived at through the discursive redemption of validity claims. Moreover, at its best this dialogue takes seriously the contribution of tradition, but not in a reified understanding. The tradition itself must be subjected to a respectful and sensitive but thorough hermeneutical analysis and historical investigation, if it is to be able to speak in the discourse of the current community. So-called historical theology exercises this work of retrieval or translation with respect to the tradition for the sake of the contemporary church.

It seems as if we are at something of an impasse. Although there are, of course, good theologians among the bishops, and there are even documents of recent history that recognize the importance of historical considerations in the interpretation of scripture and doctrinal formulations of the past, the identification of bishops with magisterium is firm.[36] Yet, as we have said above, the kinds of judgments involved in examination of theological developments are the same kinds of judgments used by theologians in the development of new insights. Nor is it helpful to assert simply that the charism of magisterium is precisely that bishops are gifted with better judgment, since judgment is itself not magical and requires grounds. And, once again, the grounds for the judgment do not differ from the grounds for the theological insight.

TRADITION AS DISCOURSE

We shall make no further progress, either here or in the life of the church, so long as we persist in seeing the bishops and the theologians effectively occupying the same ground, nor indeed so long as we continue to think of tradition as a body of truths bequeathed to us by the past on the condition that we put them in glass cases and look at them from time to time. Bishops as bishops and theologians as theologians contribute equally to teaching, though the former principally to the process of teaching, the latter to the substance. And tradition *is* a bequest of the past, but one to be invested in the present so that we may reap dividends in the future.

The communication community of the church is composed of people who share equally in their inheritance of scripture and tradition, and who in principle share equally in the role of interpretation of and reflection upon that inheritance. Their share is equal "in principle" only because in practice not all have equal gifts or expertise, and consequently not all will make the same contribution.

But insofar as all genuinely engage in communicative action oriented to consensus, all can follow the discursive redemption of questioned validity claims to the degree that they are able. Understood this way, theological reflection is quite definitely the work of the whole church, though the nontheologian, the theologian, and the bishop relate to this work in different ways. Recognizing the fact that the first and third and the second and third of these categories overlap somewhat, I want to make a few remarks about the relation to theology of each of the three groups.

Nonspecialists, whether lay or clerical, are inevitably placed in a secondary if not subordinate position in the theological discourse of the church. The fact that they do not possess any theological expertise (not to be confused simply with training) does not render them subordinate, because they are as capable as the next person of insight and creative reflection on texts. The example of base Christian communities has shown us that very clearly. However, their place is secondary in the obvious sense that it is to a degree dependent on the contributions of those who do possess the expertise. Thus, for example, any Christian might in principle develop a brilliant analogy for illuminating the doctrine of the Trinity, but the ability to discriminate between what is brilliant and apposite, and what is brilliant and wrong, requires the contribution of those theological scholars who can elucidate the historical development of the doctrine of the Trinity.

While we are affirming the secondary role of the lay and clerical nonspecialist in the theological discourse of the church, it is important to stress that this discourse is not itself *the* work of the church. That, of course, is the efficacious witness to the salvific love of God at work in the world, the demonstration that God wills the salvation of the whole world. In *that* work a different division of labor is operative, and the lay nonspecialists who constitute the vast majority of those who are the efficacy of God's love of the world in the world are revealed to be the bearers of the mission. The clergy and the theologians, lay or clerical, are in this respect mere support personnel.

The work of theologians in the church is related to the substance of teaching. It is their responsibility to study and reflect upon the texts of the tradition, scriptural and nonscriptural alike, to seek to understand them in their historical context, and to connect them to the needs of today's world. They do this work for and with the church community as a whole, learning from the insight and reflections of nonspecialists, both lay and clerical, and providing the service of expertise to those lay and clerical nonspecialists who take seriously their responsibility to share in the theological discourse of the church.

Theologians qua theologians are miners, quarrying at the coal-face; bishops qua bishops are white-collar workers at the pithead, engaged in a species of quality control. In other words, the bishop as bishop is not concerned to repeat the theological judgments of the theologians upon tradition, reinventing the wheel as it were. On the contrary, the bishops' role vis-à-vis tradition and scripture is procedural. It is their responsibility to protect the integrity of tradition, understood as a process of discourse. When they teach, they teach what earlier bishops have affirmed as products of authentic discourse, or what they in their turn recognize as the outcome of the authentic continuing discourse of the church.

If we present bishops as having oversight over the authenticity of interpretations of tradition, then it is important to remind ourselves what "discourse" in the Habermasian vocabulary means. Discourse is what occurs when the flow of communicative action is interrupted because of a need to redeem one or another validity claim.

In the theological discourse of the church, the scrutiny falls upon the validity claim to truth that is relevant to the category of theoretical discourse into which theology falls. The argument here then is that tradition is best understood as a living testimony to the two-thousand-year-old process of the discursive redemption of the validity claim to truth continually punctuating the communicative action of the ecclesial community.

The role of the magisterium in the preservation of tradition is the oversight of a process that has at its core a belief in evidence and grounds for what is claimed to be true. This obviously involves rejection of a correspondence theory of truth more akin to semantic approaches to meaning. To illustrate what I mean let us consider the statement, "God is three persons in one nature." The *tendency* of semantic approaches to meaning is to look for grounds for the validity (truth) of that statement in abstraction from the concrete conditions in which it was uttered. As a matter of fact, most theories of meaning would have trouble with this particular example, but the traditional approach to magisterium would invoke authority as the ground for the truth of this statement, perhaps based in a (similarly) authoritative reading of scripture, and then defend it by requiring subsequent discussion of trinitarian theology to align itself with this disembodied phrase. The direction of speech-act or discursive approaches to meaning, on the other hand, is to seek the grounds for the validity (truth) of the statement in the illocutionary force with which the locution was uttered, thus in the intent and the context of the Council of Nicea. As a consequence, subsequent defense of this speech-act of the Council of Nicea would consist in relating the later interpretations to the illocutionary component of the original affirmation, that is, to the grounds for the assertion. At the very least then this latter understanding must be far more sensitive to hermeneutical and historical considerations.

The essentially procedural role of the magisterium vis-à-vis tradition can be expressed thus: The magisterium has as its particular charism to preserve the rules of discourse that govern the process of tradition. We should therefore not expect from the magisterium either the slavish repetition of traditional theological positions in the teeth of current reflection, or the presentation of creative theological insight on their own part. Their role is rather to identify authentic tradition as that which respects the rules of discourse, and to sanction authentic theological reflection by the same standards. Their charism consists in the insight to recognize when tradition and the church today are playing by the rules of the discursive redemption of validity claims, and to demand conformity to those rules. They are referees, to borrow the language of James P. Carse, in an infinite rather than a finite game.[37] Their role is vital and one of leadership, but it is quite distinct from that of the theologian.

A second charism of the magisterium may present further difficulties. The bishops are not only those charged with the protection of the tradition of authentic teaching. They are also those given the responsibility of teaching authentic doctrine. However, once again, if we can stand firm in our definition of tradition as a process of discourse, then we can see the bishops' teaching charism as obliging them to teach those things and only those things which have been established through a legitimate discourse involving the discursive redemption of validity claims. In this particular and perhaps peculiar sense, theologians do not teach, though the bishops may teach by repeating what this or that theologian said, perhaps word for word. Theologians may enunciate what they take to be sound theology, but they cannot be self-appointed judges of their own conformity to the canons of communicative action.

An important implication of this interpretation of the magisterium is that the bishops' judgments on the authenticity of this or that theological work must themselves abide by the canons of discourse. If I am right in my suggestion that the role of the magisterium involves oversight of the proper conduct of critical discourse and respect for the products of that discourse in the past, then they must themselves be shining examples of respect for the proper conduct of communicative action. Consequently, they cannot operate simply by an appeal to authority, even the authority of their own charism. Moreover, their pronouncements will never be the last word, and will always be open to challenge, discussion, and correction, provided that continued conversation follows the same rules of discourse.

To conclude, I want to comment briefly on several problematic dimensions of this understanding of the relationship of the magisterium and theologians. In the first place, what is the meaning of a "canonical mission" that is given to some theologians and not to others? Second, is the suggestion that magisterial pronouncements "will never be the last word" not in fact dismissive of any idea of infallibility? And finally and most important, what is the illocutionary force of a magisterial assertion of truth, as compared with a theologian's enunciation of the same proposal?

Earlier, I said something about the concept of a "canonical mission" to teach Catholic theology, and in any case many if not most of my readers will already have been quite familiar with the idea. I tried to show that contradiction and confusion were built into the idea if we tried to compare the judgment a theologian and a bishop would be making about theological insights. I also suggested that it would be still more so if we tried to suggest that a theologian with and a theologian without such a mission were either doing something different from each other, or that the possession of the mission guaranteed the more successful accomplishment of the same activity as the one without the mission was engaged in. But if we now look at canonical mission in the light of tradition as discourse, the problems may begin to disappear.

We are concerned with three groups of people in the community. Bishops exercise the magisterium, some people (most if not all of them clergy) hold a canonical mission to teach Catholic theology, and some people study and teach theology without such a mission. The canonical mission is not a license to be a part of the magisterium, nor is it necessarily linked to superior theological expertise, although one would like to believe that this is one criterion for the awarding of such a license. Rather, a canonical mission indicates the task of accurately representing the tradition of the church and faithfully teaching the teaching presented by the magisterium, both of the past and the present. Regarding at least the past teaching, of course, it does not preclude the necessary process of interpretation and historical contextualizing without which it would not be *teaching* at all. A canonical mission is therefore only going to be given provisionally, and its granting has to indicate a measure of trust in the good sense and good faith of the possessor, as well as a certain humility before the tradition. It is absolutely correct to distinguish the possession of this mission from the charism of theological research and creativity. A canonical mission says nothing about creativity. It is, however, facile to imagine that anyone teaching theology with such a mission in hand could altogether separate the fruits of research

165

and creativity from the accurate portrayal of the tradition and the magisterium.

The fundamental issue with the canonical mission is that it involves teaching not simply the content of tradition or the words of the magisterium, but the idea of tradition as a process and respect for the procedure by which the magisterium has to abide if it is to be faithful to this process of tradition. So someone who teaches with a canonical mission must be able to recount the tradition faithfully, and show how the tradition has been faithful to the canons of procedural rationality. He or she must be willing and able to expound the position of the magisterium and show how the magisterium has itself been faithful to these same procedural regularities. But he or she must also have the right, as does any theologian, or any Christian for that matter, to challenge the improper application of these canons of procedural rationality, whether noted in the writings of a thirteenth-century pope or in the latest words of the Congregation for the Doctrine of the Faith.

It may seem as if the account above does not differ much from the traditional approach, apart from the substitution of Habermasian terminology. There is, however, a significant change. Matters of dispute between magisterium and theologians, or between theologians themselves, are adjudicable not in terms of the authority of the magisterial or theological charism, but through the discursive redemption of contested validity claims. Since we have reinterpreted the magisterial charism as one of oversight of commitment to procedural rationality through the exercise of procedural rationality, if it is not to be self-contradictory it must be ready to engage in the discursive redemption of its own claims. Moreover, the possession of this charism cannot possibly *guarantee* right judgment, since the charism itself is exercised only in a process which of its nature is open-ended.

What then, finally, is a canonical mission *for*, and *who* should have one? Since all theologians within the tradition cannot be good theologians without showing the same respect for the tradition that the bishops themselves must have, the granting of a canonical mission only makes sense for those designated as official spokespersons for the magisterium. This more or less corresponds to the present reality, where those who teach in seminaries and pontifical universities, or in departments in other universities attached to the Vatican (as in the department of theology at Catholic University), must hold the canonical mission. It in no way corresponds to the extension of the idea that the Vatican is promoting, where everyone teaching theology or scripture studies in any university claiming to be Catholic ought to have a canonical mission. This is to make a canonical mission into a vehicle of control over the theologian, whereas we have seen that in reality it exists to designate official spokespersons, and even with those persons delimits only a part of their theological activity. As to *who* should be eligible for such a mission, there is of course no way of tying the idea of being an official spokesperson for Catholic teaching to gender or ordination. It simply requires knowledge and wisdom, the exclusive possession neither of men nor of the clergy.

I want to turn now to the difficult question of infallibility. My focus will not be on that cause so close to the heart of Catholics on the extreme right, namely, the infallibility of the noninfallible magisterium. The issue I want to address is whether and how we can make sense of the idea of infallibility within the context of magisterium understood as oversight of the tradition's faithfulness to those canons of procedural rationality without which human communication is made mockery. Clearly, infallibility is one form of authority, and if we cannot find a place for it in the framework I have presented, then there will be problems with the acceptability of this framework for the Catholic tradition.

The usual mistake in discussion of infallibility is to restrict consideration to the exercise of papal infallibility. In fact, infallibility can only really be understood when papal infallibility is placed beside two other forms of infallibility, the infallibility of the whole body of bishops, and the infallibility of the whole church. *Lumen Gentium* refers to all three, and all three derive from the same source, namely, the promise of the Spirit to guide the church into all truth. The differences correspond to the different charisms: Thus the infallibility of bishops and of the pope as their head is related to the charism of teaching. The infallibility of the whole church, the so-called *sensus fidelium*, attaches not to the charism of teaching but to the gift of faith. All three, then, pertain to revelation which, as the Council said, "under the guiding light of the Spirit of truth is religiously preserved and faithfully expounded in the Church."[38]

There is no new revelation, not even from the lips of a pope. Even infallibility is tied to the proclamation of those doctrines which are affirmed always to have been held in the church. The infallible declaration of a doctrine amounts to an assertion that it has always been believed by the church as a whole, if not by every single member of the community. The exercise of teaching infallibility, then, is not the proclamation of a "new" truth, but a judgment that tradition as discourse—that is, tradition as a process of communicative action and the discursive redemption of disputed validity claims—has been constant in its attachment to, say, the trinitarian understanding of divinity. The *sensus fidelium* is simply the living demonstration that the judgment of the magisterium is correct. It follows that the magisterium cannot teach something infallibly which the great majority of the members of the community simply have not believed and do not believe, for then the judgment that a given doctrine had always been part of the discourse of the church would clearly be in error.

It is not clear that linking infallible magisterium to an understanding of tradition as discourse solves all the problematic aspects of the idea. Why should it be less controversial to assert that the magisterium is infallibly able to judge the commitment to discourse in the tradition than that the magisterium can make an infallible judgment on the "objective" truth of a doctrine? Second, do there not seem to be some doctrines that apparently precede discourse, or that discourse, while examining and defending them, cannot deny? That is, are there not some teachings in the Christian tradition that have a privileged position, and does this not offend against the idea of a consensus theory of truth?

Seeing infallibility in relation to tradition as discourse, actually cuts it down to size. It is not and cannot be some magical property of the judgment of any individual or group of individuals. It has to be explicable. The significant difference between the popular understanding of infallibility and the one I am presenting here is that the latter, being a commitment to discourse, must be willing to abide by the canons of discourse. That is to say, it must be able to explicate and defend its judgment that a particular doctrine has been a constant of the tradition, and cannot simply rest its claim on the authority of its own charism. The charism itself is active only when it is governed by the canons of discourse. We can then formulate the doctrine of infallibility itself in the following way: The pope or the bishops together with the pope teach infallibly when, given that they speak on a fundamental matter of faith or morals to be held by the whole church, they judge that the doctrine upon which they speak has been a constant in the discourse of the church, and they are willing and able to *defend* their judgment according to the *canons of critical discourse*. In other words, they judge infallibly when they make a judgment that is discursively redeemable. This does not reduce their authority or the power of the Spirit; it simply indicates that both their authority and the power of the Spirit must be channeled through speech-acts within the sphere of communicative action.

The issue of fundamental doctrines within the tradition that are themselves apparently not open to question can be dealt with fairly briefly. It is true that such doctrines exist, though how long the list should be is open to dispute and discussion according to the rules of communicative action. All Christians within the Catholic tradition would accept at least the following doctrines, however: the trinitarian understanding of God, the Incarnation, the redeeming power of God's grace freely given to human beings, the authority of canonical scripture. It is noteworthy, of course, that the more fundamental and generally acceptable a doctrine has been, the more discussion there has been in the tradition over its meaning. The question of the interpretation of the Trinity, or discourse about the Trinity, has been far more extensive in the tradition than discourse about miracles, though belief in miracles is much less fundamental to the tradition, and therefore presumably far more open to dispute.

The reason for the apparently a priori status of at least some fundamental doctrines resides in the fact that they are so closely linked to the very identity of the community. The Christian community has historical origins, however hazy, and the discourse of the community would no longer be the discourse of the community if it simply rejected these fundamentals. True, there would be *a* community and perhaps a better one, but it would not be *the* community bound by its common possession of a tradition of discourse. At the same time, there can be no preordained limits to the degree to which even the fundamental doctrines must be open to discursive redemption. It is simply the case that if the time should arrive at which one or more of these fundamentals fails the tests of discourse (that is, cannot redeem disputed validity claims), then the community becomes something other than what it has always been, becomes another community. *Schism* is a term used traditionally to describe what would happen when a minority in the community rejected the majority commitment to discourse. But if the whole group were to take the same step, then it would, from one point of view, be the self-destruction of the community and from another (perhaps that of Habermas) the maturation of this particular community from an essentially mythical to a rational world view. I hope that enough has been said here to suggest that tradition as discourse, particularly with reference to fundamental doctrines, releases the rational potential of the symbol that has itself emerged from the myth, without abandoning the symbol.

The final question to be considered here is that of the difference between a theological pronouncement of the magisterium and the same pronouncement uttered by a theologian who is not a bishop. The locutionary component is identical, and since we are involved in speech-acts oriented toward understanding rather than success, the question of a difference of perlocution does not arise. The issue comes down, then, to one of identifying the appropriate illocutionary force of magisterial teaching and that of theological insight. The magisterial illocution, sometimes stated openly but usually implicitly, is "We teach that x." The illocution of the theologian is more likely to be "It is my considered opinion that x." "X," whatever else it is, is some item of the tradition expressed or at least understood with full historical and hermeneutical sophistication. But, and this is most important, the "x"

171

itself is not a simple proposition, but a speech-act.

To explain further, let us look at a possible example, one that almost all Christians would accept, and which authoritative Vatican sources have also proclaimed. The formulation here is that of the 1970 Synod of Bishops in Rome: "Action on behalf of justice is a constitutive dimension of the preaching of the gospel." In the mouths of bishops, theologians, and the church as a whole, this statement would appear as follows, given the truth of our understanding of tradition as discourse:

A. Bishops: We judge that the belief that action on behalf of justice is a constitutive dimension of the preaching of the gospel is a discursively redeemable truth-claim (that is, that in principle all members of the community acting according to the canons of critical discourse could be led to accept it).

B. Theologian: I judge that the belief that action on behalf of justice is a constitutive dimension of the preaching of the gospel is a discursively redeemable truth-claim.

C. Community: We believe that action on behalf of justice is a constitutive dimension of the preaching of the gospel, and we can and will defend the validity of this claim if challenged.

The claim may of course need to be defended in a number of ways by different groups within the community. Bishops and theologians might be called on to defend its comprehensibility (explain!) or its truth (how does it fit into the tradition?). The community as a whole must defend the sincerity or truthfulness of the claim through pointing to the consistency of its own praxis with the mere assertion of the truth-claim. The community can be distinguished from both bishops and theologians (though it includes them in their basic identity as Christians among other Christians) because its speech-act has the illocutionary force of a faith-statement or truth-claim, which is simultaneously not irrational and is therefore open to discursive redemption. Bishops and theologians both second the judgment that this faith-statement or truth-claim is valid. That is, they make explicit what the truth-claim of the community leaves implicit. But bishops and theologians, except that the former at least in principle speak communally and the latter in principle alone, seem to share the illocutionary force of judgment. Are we then to say that there is no difference between their statements; and if so, where does that leave the magisterium?

There is a clue in the implicit "we" of the teaching of even an individual bishop. *Lumen Gentium* is explicit on the essentially communal character of magisterium.[39] The bishops teach not in virtue of the authority of expertise, which frankly many of them neither possess nor claim to possess, but in virtue of the charism of office that the community recognizes in them. At the risk of being tiresome, let us recall once again that the charism is not an intuitive power of identifying true propositions, but a rational ability to judge which theological pronouncements respect and further the discourse of the church, an ability exercised infallibly when it is in full conformity with the same canons of critical discourse at work in the tradition. The theologians, on the other hand, precisely because they judge individually even when they agree with one another, rest their judgment on their own expertise in theological matters and cannot in the last analysis be vested with the charism of pronouncing a further judgment upon the rightness of their insight. This last, teaching judgment resides in the magisterium through the power of the Spirit and as an expression of the will of the whole community about the necessary organs for safeguarding the process of theological discourse in the church.

CHAPTER SIX

THE ETHICAL DISCOURSE OF
THE CHURCH

I f the discourse of the church on matters theological and doctrinal fits into Habermas's category of theoretical discourse, then the ethical teaching of the church corresponds to what in Habermas's schema would be referred to as "practical discourse." Just as the focus in theoretical discourse is on the validity claim to truth, so in practical discourse attention shifts to the claims to sincerity and, above all, to the claim to rightness. The claim to sincerity cannot be discursively redeemed, since what is at issue is precisely the relationship between discourse and spheres of action. Sincerity can be proved only by the conformity of actions to the normative demands of practical discourse. This is a relatively noncontroversial claim, though it serves the useful ancillary function of drawing attention to the fact that not all communicative action is a matter of *speech*-acts. Significant action is the form of (nondiscursive) redemption of the validity claim to sincerity.

The practical discourse of the church—its conversation, research, communication, and teaching on ethical issues—receives far more attention in the church and the world at large than does the theoretical discourse. This is so for several reasons. In the first place, ethical discourse touches the lives of all members of the community more immediately than theoretical discourse is perceived to. When the magisterium pronounces on nuclear warfare, economics, abortion, or the rights of homosexuals, or when a theologian opines that contraception or abortion cannot be subjected to blanket condemnation, the lives of many people may be affected. Second, at least on a number of important issues, the ethical discourse of the church has an influence beyond the community of believers. This might be a product of the respect other religious traditions pay to the teaching of the Catholic tradition, or the outrage that they might feel, or perhaps it might be a matter of the political and economic fallout for governments of, say, the church's position on nuclear deterrence or population control. Third, ethical issues arouse much more media attention than do narrowly theological concerns. Though *Time* magazine did once run a cover story on the death of God, it has far more often filled its pages with conflicts in the church over homosexuality, abortion, contraception, freedom of speech, or revolutionary theologies. As a cause or perhaps consequence of the closer media scrutiny of ethical issues, the church has increasingly attended to its perceived responsibilities to the world beyond its boundaries, strengthened in this by the concern for church-world relations expressed in Vatican II's *Gaudium et Spes*, the "Pastoral Constitution on the Church in the Modern World."[1] In return, for all the reasons mentioned above, the world has paid more attention to the words of popes and bishops. The extensive travels of the present Pope have only increased attention to his words, for good or ill.

Ethical pronouncements, at least from the perspective of members of the magisterium, take on a different character when they are oriented particularly toward the members of the community and when they are intended for a wider audience. Most explicit notice of this variation has been taken by the United States Catholic bishops in their recent letter, *Economic Justice for All: Catholic Social Teaching and the U.S. Economy.*[2] In paragraph 27, at the end of their introductory chapter, they clearly recognize the problem:

> We write, then, first of all to provide guidance for members of our own church as they seek to form their consciences about economic matters. No one may claim the name of Christian and be comfortable in the face of the hunger, homelessness, insecurity and injustice found in this country and the world. At the same time, we want to add our voice to the public debate about the directions in which the U.S. economy should be moving. We seek the cooperation and support of those who do not share our faith or tradition.[3]

The twofold purpose of the letter is evident in its subsequent construction. Its arguments are buttressed by reference both to principles of the Hebrew and Christian scriptures, and to an anthropological vision informed by natural law which the bishops at least believe will be persuasive for those beyond the confines of the community, as well as to ideals of the United States tradition and its Constitution. The bishops are also careful to distinguish between their enunciation of "universal moral principles and formal church teaching," which they clearly believe are not open to interpretation, and their "judgments and recommendations on specific economic issues," which "do not carry the same moral authority" and over which they "expect and welcome debate."[4]

There are evidently a number of concerns to be

discussed over the right exercise of moral authority in and on the part of the church. There is, as in the foregoing chapter, the question of the relation of magisterial teaching to expertise and to the *sensus fidelium*. There is the distinction between unchanging and unquestionable principles on the one hand, and arguable applications of the principles on the other. Third, there is perhaps a more fundamental issue, that of the character of the reception of the ethical teaching expected of members of the community and that accorded to it by "all people of good will." It would certainly seem to be the case that in the realm of public discourse in a pluralistic society, the bishops would hope to persuade their fellow citizens by the force of argument, that is, that they would accept the rules of discourse in at least something like the Habermasian form. On the other hand, this is definitely not the way in which the magisterium usually expects its pronouncements to work within the ecclesial community. Thus, something other than the intrinsic rightness of the norms used for the ethical teaching is apparently brought into play within the church community. If this is the case, we should ask with what justification?

To address these issues I have divided the chapter into four sections. In the first I shall take a general look at a number of phenomena related to problematic aspects of ethical teaching in the church, in search both of attention to the canons of procedural rationality and of the "something extra" that the church seems to expect in the assent of its members. In the second, I shall outline Habermas's discourse ethics, look at one or two of its critics, and look at the way Habermas himself responds to these critics. The third section will attempt a Habermasian reaction to the range of problems we have already mentioned by examining the illocutionary force of magisterial ethical teaching. Finally, in the fourth section we will examine different understandings of the role of authority, locating them in terms of Habermas's distinction between "power" and "influence" developed in his more recent work and outlined briefly in chapter 2 above. This will prepare the ground for the final chapter, in which Habermas's critique of modernity will be discussed as a potentially valuable resource in the church's own encounter with the postmodern world.

ETHICS IN THE CHURCH

In the everyday life of the church, ethical rather than theological issues loom large, for all of the reasons mentioned above and for one more. While Catholic laypeople continue to defer to trained theologians and particularly to the clergy (whether trained theologians or not) on what are perceived to be strictly theological issues, they are far less likely simply to accept ethical teaching. I am not referring to the many who either do not understand it or do not care to make the effort to follow it, nor to the still considerable numbers who embrace rules as an escape from moral decision making, but to the sincere and well-intentioned active Christians who take seriously what church leaders say and who want to understand and follow that teaching. They are less likely to accept ethical teaching docilely, however, because they believe in many cases, and often with justification, that they know as much if not more than the clergy about the matters being taught. In *ethical* matters, the authority of expertise is far more likely to be tied to experience.

To carry conviction, ethical teaching must demonstrate a number of characteristics. In the first place, it must be compassionate and sensitive to the lives of ordinary people in the everyday world. This may not be where its truth lies, but it is a *sine qua non* for the truth reaching and convincing its supposed audience. Second, there must be a clear progression of ideas from fundamental principles that the entire community would unquestioningly accept to so-called middle axioms if not to particular applications of those principles. If this is not possible, then it should stop at the enunciation of the fundamental principles. Third, to return to Habermasian terminology, the validity claim to rightness is vitiated at the outset if the sincerity of the speaker is questionable. This is another way of phrasing the "reflexivity" of critical theory; if there is no consonance between the speech-acts of the speaker and the "action-contexts" in which they are embedded, then there is no authority to the utterance, since the authority itself, as we have already said so many times, derives principally from the commitment of the speaker to the idea of discourse.

The questions to be asked about the ethical teaching of today's church can be abbreviated as follows:

1. Is this teaching attuned to ordinary experience?
2. Is the teaching well and clearly argued?
3. Does it pass the test of the validity claim to sincerity?

The irony of such questions is that they would seem completely noncontroversial within the sphere of public discourse, even in relation to the involvement of the bishops in the public arena. In ecclesial discourse they will seem impertinent to some, and of course in the following pages I do not intend to give the impression that there is no sound ethical teaching in the church. On the contrary, much if not most ethical teaching is quite perspicuous. The problem is a different one, namely, the question whether even good teaching arrived at by a method inconsistent with a community whose action is oriented to understanding can be acceptable. When the teaching is perceived to be poor or misdirected, the problem of lack of communication and dialogue is glaringly obvious. When good, the same problem is there but hidden. The root issue is that of the character of the ecclesial community and the nature of leadership. If indeed it is true that the ecclesiality of Vatican II is that of a community oriented toward understanding, what should be the moral discourse of such a people?

a. *Teaching as the Fruit of Experience*

There is a simplistic form of the "argument from inexperience" that I would like to dismiss at the outset. It is often said that celibate male clergy are really disqualified from ethical teaching in the realm of marriage and the family, sexuality, gender roles, and similar areas in which they have "no experience," or at least in which what experience they have is not acquired in the normal course of events. A similar argument is used by different people to try to dissuade the clergy from pronouncements in economic or political issues, where they should "leave it to the experts." This is not a convincing approach to the issue.

To take but one example, it is frequently said by opponents of the official church position on abortion that clergy and perhaps even all men cannot really speak on the morality of abortion, that women alone are in a position to be aware of all the issues that come into play. Although there is an important and obvious truth here, it disguises the fact that there is a difference between reflection on the ethical issues surrounding abortion and teaching as a fruit of such reflection on the one hand, and, on the other, authentic knowledge of how you or I would respond when faced with this particular ethical dilemma. In some ways, the ethical reflection necessary to formulate principles is *only* possible when the pressures of the actual situation are not upon us. Just so long as this leisure to reflect is not confused with superior ethical behavior (which can only be adjudged when an individual has to make a choice), it may be that lack of experience could be a positive advantage.

I may at this point be revealing my own biases, but I see a correlation here between the innocence-experience issue on the one hand, and the division between "personal" and "social" ethics on the other. On the whole, I believe, the official teaching of the church on social ethics, though there are serious problems with the way the teaching is arrived at, is exemplary, and the failure of the church as a whole to embrace it is a deplorable lack of courage and compassion. The teaching on "personal" (predominantly sexual) ethics, in my opinion, leaves a great deal to be desired, for reasons I will go into below. Thus, the strengths of the teaching lie in those realms where our inhumanity to one another and our self-concern cloud our judgment (for example, capital punishment, "defense" spending, racism and sexism), while the weaknesses of the teaching cluster more commonly where dilemmas marked by a real struggle between competing "goods" are subordinated to the proclamation of unrelenting principle.

In another sense the divorce of the clergy from everyday experience is much more problematic. The problem is not that they have never had to raise a family or that most of them have not had to share a decision about an unwanted pregnancy, but rather the general moral unaccountability of the clerical life-style. I am not suggesting that the clergy are any more or less moral than anyone else, but that the received structures of the clerical life in fact insulate the clergy from most of the more insistent pressures of "ordinary" life. The usual defense of this situation is that it is thus that the clergy are freed to be of more generous service to the whole community, and obviously in many cases that is the result. At the same time, it does not promote familiarity with the experience of moral choice.

The weakness of putting ethical teaching in the hands of a male celibate clergy is then not that they have not had this or that experience, but that the experience of moral choice itself is considerably less familiar to the clergy than to the majority of laypeople. Obviously this is a generalization, and there are many heroes and heroines in clerical circles and in the religious life to whom none of these strictures apply. But *real* moral choice is of course not a matter of choosing between good and evil so much as between two imperfect options, both of which have much to recommend them. For the great mass of the laity, this kind of moral choice is forced on them by the pressure of circumstances, while for the great mass of clergy, moral choice is rarely forced on them. It is not that they are immoral, but rather that they are not allowed to be moral.

Although the separation from the experience of this or that moral dilemma may in certain circumstances make it easier to present objectively the ethical principles which bear upon the case, lack of familiarity with balancing such principles under pressure can adversely affect the tone and thus the effectiveness of the teaching. Choices about abortion, artificial insemination, *in vitro* fertilization, care of handicapped children, or terminally ill parents, decisions about the morality of this or that form of employment, choices about marriage, divorce or remarriage and so on, are most frequently made under severe emotional and psychological stress, and often under considerable financial pressure. Clergy are excluded from most of these decisions for most of the time, and especially from the financial pressures attendant upon them.

Obviously, the experience of ethical choice does not change moral principles, but a system which excludes those who bear the brunt of moral choice from the formation of ethical teaching is missing some very important dimensions.

If teaching, then, is at least partly strengthened by being the fruit of experience, it seems as if the formation of the church's teaching and the consequent refinement of its ethical conscience and sensitivity need the contributions of the laity, excluded to date from any real participation. In a fashion parallel to the argument of the last chapter, we can say that while the magisterium retains and should retain the charism of judgment about the commitment to the discourse of the moral tradition, that discourse over which they exercise their charism must become a discourse of the whole church. In the moral discourse of the whole church, because it must incorporate the fruits of experience, ethicists both clerical and lay will contribute their logic and learning, but the brunt of discussion must be shouldered by the whole communication community.

b. *Teaching as Argumentation*

Ethical teaching exhibits a blend of three levels of statement: fundamental principles, middle axioms, and particular applications, Thus, for example, there is the fundamental ethical principle that all human life is sacred. A middle axiom deriving from this would be the claim that therefore no one may do anything to interfere with or terminate a life once begun, from the moment of conception to the deathbed. One of many particular applications of this is the ethical teaching of the immorality of abortion. An alternative application of the same principle could be complete pacifism or opposition to capital punishment.

Generally speaking, there is little dispute over fundamental moral principles. They are few, universal, and abstracted from particular contexts. They are on the whole unexceptionable. Middle axioms are key because they are the source of rules for applying principles to real-life situations. Although they may be quite acceptable as general guidelines, problems arise when they become affected by a creeping absolutism that surreptitiously raises them to the rank of moral principles. Middle axioms, however, because they can be explained only in terms of something more fundamental to which they refer and on which they depend for their meaning, are always revisable, where moral principles are not. To ask why human life is sacred is to step outside the rules of the game; to question a middle axiom is to seek clarity about the rules of the game and its possible outcomes.

In the Habermasian categories of chapter 5, the fundamental moral principles correspond to defining characteristics of the particular communication community, *principia* of the lifeworld without which this particular community would cease to be. The moral discourse of the communication community operates against the background of the lifeworld to pursue normative agreement. The search for normative agreement involves discourse about middle axioms, as a result of which the community can lay down boundaries for what is acceptable and unacceptable conduct. But this is not to say that norms must be of the kind exemplified above, which are really ways of linking in a smoothly running chain the fundamental principles to real-life situations in order to circumvent the need for moral discourse.

If one of the weaknesses of the magisterium is that those who teach suffer from a kind of structurally reinforced inexperience, then a second and perhaps related problem is the apparent preference in the teaching for unequivocal principle and absolutized middle axioms to existence within the gray area of more or less good alternatives in which moral choice must actually take place. This seems to derive from a fear or suspicion of the experience of moral choice, and even more from the unwillingness to proclaim unequivocally that moral choice is ethical, and that of itself mere assent even to authoritative teaching is at best morally neutral. The promotion of a rule-based morality, particularly one whose principles derive from some arbitrarily espoused theoretical framework (such as, notoriously, so-called natural law) is in fact a form of ethical fundamentalism. It derives from a fear or unwillingness to occupy the space of moral choice, and exhibits a preference for obedience over discernment. I do not wish to argue that there is no place for ethical principles, but rather that where there is no conflict of ethical principles, there is no moral dilemma.

There are two models operative in current ethical teaching in the Catholic church, one frankly insensitive to the demands of communicative action, one at least more sensitive. The first or "way of authority" model is unfortunately the majority position, utilized throughout official Vatican documents and in much episcopal teaching. The second or "way of consensus" approach appears in *some* episcopal teaching, and most clearly in the recent writings of the United States Catholic bishops. Once again, let me stress that the objective validity of the ethical insights expressed is not tied to one model rather than another. The process of the former, however, must in the end reduce the effectiveness of the teaching.

The recent letter of the Congregation for the Doctrine of the Faith "On the Pastoral Care of Homosexual Persons" is a useful illustration of the "way of authority" for a number of reasons.[5] In the first place, the document, despite its shortcomings, does show considerable compassion, and so cannot be accused of being one of the worst examples of magisterial teaching. Second, homosexuality is not something from which the clergy is insulated in the same way as, say, it largely is from abortion or contraception. Third, and despite the first two considerations, the document shows a remarkable preference for abstraction over experience. A distinction is made between homosexual activity and what the Congregation quaintly calls the "homosexual condition." Most criticisms of official church teaching on homosexuality understandably focus on the teaching about the "unnaturalness" of same-sex sexual relations, as just one more misapplication of an outmoded and in any case wooden understanding of natural law. The real weakness of the teaching, however, is that while it apparently believes that both homosexual activity and homosexual orientation are "unnatural," it operates with a division between the two kinds of unnaturalness by which the unnatural act is sinful and the unnatural "condition" is not. The more important issue for our particular purposes, however, is that the teaching is arrived at through the repetition of scriptural and historical argumentation alone, without any attempt to reflect the discourse of the ecclesial community, in which at the present time homosexuality is neither approved of nor utterly condemned, but in which understanding and compassion are undoubtedly growing.

Similar comments could be made on a whole variety of other teachings: For example, how many women who have had abortions have been heard in preparing teaching on abortion? how many married couples are listened to in the formation of church teaching on birth control? how many childless couples when the teaching banning artificial insemination is considered? how many women when telling women what their rightful place in society is? It is not that any of these groups has the last say on any of these issues, but that the absence of those most centrally involved from the discursive formation of the particular teaching detracts from that teaching's acceptability even when it is objectively correct.

For an example of the "way of consensus" model of teaching, I turn back to the United States Catholic bishops' document, *Economic Justice for All: Catholic Social Teaching and the U.S. Economy,* which was mentioned briefly at the beginning of this chapter. Though one can carp at some aspects of the letter, its publication was an important event. It summons the church to an examination of relatedness. It calls for an integral approach to economic, political, social, and religious realities, a radically different way of looking not only at the economic realities of daily life, but also at the relationship of religious belief to those economic facts of life. The world the bishops depict is one in ever-present danger of what Dorothee Soelle has called "death by bread alone." The proposals they make in the milieu of a pluralistic society illustrate the truth of Soelle's remark that religion can be seen as "one way of naming the activity of taking sides with life."[6] Overall, the document presents a Christian reflection on and response to the current United States economy in relation to the world economy as a whole. It is both a teaching document addressed to members of the church and a position paper from the perspective of the Catholic tradition in social ethics intended as a contribution to public debate.

This document differs in a number of respects from most others in the tradition of Catholic Social Teaching. In the first place, though it is of course true that most if not all of the organizing ethical principles of the document are drawn directly from previous teaching in social ethics, perhaps especially from that of the present Pope, the self-understanding of the document differs widely. As a reflection on the *national* implications and repercussions of a world problem, it is much more like the kind of document Paul VI advocated in *Octogesima Adveniens*[7] in 1972 than an attempt at a universal solution favored, apparently, by John Paul II. Second, the consultative model employed in composing the document, parallel to the earlier 1983 document on nuclear deterrence, with its published drafts and opportunity for church-wide comment and consultation, differs spectacularly from all that has gone before in instruments of church teaching, as well as from most of what has followed. These two divergences from traditional approaches mean, of course, that this kind of document is at one and the same time more in touch with the experience of the wider church community and more tentative in its conclusions. Its plurality and ambiguity are a surer indication of the complexity of the issues it discusses. The openness of the process that led to its publication, by the same token, opens it more to the influence of interest groups. The tone of honest searching in the document testifies to the former, while what some have perceived as the oversensitivity to American sensibilities introduced into the third and final draft of the document could be explained as a response to the pressure the bishops undoubtedly felt from the signatories of the "lay letter" produced to coincide with their first draft two years earlier.

That the document explicitly sets out to be both a teaching instrument for Christians and a contribution to a public debate explains one of its chief polarities, the "twin-source" approach to ethical teaching. In a departure from the almost exclusively natural law approach of Catholic Social Teaching, the bishops give a great deal of attention to biblical sources for ethics, far more than did John Paul II in his brief references to Genesis in *On Human Work* (1981). On the face of it, this would seem to make it harder to gain recognition for their position in the arena of public debate. In a pluralistic society arguments that derive from Hebrew or Christian scripture must be set aside.

Attention to Scripture seems to me to have at least two advantages now in the American arena. First, the use of scripture uncovers ethical principles that have to be applied in the world, it does not find easy answers to dificult moral problems. It is thus a corrective to the fundamentalist biblical vision, itself an important part of national public debate. Creation is the foundation of human dignity, covenantal justice highlights the plight of the poor and oppressed, and discipleship is an "imitation of Christ" ordered more to loving service of the needy and dispossessed than to the disembodied pieties of an earlier age. In the second place, the Christians are invited by the bishops' scriptural arguments into a position where they will be more likely to take seriously the radical character of the ethical norms which follow. Justice in solidarity, say the bishops,

> demands the establishment of minimum levels of participation in the life of the human community for all persons. . . . Minimum material resources are an absolute necessity for human life. If persons are to be recognized as members of the human community, then the community has an obligation to help fulfill these basic needs unless an absolute scarcity of resources makes this strictly impossible. No such scarcity exists in the United States today.[8]

The document does not allow the reader to conclude that these levels of participation can be met by private initiatives alone. Perhaps the connection to Scripture is intended to sweeten what to most political conservatives and economic capitalists must seem quite a bitter pill to swallow.

The way in which the community was involved in the composition of this document clearly places it closer to the perspective of communicative action and discourse. Thought it can possibly be considered a first step in the right direction, however, it is not as it stands a product of discourse ethics. Most of the consultation prior to the first draft consisted in hearing expert testimony, and what we might call the "committee stage" was principally focused on matters of organization and structure. Moreover it was pointed out more than once that although the document concerned itself in large part with the plight of the poor, and though it called a number of experts on poverty to provide testimony, it did not actually call on any of the poor themselves for their input.

More important than these considerations, the ineffectiveness of this document (like that of the earlier document on nuclear armaments) is directly related to its divorce from the discourse of the community it is intended to teach. Its content did not issue from community consensus, and since there is no process of discourse in the church, that can come as no surprise! Its teaching has not reached the vast majority of the community, because there is no grassroots structure of community discourse into which it can be inserted. So hierarchically structured is the church that dissemination of information from the top downward, so to speak, is always in the form of directives, and from the bottom upward, where it exists at all, in the form of commentary on draft directives. There is no forum in which all the members of the church meet absolutely equally as ethical actors or as humble listeners to the gospel. Thus, despite the step forward it represents, the bishops' approach continues to suffer from many of the weaknesses of the more rigid traditional model of teaching.

The clear confusion of this discussion of the two models

of ethical argumentation in formal church documents is that the effectiveness as opposed to the truth of the teaching is seriously at risk because it lacks both the foundation in the ethical discourse of the community and the base for its further discussion and dissemination in that same community. There are hopeful signs in the recent practice of the United States bishops and others, but until ethical teaching becomes the exercise of the charism of judgment over the moral discourse of the whole community, it will carry conviction only for those who agree with the position it takes, and it will be unable to reach those roots of the ecclesial community where individual Christians make moral choices and influence the society in which they live.

c. *Teaching by Example*

The *moral* force of teaching does not depend solely or even principally on the abstract truth of its arguments. The moral force has much more to do with the example the teachers set of their own willingness to live up to their standards, and the authenticity that is consequently brought to teaching by the witness of the lives out of which it issues. There is nothing new about this insight; it is as old as the injunction to practice what you preach, though it has been given fresher impetus by critical theory's insistence on the reflexivity of critique, by hermeneutical insight into the bankruptcy of subject-object dichotomies, and by Habermas's description of the validity claim to sincerity in terms of speech-acts and their relationship to "action-contexts."

A shining example of sincere ethical teaching can be found in the document "The Poverty of the Church" issued by the Latin American Bishops' Conference at their Medellin meeting in 1968.[9] The bishops not only recognized their responsibility to reorient the church toward the needs of the vast number of poor and oppressed people in Latin America, but they also saw that such a shift in perspective would require the church to become poor itself, both as a sign of its commitment and in order to be able to see the world from the point of view of the poor. More important still, in quite a number of Latin American countries this ethical teaching was put into practice, and the church became a church of the poor and expressed that preferential option for the poor that Vatican documents have more recently adopted.[10]

The requirements of the validity claim to sincerity are easy to see, if they are not always easy to practice. Documents on the pastoral care of homosexual persons are as sincere as is the personal commitment to those pastoral directives on the part of homosexual bishops and clergy. Teaching on liberation is sincere if the teaching body is itself committed to structures of freedom rather than oppression. The rights of women in society are sincerely proclaimed only if the rights of women in the church are genuinely recognized and protected. Teaching on the rights of labor is hypocritical if church institutions themselves, from the Vatican to the parochial school, are not *the* examples of humane practices and outstanding working conditions.

The validity claim to sincerity is not identical to the claim to rightness. The magisterium, or anyone else, can be sincere about a wrong teaching and teach rightly while being insincere. The majority of lay Catholics in the United States seem to think that the church's teaching on birth control is wrong, but few doubt its sincerity. While sincere, church teaching on artificial insemination of a woman with her husband's sperm, hinging as it does on the illicitness of masturbation as a means of collecting the sperm, seems to most people almost unimaginably remote from reality. On the other side, Catholic elementary school teachers may well applaud the rightness of teaching on economic justice while suspecting the sincerity of an institution that has never paid them a living wage. In all such issues, the sincerity of teaching is relatively easy to defend, and even easier to disprove where necessary.

The previous discussions of ethics and the fruit of experience must not be forgotten at this point. While it is true that the sincerity of ethical teachers has an enormous impact on their effectiveness and authority, if ethical teaching is construed as the charism of judgment exercised over the ethical discourse of the whole community, then the requirement of sincerity is displaced from the magisterium alone and imposed on all of us. It is the practical discourse of the entire communication community that is subject to the requirement of sincerity, it is its validity claim to sincerity that is open to challenge, and it is the communication community as a whole that must vindicate that sincerity in the demonstration that there is a consonance between its discourse and the action-contexts. Thus, on this understanding, we expect no more but no less of bishops than we do of everyone, because they are participants in the moral discourse of the community before they are judges over its conformity to the rules of discourse which guard the ethical tradition of the church.

HABERMAS'S DISCOURSE ETHICS

Just as Habermas's consensus theory of truth emerged in the discussion of theoretical discourse, so a "discourse ethics" arises under the rubric of practical discourse. For Habermas, the reader will recall, truth lies not in some proposition abstracted from the field of communicative action, but in the consensus that interlocutors could arrive at as a result of investigating the cogency of a particular truth-claim. That is true which can command the assent of reasonable people in open-ended and uncoerced communication. The sphere of the ethical is subjected to similar discursive testing.

"Practical discourse" is that process of discursive examination which occurs in communicative action when norms of rightness are under scrutiny. Habermas's earliest and most compact treatment of this process is to be found in *Legitimation Crisis*.[11] The validity claim of a norm, says Habermas, lies in its "binding character." This cannot be explained "without recourse to rationally motivated agreement or at least to the conviction that consensus on a recommended norm could be brought about *with reasons*." In the communication community, "The validity claim of norms is grounded not in irrational volitional acts of the contracting parties, but in the rationally motivated recognition of norms, which may be questioned at any time."[12] This proceeds through the use of "substantial arguments," which "are based on logical inferences" but "are not exhausted in deductive systems of statements."[13]

Discourse ethics has to do with the establishment of norms governing "generalizable interests" or "needs that can be communicatively shared."[14] This is an ethic that "has no need of principles" because "it is based only on fundamental norms of rational speech that we must always presuppose if we discourse at all."[15] Fundamentally, therefore, it operates on the belief that there are some interests that a particular communication community can universalize, and that unconstrained and deception-free discourse is the way to uncover what they are. *What* they are is not at issue for discourse ethics. Just as the consensus theory of truth found the truth in the reasons offered, through which the consensus came about, so discourse ethics finds the ethic in the "rational will formation" that occurs through practical discourse, not in this or that ensuing value. In this way, discourse ethics is at once universal and pluralistic. It expects that what is ethical will always and everywhere be decided in the same way, through rational will formation proceeding according to the discursive redemption of the validity claim to rightness. But it does not make judgments about the content of this or that ethical code. In Habermas's words, "Ethical universalism does indeed have a utopian content, but it does not *sketch out* a utopia."[16]

In a conversation with another human being, or in the life of the ecclesial community, agreement on norms is for the most part implicit. Certainly such fundamental agreement is necessary if the consensus community is to be genuinely possible. But as the foregoing discussion tried to make clear, it is the normative dimension in ethical discourse that is both the most controversial element and the heart of the ethical.

Discourse ethics, though articulated in procedural categories, takes place only within particular communities, and will inevitably be set against the background of the lifeworld. But discourse ethics is not identical with the discussion of which courses of action to consider adopting in a particular circumstance. Of course, even in this discussion, one would hope, procedural rationality of the kind Habermas is concerned with will play a part if proper conclusions are to be reached. But the locus of discourse ethics is in discussion of the norms that bind the universal will formation. Indeed, this is an important and often forgotten distinction. Ethical discourse, and in consequence, it would seem, ethical teaching, belongs in the realm of the discussion of norms of rightness, essentially formulating and defending the "middle axioms," which mediate between fundamental moral axioms and concrete situations. The fundamental principles themselves lie beyond ethics in the largely unthematized content of the lifeworld, and the concrete situations in which norms must be applied are too numerous for teaching to cover them. Although the ideal of ethical discourse takes place in a community or between a number of interlocutors, in the real world there may be a kind of personal, internal discourse as it were, corresponding to the fact that ethical choice is very often a matter for the individual, and indeed that time does not always allow the individual to consult the community. Now, of course, to the degree that the communication community is a living reality, the pressure on the individual to meet moral dilemmas alone will be correspondingly reduced, but such situations will always occur, perhaps even often. The difference between the individual placed in such a situation under discourse ethics, and one situated similarly under a more traditionally authoritarian ethical system is that in the former the individual is bound only to the practical discourse in which he or she has already in principle been a participant, but in the latter the individual is open to oppression by a moral vision essentially imposed from without.

In a recent essay referred to already in chapter 2, Habermas formulated his universalizability principle in a manner that makes it possible to see how it can be applied by the individual as well as in the ideal case of the communication community. It will be helpful to repeat it here: "The consequences and side-effects which would foreseeably result from the universal subscription to a disputed norm, and as they would affect the satisfaction of the interests of *each* single individual, could be accepted by all *without constraints*."[17] The individual employs norms in making choices, and is not always or even often in a posture of discursive defense of the norms applicable in a particular situation. But the norms employed are either the product of discourse or, if they are defensible, open to the constraint-free consent of every individual. What preserves this position from a Kantian formalism is its location within a communication community that shares and may invoke the lifeworld, and its essential subordination to the discourse of the community.[18]

THE WAY OF AUTHORITY AND THE WAY OF CONSENSUS

In order to use Habermas's discourse ethics to inform our understanding of the relationship between ethical discourse and ethical teaching in the church, I want to ask about the illocutionary force of moral teaching. When an official organ of the magisterium pronounces a locution with an ethical content (assuming that it has no strategic perlocutionary intent), what is the implied but unspoken addition to this statement that makes it teaching rather than opinion? In the last chapter we considered a similar but more narrowly doctrinal issue and concluded that the illocution had to do with a judgment on the appropriateness of this or that insight to the tradition viewed as discourse. Now we must consider the question of whether any new factor is added by the ethical circumstances in which the teaching is proclaimed.

The illocutionary force of teaching implies a claim either to some special expertise or to some authority, or a mixture of both, on the matter to be taught. In the ethical field, this is either a matter of special insight into what ought to be done, or a mandate to proclaim what ought to be done, or a mixture of both. As we saw above, this teaching is always a mixture of the enunciation of principles, the extrapolation of middle axioms, and the application of principles and derived axioms to concrete situations and circumstances. Expertise and authority are differently related to each of these stages.

In ethical teaching in the Catholic tradition, the enunciation of ethical principles is always a matter of appeal either to revelation or to supposedly unchanging principles of natural law. Reference to revelation for ethical principles, however, always arrives at principles that are taken to be a part of that natural law. That is to say, the ethical principles are at least understood by the magisterium to be principles that command the assent of all human beings, that do not derive, in other words, from revelation even if for the Christian tradition they have their first and privileged expression in revelation. It did not become wrong to take human life at the moment at which the injunction against killing appeared in the Decalogue. On the contrary, the Decalogue contained a ban on killing because it was and always had been wrong to kill, whether or not killing had previously been a way of life.

Fundamental ethical principles are hard to argue, because there is a certain self-evident character to them. They are, by their nature, beyond dispute within any particular community. Those who deny the right to life, to liberty (however understood), to fulfilling human relationships, and to membership in a community place themselves beyond the ethical, because they put themselves outside the boundaries of discourse. At the furthest extreme, in the realm of the largest possible communication community, that of the human race, refusal to recognize the most basic of values, including the validity claims of rational communication, literally precludes genuine human interchange. There is no way to argue with someone about the *relative* merits of the right to life or the lack of such a right. Another way to say this is to say that fundamental ethical principles are the defining characteristics of the community, and that discourse can occur only within the community, or between communities open to the logic of communicative action.

If fundamental principles are not the subject of ethical discourse, then neither is discourse appropriate to the concrete circumstances of this or that particular ethical dilemma. For one thing, the ethical situation is intensely particular; only the particular individual or individuals involved are able to make the ethical decision, though no doubt in principle many others could advise them. But furthermore, the ethical situation is also one requiring choice or decision rather than discourse. Of course, the capacity to make the right decision is at least partly a product of moral education, which is a matter for the community and its discourse, and is the principal way in which the community enters into the individual's choice. But in the last analysis, as even the traditions of the church recognize, the weight of authority, moral leadership, and moral education must bow before the responsibilities of the individual conscience.

In fact, discourse occurs only in discussing middle axioms, coming to consensus on how norms shall be derived from principles, and in discussing whether and how a norm or norms apply to this or that particular circumstance. It is exactly at the point where revelation and natural law leave off that ethics become necessary. Revelation is a narrative account of human teleology, and natural law is an extrarevelatory systematization of this narrative in anthropological terms. Revelation tells the story of human destiny. It shows how God's initiative creates the conditions in which it is possible for human beings to overcome sin and achieve eternal happiness. The derived anthropology lying behind natural law sees human fulfillment as intimately connected with three principles: the acceptance of one's own contingency, the recognition of the dignity of the individual human being, and the essentially interpersonal and communal structure of human existence. Ethics is the discourse that takes up this vision of the human and fashions a response to the question: So how shall we live?

Because ethics and consequently ethical teaching only come into existence at the level of discourse on the relationship between principles and their mediation to concrete circumstances, there is no appropriate direct application of scripture or revelation to ethical discourse. The ethical vision of the Mosaic law or the Sermon on the Mount can teach us a great deal about what a sensitive and contextualized ethical application of fundamental principles might look like, but neither can be transferred directly to our own times. Of course many of the insights of the Mosaic law and of Jesus remain applicable in our own day, but this is because our circumstances continue to make them relevant, and a judgment about which insights remain appropriate and which do not (and there are many, even in Jesus' teaching, that do not receive assent today) itself involves complex theological, historical, and ethical considerations.

The ethical teaching of the magisterium seems to be a combination of two components. In the first place, its authority and expertise, as in the case of strictly theological judgments, are connected with the charism of judgment. But this charism of judgment is not exercised in discerning fundamental ethical principles. These are "pre-institutional," one might almost say pre-historical. Rather, the charism of judgment is applied to assessing which ethical discourse in the Christian community represents a response to fundamental ethical principles and the narrative of revelation consistent with, though not identical to, the response contained in scripture itself. This first component, then, is closely connected with tradition, but specifically with the tradition of ethical or practical discourse, rather than theological or theoretical discourse. Just as in the case of theological discourse, the teaching function operates within the perimeters of the work of the expert and the conversation of the community.

In ethical discourse the notion of the expert has to be modified. Experts on moral decision making are those who have most frequently experienced the need to make ethical choices. This is why earlier it was suggested that authority and expertise are more closely identified in the ethical field than in the theological field with experience itself. Although it is not possible to deny a role to experts in the more traditional sense, to those professionals who have specialized in philosophical or theological ethics, in logic or in the social sciences, their expertise is not precisely *ethical* expertise, but expertise about ethics, which is by no means the same thing. They are, therefore, support personnel to the ethical discourse, which cannot be limited by perimeters narrower than those of the entire community. It is in the community itself that ethical expertise is properly located, in moral caliber and leadership that, because it must be directly linked to experience, cannot be simply identified with the charism of the magisterium.

Ethical discourse *within* the church is then a bridging conversation, adjudicated by the magisterium, whose role it is to see that in the formulation of those middle axioms, which make the fateful transition from eternal truths to concrete circumstances, the conversation partners proceed according to the principles of communicative action, and faithfully follow the rules for the "redemption" of disputed validity claims when these arise. Eternal truths can be proclaimed, and the magisterium can proclaim them. Middle axioms must be negotiated, in the dialectic between eternal truths and concrete situations. Ethical decisions can only be made, and in the last analysis made only by individuals, even when they emerge as a community consensus on a public policy matter.

It is time to return to the question with which this section began, that of the "illocutionary force" of ethical teaching. For it remains true that the church's magisterium does as a matter of fact engage in a considerable amount of ethical teaching, and does not simply restrict itself to the charism of judgment over the ethical discourse of the whole community. The force of its teaching seems to be a claim to an authority precisely to teach, and moreover one that the community as a whole recognizes, though not as an ultimate right over the informed conscience of the individual. Additionally, it seems clear that the "sense of the faithful" on at least some issues leads it not to accept fully every single ethical teaching (the teaching of the Vatican on birth control is the most spectacular example). Are there rules that can govern this situation, or are we bound to shifting opinion and liberal illusions?

The illocutionary force of ethical teaching implicitly claims an authority the community recognizes. However, the authority does not rest on the claim to it, as we have already noted. Rather it depends on three factors. First, the authority claimed is an authority that must be exercised in the light of the discourse of the whole community. This does not mean that the magisterium is bound to the enunciation of majority opinion on ethical issues, but that it is indeed bound to teach what has emerged and continues to emerge from an ecclesial discourse governed by the desire for understanding and consensus. Second, the authority emerges from the discourse of the community in the sense that those exercising it must recognize that they must also and even primarily take their place as members of the discourse community, *equal* partners in the discourse of the church. Finally, the authority evaporates if those exercising it are not seen to be as deeply engaged in making ethical choices as they are in teaching ethics; in other words, the authority is tied to sincerity.

The second component of the ethical teaching of the magisterium is their voice as conversation partners in the consideration of ethical issues within a pluralistic world. Although this has been most explicitly affirmed in the documents of the American Catholic bishops, from the time of *Gaudium et Spes* it has implicitly been a dimension of the church's self-understanding. In this context, the word "teaching" can only be used with great caution. Obviously, all teach one another in any seminar setting, even if one or another participant has more theoretical knowledge, and one is more saintly than the rest. But the authority with which one or another conversation partner speaks is directly related to the cogency of their arguments and the confidence they inspire in others that they act upon their beliefs. In dialogue in the wider world, in other words, whether that of ecumenical, interreligious, or secular character, the sole basis for any authority the magisterium might possess is that of expertise, both theoretical and practical. In the public sphere they must earn authority; they cannot simply claim it. Of course, because we have also seen that the experience of moral decision making is intrinsic to the notion of ethical authority, to a degree this claim to authority must also be earned within the church.

The charism of authoritative teaching in the ethical sphere in the church is then somewhat circumscribed and dependent for its validity on the simultaneous existence of a vigorous moral discourse in the community as a whole. There is no way for the magisterium to determine on its own account the "universal will formation" needed for the recognition of generalizable interests. That requires a discourse shared by the whole community. Generalizable interests are only those which either are agreed upon by the community, or could be agreed upon by the community. All other matters are governed by compromise, which while itself a function of discourse, is not strictly within the realm of the ethical, at least as Habermas defines it. The erroneous exercise of magisterium occurs when the charism is assumed to be one of informing the community which interests are generalizable, when the determination of this is only possible through discourse. The correct exercise of magisterium occurs when judgment is offered on the conformity of discourse to the tradition of discourse, that is, when errors in commitment to the canons of procedural rationality are pointed out, and when the consensus of the community upon its generalizable interests is affirmed as consistent with the discourse of tradition.

AUTHORITY, PRESTIGE, AND INFLUENCE

In the second volume of *The Theory of Communicative Action*, Habermas recognizes, as we saw in chapter 2, the emergence of "relief mechanisms" by which society releases itself from the constant need to "steer" everything through discourse. If every choice in society had to go through a process of communicative action and await the emergence of consensus, nothing would ever get done. Instead, those everyday choices and operations that form recognizable patterns and follow predictable courses— what Habermas calls "generalized action orientations"— are coordinated through the functioning of "prestige" and "influence."

Prestige and *influence* are terms denoting two bases for the exercise of authority or leadership in society. The former is a matter of personal attributes, the latter of the power of disposition of resources. Habermas lists the defining characteristics of prestige and influence in a table that indicates the potentially valuable and potentially harmful variants of both.[19] Empirically, prestige is a matter of a mixture of strength, know-how, and physical attractiveness; rationally, it is based on responsibility. Influence, on the other hand, is empirically based on "property," rationally, on knowledge. The empirical, corresponding to the system, works through various forms of inducement. The rational, that of the lifeworld and of communicative action, is based on trust.

The political systems of present-day Western democracies provide a very good example of the exercise of prestige and influence empirically. The role of "image-makers" in the United States presidential stakes is probably the most notorious instance of the system's recognition, even management, of how and why voters vote. "Charisma" and financial resources consistently win over responsibility and trust. Political life has become detached from the community (lifeworld) and attached to the system. Restored to its rightful place, it would still involve a mechanism for selecting a leader who would foreshorten the daily process of discourse, who would in other words govern in the name and according to the values of the community. But in the present situation, discourse has been abandoned to government, not placed in trust.

One way to express the possibilities and limitations of ethical teaching and leadership in the church is in the same language of system and lifeworld, prestige and influence. The recognition on the part of the ecclesial community of the charism of authoritative teaching is a possible appropriate "relief mechanism" by which the community is not endlessly involved in reinventing the ethical wheel. However, the "rational" rather than the empirical must apply: That is, *in the last analysis* this teaching must rest not on its own claim to authority but on the conformity and openness of the teaching to the discursive redemption of its validity claims. Teaching, in other words, rests on communicative action and discourse, it does not displace it.

Recent problems in the institutional exercise of ethical teaching authority can be characterized, I believe, as attempts to operate on the empirical, systemic level. Teaching is then an exercise of authority on the assumption that there is no significant moral discourse of the whole community within which this teaching takes its place. Rather, the teaching is gratefully received by a community that does not see or perhaps would not welcome a role for itself in the formation of moral teaching. If I am right, the term "dissent" is itself obsolete: For the tradition language of "teaching" and "dissent from teaching" simply does not recognize the reality of the discourse community. To use the proper terminology, I believe, would be to talk not of teaching and dissent but of teaching and discourse. Teaching and discourse are always going on, and the former is always adjusting to the new insights acquired through the latter, just as the latter is always aware of the perimeters laid down by the former. Of course, these boundaries are not so much limits that the teaching itself expresses as they are limits of the tradition of discourse to which the teaching is itself held accountable.

Let us take an example or two from current ethical issues. On the one side, there are those issues like abortion, artificial insemination, "test-tube" babies, birth control, homosexuality, and so on, where the apparent dynamics consist of a somewhat entrenched or at least static magisterium, and an ecclesial public that is to a degree more flexible. Here the role of the magisterium is predominantly and rightly conservative, not in the sense that it should preclude discourse, but that it should require such discourse to conform to canons of communicative action, and that it should be open to the possibility of a developing understanding and, consequently, a modified teaching if that authentic discourse arrives at new insights. On the other side, there are issues such as capital punishment, world hunger, economic rights, and homelessness, where the dynamics are quite different. Here, the magisterium is more progressive than the community, and its role is the same role of overseeing the tradition of discourse, but the exercise of that role is one of challenging the community to free itself to practice genuine discourse. The so-called seamless garment approach to right-to-life issues is a classic example of a call for the discursive redemption of validity claims. How, consistently, can communicative action oppose abortion, do nothing serious about starvation at home and abroad, and actively support capital punishment?

The preceding two chapters in particular have mapped out an understanding of the role of the community and the charism of authoritative teaching that promotes freedom, responsibility, and discernment. Such a church, come of age in a world that too often seems wrapped up in selfish irresponsibility, could have an enormous impact, not perhaps in a way that people would recognize as directly religious or evangelical, but in providing a working model of a community dedicated to discourse and communicative action. That this does not look much like the public face of the Catholic church today is both a tragic missed opportunity and evidence of a distorted colonization of the lifeworld by the system, in this case of the community by its institutional elements. But the resources are undoubtedly present in a way that they are not in the world at large, and in the next and final chapter I shall address the question of how this role for the church, if put to work, could have an impact on our postmodern society.

CHAPTER SEVEN

CATHOLICISM AND POSTMODERNITY

The principal objective of the foregoing chapters has been to show that Habermas's ideas of communicative action and discourse support in a number of ways postconciliar Catholic ecclesiology. They provide a mechanism for the diagnosis and treatment of problematic elements in the tradition of social ethics. They offer a corrective to the authoritarianism of everyday praxis. They enable a new and helpful articulation of the important concept of tradition. Taken all in all, while they do not impinge upon the mystery of the sacramental reality of the church, they assist immensely in clarifying both the internal dynamics of the ecclesial community and its outlook on the world.

It remains to ask if critical theory can assist in elucidating the overall relationship of the church to the world, and, in the concrete, to our own "postmodern" world. It is axiomatic in contemporary Catholic ecclesiology that the church exists not for its own sake, nor even for God's, but for the sake of the world that is saved through Christ's redemptive act. The church indeed has a mission to the world, if not necessarily one to be perceived solely in traditionally missionary fashion as the aggressive proclamation of the gospel or the equally aggressive offer of baptism. It is a mission to be distinguished, among other things, by the recognition that "action on behalf of justice and participation in the transformation of the world fully appear to us as a constitutive dimension of the preaching of the gospel."[1]

The optimistic and indeed "upbeat" tone of most social teaching from the Vatican can be a problem. It is of course a natural outgrowth of a salvation-historical, incarnationalist theological perspective. If "God so loved the world," then its problems cannot be beyond resolution and its destiny cannot be to become a dead planet murdered by the human race. But this strength can sometimes be a weakness. Where Protestant traditions more comfortable with the dialectical imagination or more attuned to apocalyptic visions of reality can either live with the ambiguities seemingly endemic to our present condition or deny the ultimate significance of the world, Catholicism struggles to cope with its theologically and perhaps even ideologically rose-tinted lenses. The cosmic Christ and the redemption of the whole of creation can be obstructed through human imperfection and perhaps slowed by genuine evil, but not finally bested. Christ has conquered once and for all. And though Protestant traditions are as firm in their faith in redemption, they are on the whole less concerned to take the *saeculum* with them into the reign of God, or to find the reign of God here and now in the world.

It is because of this conviction of the goodness of the whole created order that the chaotic, contingent, and threatened status of what is increasingly often referred to as our "postmodern" world becomes for Catholics a particular theological problem. The real possibility of nuclear annihilation, the apparently major threat of global warming or the depletion of the ozone layer, the scale of the AIDS epidemic are frightening challenges to human goodness and ingenuity. But in some ways they present far greater challenges to the religious imagination, and in particular to one marked by an upbeat attitude to human history. Theology may have to think the unthinkable. For example: Is it possible that the human race could defeat the divine purpose? Or is it possible that the scale of redemption has been misconceived by the human race, that "our" story may be but a detail in a much larger picture, one that incorporates not only the nonhuman world of our own planet but also the unknown reaches of the farthest galaxies? Perhaps the redemption of the race, as of the individuals within it, somehow involves not only the acceptance of contingency but also the abandonment, finally, of our anthropocentric vision of reality.

In facing up to the horrendous scale of today's problems, it has already been argued above that critical social theory could provide support in the formation of an appropriate theoretical background. In this final chapter I want to pay somewhat closer attention to Habermas's theory of modernity, whereas more attention has been given to the structural value of communicative action theory in the praxis of the ecclesial community heretofore. A theory of modernity, and Habermas's in particular, is especially crucial to the church now that the world itself seems to have outgrown the easy optimism of the developmentally inclined sixties.

It will be necessary to begin with a few comments on the language of "modern and postmodern" used in such a bewildering variety of ways by those engaged now in cultural criticism. Following this, Habermas's theory of modernity will be outlined. This will leave three questions to be answered. First, is Habermas's theory of modernity a suitable tool for a better understanding of the character of the postmodern world? Second, how can the ecclesial community be perceived as a point of entry of communicative action into this world? Finally, can this role for the church legitimately be understood to be an important part of its redemptive, transcendent significance? The discussion of the value of critical theory for the work of the church we conducted earlier thus passes over into a consideration of critical theory as a more fundamental theological resource.

MODERNITY AND POSTMODERNITY

Nowhere is terminology more confusing than in the debate over the nature of modernity. The word *modern*, originally intended to identify the postclassical age, was also consciously adopted by the confident age of steam, and is still used today in common parlance to refer to anything perceived to be "up-to-date." "Modernity," on the other hand, is a theoretician's label for the "modern age." Further and more confusing, "Modernism" refers principally to that movement within the arts that sought what it perceived to be a purer and more disciplined approach to the object than that advocated by its immediate artistic antecedents. None of these terms is in itself positive or negative, all are used in both ways by different thinkers.

If anything, the term "postmodern" and its cognates "postmodernity" and "postmodernism" are even more confusing and ambiguous. If this is the postmodern age, does that mean that the modern age is over, or simply that it is in decline? Is postmodernity the defeat of modernity or its development? Would it be correct to see postmodernism as a conscious retrieval of the classical past from beyond Modernism, or as the latest challenge to the impoverished everyday imagination, as a challenge to Modernism or as a challenge to those who identify Modernism as the enemy of the modern age? Any and all of the above, unfortunately, is the answer. The currency of the label "postmodernity" to characterize our age may itself be revealing. In the first place, it betrays the uncertainty of the age, which defines itself by what it is not, or by what it succeeds. More significant, it allows for a multiplicity of interpretations. The postmodern world may thus be construed to be one of the many things that is *not* modernity, or it may be a time and place in which the modernity of the recent past is somehow an issue. This latter more controllable possibility is further subdivided by Hal Foster, when he writes of two opposed postmodernisms, one "which seeks to deconstruct modernism and resist the status quo," and another "which repudiates the former to celebrate the latter." They are, he says, "a postmodernism of resistance and a postmodernism of reaction."[2] This distinction will be utilized below at some length.

While Modernism and Postmodernism (particularly in this capitalized form) were initially and remain predominantly aesthetic labels, though even here there is no consistency with which the terms are interpreted, "postmodernity" is a term increasingly used in the contexts of philosophy and the social sciences.[3] Thus, Habermas identifies a form of postmodernism with the neoconservatism that celebrates "modernity" while rejecting "modernism."[4] Fredric Jameson suggests that two important features of postmodernism in the arts—"the transformation of reality into images, the fragmentation of time into a series of perpetual presents"—reinforce "the logic of consumer capitalism."[5] And Charles Newman has devoted a whole work to the relationship between avant-garde literature and the economics of publishing.[6]

As it stands, of course, the term "postmodernism" is value-free, but as Foster pointed out, there are two ways at least that it can be used, two possible underlying sets of assumptions. A "postmodernism of reaction" rejects the recent modernist past, perceived as the source of the ills of today's world. Modernism is accused of being the origin of hedonism, atheism, "secular humanism," the antisocial, and the socialist. Thus, on this view, the postmodern world is the world come to its senses, returned to the straight and narrow of "family values," God and country, security and prosperity, the "good citizen," and the capitalist system. A postmodernism of resistance, on the contrary, is really the persistence of a strain of modernism into a world that is believed to have become essentially antihuman. The problems of today's world, and above all the introjection of the instincts of the system into the hearts of the citizens, are perceived to demand a countermovement in the name of genuine community and sociality. What is distinctive about this postmodernism of resistance is the formation of a social theory that gives a pronouncedly political interpretation to cultural phenomena.

In noting the frequency of the prefix "post" in much current terminology, Stephen Toulmin refers to "the world that has not yet discovered how to define itself in terms of what it *is,* but only in terms of what it has *just-now-ceased-to-be.*"[7] It is perhaps best to settle for this unjudgmental interpretation of the word "postmodern." It can be descriptive or prescriptive, laudatory or condemnatory, matter-of-fact or highly emotional. But undoubtedly, all those who use the term in whatever sense agree in their uncertainty about a positive label for our times. Maybe that was almost always the case. Perhaps the judgment of history must be awaited for the appropriate name; certainly, the classical and the romantic ages never knew they were classical or romantic. But the "modern age" was an exception. The late nineteenth and early twentieth centuries were filled with a passionate conviction of their own modernity, confident in unraveling the final mysteries of the universe. Perhaps the postmodernism of reaction preserves something of that self-satisfaction, even as it rejects the aesthetic modernism that accompanied the later stages of the modern age, but it has still to find its own identity.

It takes no great depth of perception to see that different forms of religion might be attracted to one or another of our categories of postmodernism. The world as perceived in a postmodernism of reaction would be readily embraced by many fundamentalist groups. Indeed, in many respects television evangelism and television evangelists are important representative phenomena of postmodernism. On the other hand, the critique of the postmodern embrace of mass consumerism and its celebration of the capitalist system fits well with more prophetic strains in Catholicism and mainstream Protestantism. The postmodernism of the former overlaps the embarrassments of the recent past to form a union of the present time with an ahistorically appropriated scriptural message, while the latter sets religion in a posture of what Johann Baptist Metz has called "productive noncontemporaneity," the peculiarly prophetic capacity of religion to stand aside from the prejudices of its own or any other time.[8]

Beyond the more or less instinctive affiliations of religious traditions with one or another attitude to modernity, there are serious theological questions to be asked about the role of Christianity in a postmodern world. This world can be characterized by notions from both the forms of postmodernism sketched out above. The postmodernism of reaction, in its religious dress, is either in search of certainty and security, finding it in an ahistorical clinging to biblical literalism, or, more subtly, settles for a privatized religion by espousing some kind of liberal cultural Christianity. The postmodernism of resistance can go in at least two directions, either toward a sophisticated neo-orthodoxy that in effect rejects the mediation of the gospel to the world, or to a radically political gospel that seeks to "redeem the time." Some at least of these possibilities have been illustrated in a number of recent writings. Both fundamentalism and liberation theology have been looked at in the light of postmodernity by Harvey Cox.[9] The powerful challenge of neo-orthodoxy is forcefully expressed by George Lindbeck.[10] The work of Richard Neuhaus is a primary example of cultural theology.[11] Finally, recent works by Mark C. Taylor[12] and Charles Davis[18] in their different ways press the challenge of postmodernity to all forms of religious belief.

Cutting across the perceptions peculiar to each of these directions is the evident fact that the church in its many forms sees itself as somehow involved in the mystery of redemption, either as its privileged though unworthy recipient, or as its equally unworthy agent to the world. The Second Vatican Council clearly demonstrated a preference for the second formulation. The mystery of the church, understood as People of God, as sacrament and servant in and for the world, is essentially bound up with its missionary role to be the loving presence in the world of Christ's redemptive act. The struggles within the Catholic church since the time of the council can be explained as the conflict of this new, council-sanctioned model with the older and more institutionally minded conception of the church as oriented to success.

The form of the challenge to be discussed from here on, then, is that posed by postconciliar Catholicism. How is it possible for the church to realize the loving presence of God in the postmodern world? What meaning can be given to the idea of salvation in a world that is mostly either non-Christian or post-Christian, for a world whose severe social and environmental problems are the heritage of Christian "civilization," and by a world that is either unimpressed by or hostile to what it perceives as the authoritarian institutionalism of the Vatican? Obviously, we leave behind here the discussion of the internal inadequacies of ecclesial procedure that has occupied so much space earlier. This final, soteriological question is crucial to the church, because it is equivalent to asking if the ecclesial community retains any relevance at all. But any attempt to answer it is predicated on the assumption that the difficult issues of tradition, teaching, and authority are within the capacities of the community to solve. If this assumption is mistaken, then the irrelevance of the church to the contemporary world is ensured.

HABERMAS AND MODERNITY

a. *Modernity and Postmodernity*

In *The Philosophical Discourse of Modernity*, Habermas presents through a dialogue with the philosophical tradition the account of modernity that he worked out in conversation with social science in the two-volume *Theory of Communicative Action*. Though not necessarily any clearer or more important than the earlier work, *The Philosophical Discourse of Modernity* has the advantage for students of religion of being in conversation with thinkers with whom, on the whole, they are more familiar. It also has the advantage of beginning with the point at which Habermas has arrived, and to which it is now apparent all of his earlier work was directed, a thorough and substantial theory of modernity.

The problem of modernity thinks Habermas is to ground itself, and it finds its norms in the principle of subjectivity, supremely in the work of Kant. Subjectivity can divide the world into autonomous realms, but cannot find within itself the means to the restoration of harmony and unity. This is why it is Hegel rather than Kant who occupies Habermas's attention, for Hegel sees the need to expand rationality into reason. Through the exercise of reason, Hegel uses a principle of the Enlightenment in a critique of the Enlightenment's commitment to a fragmenting subjectivity, and thus seeks to ground modernity in reason. According to Habermas, the young Hegel looked at the harmonious exercise of reason in the "communicative mediation of subjects" of the early Christian commune and the Greek *polis*, but unfortunately he did not finally embrace this. Seeing these earlier moments in history as irretrievable, Hegel looked elsewhere for his solution. In modernity, art was "sublated" into religion, faith into philosophy, and civil society into the state. Particularly in the last, thinks Habermas, it is evident that Hegel's solution only works "under the presupposition of an absolute that is conceived on the model of the relation-to-self of a knowing subject":

> If the absolute is then thought of as infinite subjectivity that is eternally giving birth to objectivity in order to raise itself out of its ashes into the glory of absolute knowledge, then the moments of the universal and the individual can be thought of as unified only in the framework of monological self-knowledge.[14]

Reason as absolute knowledge has replaced fate and "knows that every event of essential significance has *already* been decided." So, "Hegel's philosophy satisfied the need of modernity for self-grounding only at the cost of devaluing present-day reality and blunting critique."[15] Modernity is grounded, but the present doesn't really matter any more.

By far the greater part of *The Philosophical Discourse of Modernity* is about what happens after Hegel. The battle lines of modernity are drawn up around the Hegelian legacy. All attack Hegel's grounding of reason in the absolutization of subjectivity, since it replaces visible oppression with the "unassailable domination of rationality."[16] But three distinctive responses to this "positivism of reason" emerge. Left Hegelians remained the most faithful to Hegel's project of the self-grounding of modernity, but turned to the practical and revolutionary potential of reason stored up in historical forces for blowing apart the one-sided rationality of the bourgeois system. Right Hegelians wanted *only* the dynamism of bourgeois society. Nietzsche and those who followed him attacked both and "struck the subjective genitive from the phrase 'critique of reason' by taking critique out of the hands of reason."[17] All three responses continue into the present day, the first in praxis philosophy and the neo-Marxism of the Frankfurt School, the second in technocracy, positivist social science, and the neoconservative critique of culture. But it is with the third, the legacy of Nietzsche, that Habermas is most concerned.

Nietzsche's frontal assault on reason places him at the entry into postmodernity. His work oscillates between "an artistic contemplation of the world carried out with scholarly tools but in an anti-metaphysical, anti-romantic, pessimistic and skeptical attitude," and "a critique of metaphysics that digs up the roots of metaphysical thought without, however, itself giving up philosophy."[18] The former leads to Bataille, Lacan, and Foucault, the latter through Heidegger's philosophical critique to Derrida. With all of these, in separate chapters, Habermas takes issue. "If it should turn out," he says, "that this way also does not seriously lead beyond the philosophy of the subject, we would have to return to the alternative that Hegel left in the lurch back in Jena—to a concept of communicative reason that places the dialectic of enlightenment in a different light."[19]

To summarize a lengthy and complex argument, Habermas concludes that the critique of subject-centered reason, whether in the Heidegger-Derrida or Nietzsche-Foucault direction, does not succeed in changing the paradigm. Genuine critique of subject-centered reason has to transcend the limits of the subject. Thus Habermas proposes returning to the crossroads at which Hegel stood, and following the other path to the changed perspective of a radically intersubjective communicative reason. Reason would thus be tied to the linguisticality of the intersubjective process rather than to the power of the subject over what there is to be known. Materialism and idealism are intertwined, since the unconditionality of the validity claims always implied in communicative action are at the same time "always raised here and now, in specific contexts . . . with factual consequences for action."[20] If this choice is made, thinks Habermas, neo-Marxist thought is rehabilitated through the replacement of "labor" by "communicative action," the system's "colonization of the lifeworld" is challenged and controlled by the specifically interpersonal rationality of communicative action, and the abolition of reason stemming from Nietzsche is countered by a notion of reason located in material reality, and thus not susceptible to absolutization. Communicative rationality provides the normative context for the self-grounding of modernity.

Although much theology is going to have problems with the notion of the *self*-grounding of modernity—isn't all history grounded in the creative and providential reality of God?—theologians and religious ethicists will be able to travel quite a long way with Habermas's reconstruction of post-Enlightenment Western culture. Many of the principal contemporary statements of American religious groups on public policy issues concur with much of what Habermas has to say about technology and about the cultural consequences of the philosophical flight from the self, even if some would not feel so comfortable with his rehabilitation of Marxism or his trenchant critique of neoconservatism. Moreover, almost all the statements emerging from liberal Protestant and Catholic churches would benefit from the explanatory framework he provides. Too often these public policy documents consist of isolated truths and insightful observations on the "signs of the times," which are then immediately referred to scriptural explanation. What is missing is a more deeply historical answer to the question, Given these disturbing historical phenomena, what is actually going on in today's world?

The philosophical discussion conducted in this recent work closely parallels the diagnosis of social systems in volume 2 of *The Theory of Communicative Action*. *The Philosophical Discourse of Modernity* finds hope in a re-thought neo-Marxism in the Hegelian tradition that focuses on communicative reason. The philosophical tradition seems on the whole to have preferred, however, right Hegelianism's fascination with the system of bourgeois society, or a self-destructive nihilism that never finally escapes the philosophy of the subject. In the terminology more commonly used in this present work, the world can coopt the lifeworld or reject it. Neither option leads to satisfying human life, because both essentially ignore the fundamental reality of communicative action.

In a brief but much-quoted and influential article,

Habermas places essentially the same argument in the context of cultural criticism.[21] He begins from the perception of the waning vitality of aesthetic modernism, and the neoconservative determination to eradicate its dominance. The neoconservatives seek an answer to the following questions:

How can norms arise in society which will limit libertinism, reestablish the ethic of discipline and work? What new norms will put a brake on the levelling caused by the social welfare state so that the virtues of individual competition for achievement can again dominate?[22]

Habermas illustrates the neoconservative predicament from the work of Daniel Bell, and refers in passing to Bell's belief, in which he is not alone, that the solution must lie in some kind of religious revival.[23]

More important to Habermas than neoconservatism as an explanation for the problems of modernity is the fragmentation of the unity of metaphysics and religion into the specializations of science, morality, and art that he, following Max Weber, believes to characterize the advent of cultural modernity. Habermas thus locates one source of the crisis of modernity in the impulses of modernity itself. Because of this phenomenon of the professionalization of the cultural tradition, he says, "The distance grows between the culture of the experts and that of the larger public," and the lifeworld is progressively impoverished.[24] He focuses his explanation on the phenomenon of the arts, arguing that aesthetic modernity's flight from notions of beauty and alienation of art from life are a clear example of the problems arising from fragmentation. The problems of modernity need to be overcome through establishing a new unity residing no longer in metaphysics and religion but now in communicative rationality, which has the tasks "of passing on a cultural tradition, of social integration and of socialization."[25] The "relinking of modern culture with an everyday praxis" requires change in the processes of societal modernization, and this returns the argument finally to the confrontation with neoconservatism: "The lifeworld has to become able to develop institutions out of itself which set limits to the internal dynamics and imperatives of an almost autonomous economic system and its administrative complements."[26]

b. *Habermas and Peukert*

The inadequacy of Habermas's handling of religion has been the subject of considerable commentary.[27] Where he discusses religion, he sees it as an evolutionary stage between mythical and modern world views.[28] Where current religious thinkers are referred to with respect, it is only to show that they represent the natural evolution of theology into communicative action.[29] Although much of what Habermas says about myth and modernity is quite acceptable, theologians may want to question where he locates the fundamental impulse of religion. If it is magical merely, then of course the decline of myth is the decline of religion. But if it promotes the unity of human life and is deeply interested in the emancipation of human beings, then it may be of more help than Habermas suspects in finding those ways to heal the lifeworld which he argues are needed, but about the particular form of which he apparently has nothing to offer.

Helmut Peukert's book, *Science, Action, and Fundamental Theology*,[30] is a very impressive attempt to relate theology to critical theory, and indeed to suggest that Habermas's thought stands in need of a religious dimension to remedy some of its deficiencies. Peukert's project works at a number of levels. On one he is engaged in demonstrating how twentieth-century natural and social sciences have moved beyond a positivist stance to a more pragmatic position in which the consensus of the scientific community is vital. On a second level he tries to show a similar movement taking place in twentieth-century theology. On a third he argues that the human solidarity required for the cogency of a theory of communicative action does not make sense outside a religious framework. On a fourth and final level, consequently, he can be seen as engaged simultaneously in a critique of Habermas's communicative praxis theory and a reconstruction of contemporary theology in conformity with critical social theory.

Peukert's book starts with a discussion of the directions a twentieth-century theology must take. Obviously, this means responding to the challenges of social science, and Peukert identifies two such challenges. First, social science tends to explain the role of theology as having a particular function in the evolution of society, and thus to interpret it as "theory," which is now superseded by the social scientific "metatheory." Second, after Hegel and Marx the entire structure of social relations and the mechanisms of society are open to change. Included among these is the idea of consciousness, "which had formerly given us the final guiding categories of our understanding of reality."[31] A theology which takes these two challenges seriously will then have to be a "political" theology, at least in the sense that a theology which takes seriously its role in political society and the implications for its own self-understanding in that society can be accounted "political."

In outlining the shape that a theology adequate to the new world must take, Peukert draws it into close relationship with critical social theory. For example, he argues that the first general problem is the same, namely, the transformation of false consciousness and its illusions into true consciousness. Because it is the purpose of the kerygma to liberate from false consciousness, a modern theology has both to make explicit the ways in which the hold of false consciousness can be broken, and at the same time to recognize that its own human and historical starting point is within the hold of that same false consciousness. Theology does not have a privileged starting point outside or above history.

If theology is to begin from within the false consciousness and illusions of history, then how can it speak of God as the Lord *of* history? Only as the one who is to come, as the Lord and eschatological judge, says Peukert, adding: "The throne of history cannot be occupied by a mythical construct." `Adequate theology must then be negative theology, resisting the objectification of God. Thus, "Reaching outward toward an undominated future and protesting against what is historically actual first opens up the very possibility of the discourse about God as Lord and Meaning of history." In consequence, discourse about God seeks the "mediation of the freedom" that changes the actual and "renews lost freedom." The discourse seeks liberating action, and "free action therefore entails a primacy over the thinking that informs it."[32]

A further question brings theology into direct relationship to communicative action. In such a "negative theology," what is the relationship of the "historically significant saving event" to subsequent history and to the future? Peukert suggests that it "would have to consist in making possible the anticipatory grasp of the novelty of the future and the possibility of the transformation of the present in the direction of this future."[33] It must therefore be recalled, in Metz's phrase, as a dangerous memory. However, "memory" is subject to false consciousness, either "blocked by one's own history or collectively blocked by sedimented social relationships."[34] And so, "A theory of rectifying speech belongs . . . to a society-oriented theological hermeneutics."[35] Communicative action emerges, consistently with the views of Habermas, as the substructure of the emancipatory interest that grounds human autonomy and responsibility. It does for modern times as much as modernity can accept of what metaphysical explanations of reality achieved for a younger world. In Peukert's own words,

It is the binding anticipation of a humanity in communicative practice that, in conflict with nature and in ever further pursued reflection on its situation and its possibilities, grasps that in its free historical movement it projects for itself at every moment that horizon within which all questions must be decided.

However, in the search for transcendence, for what Peukert calls the "utmost idea achievable," humanity seems unable to go beyond "freedom in universal solidarity, to be realized in history."[36] Of course, while this is by any standards an admirable social and political target, it is not an evidently transcendent objective. In the language of the Vatican, it would be labeled "historicist immanentism."[37] Indeed, as it stands, the notion of "freedom in universal solidarity, to be realized in history," perfectly exemplifies what the Vatican takes to be the vision of salvation and Kingdom espoused by the theologians of liberation.

If Peukert stopped here, we should have our work cut out defending the *theological* significance of his views, and they might be accounted just another demythologization, or, in Habermas's terms, an exercise in "the linguistification of the sacred." However, it is at just this point that Peukert's fundamental aim becomes clear. He wishes at one and the same time to subject the theory of communicative praxis to a critique while reaffirming the significance of fundamental theology. Indeed, he suggests that critical theory needs the dimension of transcendence for its completion. Peukert believes that communicative praxis suffers from an "elementary aporia," and that this deficiency can only be met by a reassertion of fundamental theology. Following Walter Benjamin's views on the unclosed nature of the past, Peukert speaks of history as a "form of emphatic memory," through which "we have an experience that prohibits us from conceiving history completely nontheologically."[38] A theory of communicative action in which a notion of universal solidarity is implicit faces a radical challenge in the problem of the dead who have suffered, of those past "generations of the downtrodden," in Benjamin's phrase. Peukert allies himself with Christian Lenhardt's view that much of the work of the Frankfurt School is open to the challenge of what Lenhardt calls "anamnestic solidarity."[39] In any hypothetical present moment in which a measure of freedom has been achieved, history becomes a paradox, in which the joyful possession of emancipation can be maintained only by forgetting that the unsuccessful struggle of former generations paved the road to liberation. Peukert asks, "Is amnesia, the utter loss of historical memory, the presupposition of happy consciousness?"[40] He concludes:

> The normative implications of a theory of communicative action for the identity of subjects, as well as for the structure of society, end in aporia at the point where the attempt is made to conceive of the historical constitution of humanity united in solidarity.[41]

The aporias are to be overcome by taking seriously Benjamin's "theological" reflections on the unclosed past.

At the same time, this is no simplistic polemical attack on secular theory. The reality of God for Peukert is only identified and named within communicative action:

> [This] reality disclosed in communicative action, asserted as the saving reality for others and at the same time as the reality that through this salvation of the other makes possible one's own temporal existence unto death, must be called "God". . . . In this way, the basic situation of the disclosure of the reality of God and its identifiability, and hence at the same time the origin of possible discourse about God, are given.[42]

Peukert sees fundamental theology "as a theory of communicative action in universal solidarity." Such a universal solidarity must include the dead as well as the yet unborn. The scriptural warrant for this is found in the universal solidarity *in relationship to God* of the covenant community of Israel, and the universal solidarity achieved in the Christian tradition through faith in the Resurrection. To live a life of communicative action in solidarity with the dead within the Judeo-Christian tradition, is then "factually the assertion, in this action itself, of a reality that does not simply allow others to become an already superseded fact of the past." Peukert thus accepts the Habermasian emancipatory interest expressed in communicative action, but argues that it cannot be authentic unless it operates with a view of the unclosed nature of the past, and that this in its turn requires a religious vision.

Peukert's principal concern with the reassertion of a fundamental theology that takes communicative action more seriously than it takes itself has a fairly immediate and obvious bearing on ecclesiology. Peukert sees that his foundational theology "must in turn be able to be unfolded in the dimensions of its central problem constellations," and names these as "a theory of the subject, a theory of society, and a theory of history."[43] The church as a community in history is obviously implicated in these reflections. For example, the assertion of the universal character of solidarity, and of the implied universalism of communicative action, offers possibilities for a reconstruction of the classical theological notion of the church militant. Just as Peukert has demonstrated that communicative action is not complete without the universal solidarity of the believing community, so it ought to be possible for us to show that without sound communicative praxis the church of today is neither prefiguring the Kingdom nor remembering the dead, nor indeed acting out of a full theological understanding of the richness of faith in the Resurrection. Further, a reconstruction of the related notions of prayer for the dead, the myth of purgatory, and the communion of the saints ought not to be beyond our grasp. Above all, the relation of church and Kingdom might well be expressed in terms of the relation between the "now" of anamnestic solidarity and the "then" of a full presence of all with God.

COMMUNITY AND ECCLESIOLOGY

Some recent Roman Catholic ecclesiology constructs models of ecclesial community compatible with Jürgen Habermas's idea of the consensus community, though not all of it is written in conscious dialogue with Habermas. These Catholic ecclesiologies, unlike the postliberalism of George Lindbeck, envisage the church not as a ship of salvation dangerously close to foundering in the stormy seas of postmodernity, but rather as a craft built to stay seaworthy in just those unsympathetic currents. Three of these visions of the church suggest elements that need to be included in the Habermasian ecclesiology to be sketched out here in our final section.

a. *Juan Luis Segundo*

The principal ecclesiological work of the Uruguayan Jesuit Juan Luis Segundo is to be found in *The Community Called Church,* and in a more recent essay, "Capitalism-Socialism: A Theological Crux."[44] Together they present a postconciliar vision of the church as a "sign-community" and as a servant of the world.

The Community Called Church is much exercised over the relationship between the universality of the offer of salvation and the relatively small number of people who are members of the church. Segundo distinguishes between the church as the "community of revelation" and the world as the "community of redemption." The Christian is the "one who knows" the secret of the divine plan that in fact encompasses everyone in the world. Where faith in the gospel is not possible, love is a "preparation for the gospel." The role of the church is thus to be a sign of the redemptive love of God in Christ for the world, and to be this sign effectively it is necessary to be servants of the world that does not know God or Christ.

The vision of the church as sign to and servant of the world is simply an exposition of the teaching of the Second Vatican Council. Segundo becomes more original and undoubtedly more controversial when, reflecting on the fact that the nature of the church is to be a sign to the world of God's redemptive love, he argues that lukewarm members of the church impede the efficacy of the sign-value and, by not committing themselves whole-heartedly to the mission of the church, reduce their own chances of salvation. Those, in other words, who cannot at least strive for full commitment would be better off outside the church, where their salvation would depend solely on the reality of love in their lives, than within the ecclesial community where their position requires more of them. Moreover, if these people (the majority, one has to think) were outside the church, the church itself would be better able to perform its function.

Although there is much in Segundo's vision of a scaled-down church to cause disquiet, he points to one very important truth. To be the church, the community must be at work in the world as an efficacious sign, through sacrificial service done out of love, in imitation of Jesus Christ. He is also quite correct in his assessment that the church has historically expended almost all its energies on catechizing and regulating the lives of its own members, with missionary activity (usually seen very narrowly) understood as an extra, albeit an important extra. To most members of the church, membership has been attractive because it has been thought to make salvation more likely. Segundo's opposite stance is at least food for thought.

In "Capitalism-Socialism: A Theological Crux," Segundo carries further the analysis of the church-world relationship, with particular reference to the kind of significance to be attached to the sacramental and institutional life of the church. The fundamental question is a simple one: Theologically speaking, which is of absolute and which of relative significance, the struggle for justice within history, or sacraments within the worshiping community? The answer he proposes enrages many: It is the historical struggle that is absolute, the benefits of the church that are of instrumental value.

Segundo justifies his argument for the priority of the concrete historical struggle for justice by raising again the question of the mission of the church. If the mission of the church is to be for the world in the way that he outlines in

The Community Called Church, then that mission is carried out in caring and service in solidarity with the world, in the world, not in the worshiping community. The sacramental life of the church has instrumental significance. It is vitally important for Christians, the members of the ecclesial community, because it is their strength and support in the hard work of being the church in the world. Those who identify the sacramental life of the church as *the* "way to salvation" invert the proper order of things and abort the essentially missionary role of the church. Then the historical struggle becomes instrumental, secondary to the salvation obtained through participation in the sacramental life of the church.

Although Segundo's view may be as guilty of distortion as that he is attacking, accusations of what the Vatican's Congregation for the Doctrine of the Faith likes to call "historicist immanentism" are probably misdirected. Like all liberation theologians, Segundo is of course not arguing that salvation is to be identified with justice or with emancipation, but rather that salvation is encountered within the struggle for justice and emancipation carried out in history. Christian hope is for that mysterious gift of the reign of God, not for a simplistic historical utopia, but that hope is not realized through a combination of prayer and patience. "Orthopraxis" is the validation of the claim to faith. And if the reign of God is not to be found in history, well, it is not to be found in the church either.

This elaboration of Segundo's ecclesiology suggests an important characteristic for an updated ecclesiology when we look at the implications of his view for the nature of ministry, even allowing for possible exaggerations. The Catholic church has moved, thankfully, from essentially seeing only ordained ministers as engaged in ministry, to at least a good deal of talk about lay ministry.[45] However, behind the language of the universal call to ministry there remains the assumption that the ordained ministry is primary, lay ministry secondary, *because* lay ministry is predominantly ministry in and to the world, while ordained ministry is predominantly sacramental ministry within the community. But if the church is rightly seen as for the world, not for itself, then it is lay ministry that is primary because lay ministry is more central to the essentially missionary role of the church. Ordained ministry as we understand it today is supportive or instrumental to lay ministry.

b. *Johann Baptist Metz*

The most important and fascinating recent development in ecclesial structures is undoubtedly that of the so-called base Christian communities of Latin America. These were discussed above in chapter 4, and so we need not go into detail now. But it is ironic that the churches of the First World are beginning to catch on to the significance of the Latin American phenomenon of base Christian communities at precisely the time at which the Vatican seems to be winning its war of attrition against them.[46] One of the earliest "First World" theologians to recognize the importance of this development was Johann Baptist Metz in his book *The Emergent Church: The Future of Christianity in a Post-Bourgeois World,* which we also discussed in chapter 4. But his position is also valuable for a reason not considered there, namely, the case he makes for the association of religion and politics.

Metz characterizes the model of church prevalent in liberal societies as the "bourgeois church." The bourgeois mentality, thinks Metz, is the product of the individualism that emerged from the Enlightenment, and "the bourgeois individual who resulted is now capable of solidarity in only a weak and diminished form."[47] The church structure that matches the cultural dominance of the bourgeois is one that embraces the liberal separation of religion and politics, and that favors a highly privatized understanding of religion. This "supply or services church" is accompanied by a bourgeois-liberal theology, and must inevitably fall into what Dorothee Soelle has called "necrophiliac religion," the love of, attachment to, and support for an institutionalized, dehumanized, and emotionally deprived society.[48]

The base community churches emerging from the Third World provide an opportunity to respond to the crisis of bourgeois society, marked as it is by a sense of "the end of progress," the "growing probability of disaster. . . a consciousness of limits and of catastrophe."[49] The critique of values expressed in the social teaching of the episcopate shows the alarm of the church at signs of breakdown in society, but "their critique remains virtually truncated" and must "link up with a critique of social structures in society."[50] The base communities of the Third World encourage the abandonment of the liberal separation of religion and politics, and lead to overcoming that "tactical provincialism" by which we "define our political and social identity independently of the poverty, misery and oppression in the third world."[51]

Thus Metz's analysis suggests another important characteristic of a vigorous ecclesial community, though one not easily related to the peculiar case of the United States, the conscious connection of religion and politics. The United States, unlike all other liberal democracies, is both vigilant in its constitutional separation of church and state, and bedeviled by religious groups intent on only too close an association between their particular beliefs and public policy. Neither Metz nor base communities should be thought to be sympathetic to the kind of association of religion and politics that leads to single-issue lobbies opposed to abortion, favoring mandatory prayer in public schools, banning books, or insisting on creation science. But they are at least equally hostile to the cherished assumption of liberal societies that "religion should keep its nose out of politics." The base community finds strength in the gospel to engage in systemic analysis of society and protest its dehumanizing capabilities, not answers in the gospel to be applied simplistically to complex social problems.

A call for a new relationship between religion and politics is not a vote for fundamentalism or single-issue lobbying. Nor is it a challenge to the separation of church and state, understood according to its true purpose of preventing the tyranny of one group over another by constitutional means. It is, rather, a plea for the recognition that there is no true separation between religious and secular values. Religious values that are not simply the cherished anachronisms of a literalistically interpreted revelation must be explicable in secular terms. Secular values that are not the mere conveniences of a pluralistic society cannot run counter to the deepest values of Judaism, Christianity, Islam, or any other major religion. The specificity of these traditions lies in their myth and their narrative account of history. Respect for life, the dignity of the human person, human rights, compassion, and the search for truth are common because they are common to human beings. A secular society that does not respect these values is in need of correction; a religion that is not active in their defense is contemptible.

To say, then, that the ecclesial community must overcome the separation of religion and politics is to mark the community out as the place where these values must be made real, and at whose heart must be found discourse over the proper means to realize them in the world. As we saw in chapter 6, the moral discourse of the church must be focused on middle axioms. Since politics in the sense of government is normally taken up with managing society, with policies and legislation, rather than with values, the open discussion of middle axioms and the commitment to using them to actualize fundamental values cannot avoid being political, not if the church is for the world, rather than for itself.

c. *Charles Davis*

Although it is not strictly appropriate to describe the work of Charles Davis as Catholic ecclesiology, it is the third and in many ways most important exemplar of communicative ecclesiality. Two of his writings are particularly suggestive for the current project. The first, his 1980 book *Theology and Political Society*, was a thorough and extensive discussion of Habermas's religious significance as it appeared in the works published by Habermas before that time.[52] Second, in 1986 Davis published what appears to be an interim volume of reflections on Christianity, *What Is Living, What Is Dead in Christianity Today? Breaking the Liberal-Conservative Deadlock*.[53] This work owes something at least to Habermasian reflection, but its real significance is its attempt to get beyond the "parochial exclusiveness of most Christian theologians, whether Catholic or Protestant, including the representatives of political theology and the theologies of liberation."[54] It begins to raise the question, inevitable in any envisioning of religion in communicative terms, of how to treat the exclusive claims of revealed religions. In this, it is a contribution to the growing interest in the theology of religions.

A few years ago, the journal *Telos* published "Symposium on Religion and Politics" in which a series of thinkers was invited to comment briefly on the emancipatory potential of religion.[55] Davis's contribution was brief and trenchant. He distinguished between salvation, which "concerns existential anxiety, which means suffering, death and guilt, experienced as manifesting human finitude and failure," and emancipation, which "as a human ideal and project is a response to the awareness that today much human potentiality remains unfulfilled." Emancipation does not replace religion, because even in an emancipated society there would be no getting away from suffering, guilt, and the fear of death. Without openness to something transcendent, "to what is unlimited and unapprehensible,"[56] the human person is repressed and the self-reflection needed for emancipation is distorted. Nor, of course, can religion substitute for social and political liberation. But its capacity at its best for opening the individual to the transcendent tends toward the creation of "the self-reflective, critical subject, free from the dominative power of the established collectivity."[57]

Davis's distinction between politics and religion is valuable above all for the way in which it makes the transcendent the ground of politics, without politicizing religion. His views were developed out of a dialogue with Habermas, and are most clearly expressed in the final chapter of *Theology and Political Society*. There he utilizes Habermas's theory of social identity to make a case both for the deprivatization of religion and for its emergence from rigid confessionalism.

Davis recounts how Habermas's essentially evolutionary view of social history sees two significant problems with Hegel's identification of the State as the institutional expression of freedom. In the first place the classist basis of the Hegelian state does not reflect a true freedom from domination by power groups. In the second place, Hegel's concern for national boundaries can no longer be defended as the natural expression of the rational Spirit. While it is perhaps not so clear as Habermas or even Davis seems to think that Hegel has to be identified either with the particular form of Estates government in which he expressed his political thought, or that he was unaware of how individual states had to be held to the articulation of a more universal idea of freedom, it is true that Hegel could envisage no higher social structure or institution than that of the constitutional monarchy.

Davis seeks potential theological value in Habermas in his post-Hegelian theory of social identity, rather than in the much more barren fields of his occasional and dismissive treatment of religion. Habermas's theory of social identity builds upon much of the Hegelian legacy, but shifts the focus away from visible political forms like the state and nation, toward the kind of communicative action and discourse that has been the subject of much of this book, in which, says Davis, "individuals are the participants in the shaping of the collective will underlying the design of a common identity."[58] The history of religion is a "total history," which "is now entering a new phase"[59] marked by "active participation in the present shaping of a universality to be realized in the future."[60] This new history of religion is related to the old conception of religious identity as Habermas's theory of social identity is to that of Hegel.

Davis's view depends on being able to defend the conception of religion as the development of freedom. It is here that the argument of *Theology and Political Society* merges with that of *What Is Living, What Is Dead in Christianity Today?* Although religion ought to involve a private self and a commitment to strategic action to change society, at its heart, thinks Davis, is the cultivation of the "interior self," which "is the political subject par excellence, capable of entering into the communication process among free participants which constitutes the political life of society as distinct from its mere administration."[61] It was through monotheism's stress on the individual's relation to God that the idea of the interior self, the origin of modern subjectivity, was born. And modern subjectivity is the basis of that freedom at the heart of both social and religious identity. These two, thinks Davis, are the same, though the latter is the former at a deeper level.[62]

THE CHURCH IN THE POSTMODERN WORLD

The stress throughout this book has been upon viewing the church as at its best and in principle a discourse community, engaged in communicative praxis oriented to consensus. The structural principles and vocabulary for this identification have been derived from Habermas. It also has to be freely admitted that a number of the church's current problems, arising from a misunderstanding of the nature of authority, tradition, or ministry, run directly counter to the identification. The struggle between the charismatic and institutional in the life of the church is a clear parallel to Habermas's depiction of society's lifeworld-system tension.

A second, less prominent theme is indicated in my eager adoption of Habermas's sobering but illuminating analysis of modernity as a battle between lifeworld and system. This analysis is attractive for a number of reasons. In the first place, it enables the articulation of deep-seated and erstwhile badly expressed anxieties about the survival of the human spirit. Second, it does not simply blame the system. The system is a wholly necessary mechanism, but should be instrumental to the lifeworld, the home of values and convictions. Third, it fits well with the observations of the Catholic Social Teaching tradition,

238

though it is vastly superior in structure and depth of insight. Fourth, it goes beyond diagnosis to prescribe a remedy, the formation of the "protest groups" we discussed at the end of chapter 2.

What is perhaps most significant of all for Habermas's usefulness to theology is his presentation of language as inherently emancipatory, itself the basis of the entire discussion of the discourse community. Language is in principle for communication, and must therefore contain a drive toward truth understood as uncoerced consensus arrived at through a conversation to which all have equal access. The emancipatory potential of language is then clearly linked to what Habermas calls its postulation of an "ideal speech situation" as the goal in principle of all discourse. Language is itself a phenomenon which of its nature implicitly recognizes human freedom and equality, even when a particular example of language is used to pervert or obstruct that freedom. And language has perfect communication in equality as both its goal and its driving force.

These three dimensions of Habermas's critical theory correspond to three ecclesial realities: its organizational structure, its mission, and its nature. We have said more than enough in preceding chapters about the first of these three, using Habermas to clarify and purify the understanding of the internal life of the church. It remains to comment briefly on the second and third reality, both more important and both obviously meriting much more extensive treatment than a few suggestive remarks at the conclusion of a book on the first reality can provide. At the same time, the justification for concentration on that first and less dynamic reality must be that without internal respect at an organizational level for the holiness of discourse and communicative action, a sophisticated communicative vision of the mission and nature of the church would be a mere sham. The church exists not for itself or even for God, but for the sake of the world to which it is sent. The mission of the church in the world is to be an effective sign of the saving and sacrificial love of God through Christ for the whole world and all that it contains. The church cannot of itself save the world; salvation is God's work. The question of mission to the world thus comes down to this: What mission of the church to the world at the present time would be the most effective sign of God's saving love of the world? Through what activity would the church be most likely to bring hope to a troubled and depressed human community? It is my unsurprising contention, following upon the work of Juan Luis Segundo, that it would be to expend its missionary energies in work for the emancipation of human beings and, if "emancipation" can be used in this way, of the nonhuman world too. In this work, again following Segundo, lay ministry is in the vanguard, sacramental priesthood in strong support.

To suggest that the mission of the church in the postmodern world is to work for its emancipation is not, of course, to reduce the gospel to a struggle for a mundane utopia. On the contrary: The church is senseless if it does not believe that the greatest gift God can offer to individuals and to the world is that salvation which goes beyond emancipation and may exist without it, that freedom from existential anxiety which does not require social or political freedoms, and which such secular liberation may not bring. But the church at the same time cannot imagine that in its human dimension, in its decisions on how to minister to the world, it can effect in other human beings that release from existential anxiety. The church has to decide, rather, what mission will facilitate that access to God's grace which the church cannot itself control. A church devoted to the struggle for emancipation may be an avenue of God's grace not so much because of the success of its initiatives in defense of human freedom, as through the character of a community that will exhaust itself in these efforts.

Habermas has written of "defensive" protest groups, and singled out the feminist movement as the one example of a more positive force for change. To the feminist movement, I would like to add the Christian church, because like the feminist movement at its best its work involves a vision of a changed world and an invitation to all to come and share in that new community. However, to be convincing in its offer, it must be a community of emancipation, freedom, and equality. It must, in other words, be an example in miniature of that emancipated and even that saved world which its mission works toward. Metz's "basic-community church" would be such an example. Perhaps a Habermasian forward step would be for the church to learn how to blend critique, praxis, and a new hermeneutic from the feminist movement itself.

It is the nature of the church to be the eschatological community of salvation. This theological cliche can have new life breathed into it through its expression in the language of Habermasian theory. The discourse of the community is founded in the emancipatory drive of language, a drive toward an ideal speech situation which is never fully present but whose postulation is a necessary condition for the reality of that imperfect and transitory consensus achieved in the community at any given moment. Although Habermas does not use the term, his vision of the ideal speech situation is an eschatological vision. Just as I have argued that the church needs that link between language and freedom to ground its own praxis, so I would argue that critical theory needs an openness to transcendence to give credibility to the concept of an ideal speech situation. Peukert sought to bring the transcendent to critical theory through the call for universal solidarity. What I am saying is that without transcendent hope in a future realization of the ideal speech situation, that is, without grounds for hope in emancipation and even salvation, there is no reason to strive to realize the emancipatory potential of language rather than its strategic value.

In describing the church's mission as being the eschatological community of salvation, we have to be sensitive to Charles Davis's strictures on provinciality. What is lacking in Habermas's critical theory is the availability of points of reference in history to communities oriented to consensus, grounded in a universal solidarity, and struggling for the emancipation of the human community. The church, in principle and at its best, could be a particularly important exemplar, and in some parts of Latin America may already have become so. But of course the church, Catholic in particular or Christian in general, cannot claim exclusiveness as a consensus community. The lessons of history, as a matter of fact, should make the Catholic church in particular extremely slow to advance a claim to be a consensus community at all. Every religious tradition in its narrative and its doctrines is subject to the canons of discourse and must be ready to redeem all disputed validity claims. To the extent that these requirements are met, every religious tradition contributes to the struggle for emancipation.

In the late capitalist Western world that is most responsible for the set of circumstances that make up postmodernity, the Christian church remains the prevalent religious tradition. Its potential to be both a protest and an alternative may thus be crucial, not only for those who live in this world, but also for those upon whom this wealthy world visits even greater horrors. Ironically, as

Metz points out, it is in the "developing" world of Latin America, playground of the strategic and economic fancies of the North, that there has sprung up in the base Christian communities an example of how the church can be a force for emancipation and hope. The irony exhibits a tragic dimension when we reflect on the fact that the two focuses of greatest opposition to this phenomenon, the two powers that apparently find it most threatening, are Washington and Rome. The former demonstrates the system's unwillingness to allow a new flowering of the lifeworld. It is a scandal, in the true meaning of that word, that the latter seems to demonstrate the same. Not only, apparently, could the church lead a resurgence of the lifeworld in the face of the system. Within the church that same struggle is being fought. On both fronts, in our postmodern world, we have to admit that a successful outcome can never be guaranteed.

NOTES

1. THE IDEA OF A CRITICAL THEORY

1. The best currently available introduction to critical theory is *Critique, Norm and Utopia: A Study of the Foundations of Critical Theory*, by Seyla Benhabib (New York: Columbia University Press, 1986). Other particularly useful introductions among the many available are *The Origin of Negative Dialectics*, by Susan Buck-Morss (New York: Free Press, 1977); *The Idea of a Critical Theory: Habermas and the Frankfurt School*, by Raymond Geuss (New York: Cambridge University Press, 1981); and *Habermas and the Foundations of Critical Theory*, by Rick Roderick (London: Macmillan, 1986).

2. To put a positive interpretation on "heresy" requires a notion of theological creativity, itself a product of the idea of development of doctrine. For a discussion of the pioneering work of Friedrich Schleiermacher and Johann Sebastian Drey on theological orthodoxy and heterodoxy, see John E. Thiel, "Orthodoxy and Heterodoxy in Schleiermacher's Theological Encyclopedia: Doctrinal Development and Theological Creativity," *Heythrop Journal* 25 (1984): 142-47, and "J. S. Drey on Doctrinal Development: The Context of Theological Encyclopedia," *Heythrop Journal* 27 (1986): 290-305.

3. Horkheimer has to be credited with the classical statement of critical theory. See his essay "Traditional and Critical Theory" in *Critical Theory: Selected Essays* (New York: Herder & Herder, 1982), pp. 188-243.

4. Geuss, *The Idea of a Critical Theory: Habermas and the Frankfurt School* (New York: Cambridge University Press, 1981). The discussion of ideology occupies pages 4-44.

5. For an excellent account of the cultural currents in Europe from 900 to 1200, see Philippe Wolff, *The Cultural Awakening* (New York: Pantheon, 1968).

6. Quoted in Wolff, p. 77.

7. A good example of this tension is the case of usury, meaning lending money at interest, which though an essential component of economic expansion, is strictly speaking against the "natural law" as then understood. How the church accommodated itself to this fact of life is quite illuminating. See Fernand Braudel, *Civilization and Capitalism, 15th–18th Century, Vol. Two: The Wheels of Commerce* (New York: Harper & Row, 1982), pp. 560-66.

8. In *The Structure of Scientific Revolutions* (Chicago: University of Chicago Press, 1970).

9. Useful sociological treatments of the idea of secularization are to be found in *The Invisible Religion*, by Thomas Luckmann (New York: Macmillan, 1967); *A General Theory of Secularization*, by David Martin (New York: Harper & Row, 1978); and *Habits of the Heart: Individualism and Commitment in American Life*, by Robert Bellah, et al. (Berkeley: University of California Press, 1985).

10. See, for example, the extremely interesting presentation of the worldly concerns of Württemberg pietism in Laurence Dickey's *Hegel: Religion, Economics, and the Politics of Spirit, 1770–1807* (Cambridge: Cambridge University Press, 1987).

11. Fuchs, *Natural Law* (New York: Sheed and Ward, 1965), quoted in Thomas Molnar, *Politics and the State: the Catholic View* (Chicago: Franciscan Herald Press, 1980), pp. 100-101. Molnar's book is useful for a brief historical overview of the development of the classical Catholic understanding of the state, but treacherous and unreliable when the author turns to observations on the contemporary world.

12. Useful works on Hegel's significance in the development of political thought include the following: *Hegel's Theory of the Modern State*, by Shlomo Avineri (Cambridge: Cambridge University Press, 1972); *Hegel's Retreat from Eleusis: Studies in Political Thought*, by George Armstrong Kelly (Princeton: Princeton University Press, 1978); *The State and Civil Society: Studies in Hegel's Political Philosophy*, ed. Z. A. Pelczynski (Cambridge: Cambridge University Press, 1984); and *Hegel and Modern Society*, by Charles Taylor (Cambridge: Cambridge University Press, 1979).

13. See *The Tragedy of Enlightenment: An Essay on the Frankfurt School*, by Paul Connerton (Cambridge: Cambridge University Press, 1980), and "Hegel's Idea of a Critical Theory," by Steven B. Smith, *Political Theory* 15 (February 1987): 99-126.

14. See many of the essays in Pelczynski, ed., *The State and Civil Society.*
15. For a clearer understanding of Hegel's religious background, see Dickey, *Hegel.*
16. Trans. A. V. Miller (Oxford: Clarendon Press, 1977).
17. Trans. T. M. Knox (Oxford: Clarendon Press, 1942).
18. The early part of this story is brilliantly recounted by J. M. Toews in *Hegelianism: The Path Toward Dialectical Humanism, 1805–1841* (Cambridge: Cambridge University Press, 1980).
19. On this see *The Social and Political Thought of Karl Marx*, by Shlomo Avineri (Cambridge: Cambridge University Press, 1968), and *Marx's Social Critique of Culture*, by Louis Dupre (New Haven, Conn.: Yale University Press, 1983).
20. Avineri, *Hegel's Theory of the Modern State* (Cambridge: Cambridge University Press, 1972), p. 150.
21. Letter to A. Ruge, September 1843, in *Karl Marx: Early Writings* (New York: Vintage Books, 1975), p. 209.
22. *The Dialectical Imagination: A History of the Frankfurt School and the Institute of Social Research, 1923–1950* (Boston: Little, Brown & Co., 1973).
23. *Critical Theory*, pp. 188-243.
24. New York: Herder & Herder, 1972.
25. *Critique of Instrumental Reason: Lectures and Essays Since the End of World War II* (New York: Seabury Press, 1974).
26. "Traditional and Critical Theory," *Zeitschrift für Sozialforschung*, vol. 6, no. 2.
27. Ibid., p. 188.
28. Ibid., p. 197.
29. Ibid., p. 208.
30. Ibid., p. 210.
31. *Social Analysis: Linking Faith with Justice* (Maryknoll, N.Y.: Orbis Books, 1983), p. 1.
32. Hegel of course becomes the true hero, since it was Hegel, not Marx, who saw human beings sharing in some communal exercise of reason that went beyond the purpose of technical manipulation of the environment. Hegel, too, was the thinker who resisted the myth of Enlightenment, and who saw through to the questionable character of many of its assumptions. Most important, he refused to bow to the subject-object dichotomy and was deeply critical of Kant for his separation of rational activity from truth.

2. THE CRITICAL THEORY OF JÜRGEN HABERMAS

1. The major texts available in English are the following: *Communication and the Evolution of Society* (Boston: Beacon Press, 1979); *Knowledge and*

Human Interests (Boston: Beacon Press, 1971); *Legitimation Crisis* (Boston: Beacon Press, 1975); *The Philosophical Discourse of Modernity: Twelve Lectures.* Studies in Contemporary German Social Thought (Cambridge, Mass.: M.I.T. Press, 1987); *Philosophical-Political Profiles.* Studies in Contemporary German Social Thought (Cambridge, Mass.: M.I.T. Press, 1983); *The Theory of Communicative Action. Volume One: Reason and the Rationalization of Society, Volume Two: Lifeworld and System* (Boston: Beacon Press, 1984, 1988). Of major significance but so far unavailable in English translation are *Strukturwandel der Öffentlichkeit* (Frankfurt: Suhrkamp, 1974); *Zur Rekonstruktion des historischen Materialismus* (Frankfurt: Suhrkamp, 1976); *Moralbewusstsein und kommunikatives Handeln* (Frankfurt-am-Main: Suhrkamp, 1983), and the essay "Wahrheitstheorien," in *Wirklichkeit und Reflexion,* ed. H. Fahrenbach (Pfüllingen: Neske, 1973).

2. So much has been written that it is quite impossible to list it all here. In addition to those already mentioned in chapter 1, the following books include helpful discussions of Habermas: *Beyond Objectivism and Relativism: Science, Hermeneutics, and Praxis,* by Richard J. Bernstein (Philadelphia: University of Pennsylvania Press, 1983); *Habermas and Modernity,* ed. Richard J. Bernstein (Cambridge, Mass.: M.I.T. Press, 1985); *The Critical Theory of Jürgen Habermas,* by Thomas McCarthy (Cambridge, Mass.: M.I.T. Press, 1978); *On Critical Theory,* ed. John O'Neil (New York: Seabury Press, 1976); *Habermas: Critical Debates,* ed. John B. Thompson and David Held (Cambridge, Mass.: M.I.T. Press, 1982). Several recent articles provide briefer but still illuminating introductions to Habermas's critical theory: Jeffrey C. Alexander, "Review Essay: Habermas's New Critical Theory: Its Promise and Problems," *American Journal of Sociology* 91 (September 1985): 400-424; Roger S. Gottlieb, "The Contemporary Critical Theory of Jürgen Habermas," *Ethics* 91 (January 1981): 280-95; Philip Pettit, "Habermas on Truth and Justice" in *Marx and Marxisms. Royal Institute of Philosophy Lecture Series: 14, Supplement to Philosophy 1982* (Cambridge: Cambridge University Press, 1982), pp. 207-28.

3. *The Philosophical Discourse of Modernity* (Cambridge, Mass.: M.I.T. Press, 1987).

4. See for example the discussion of mythical versus modern ways of understanding the world, and closed versus open societies, in *The Theory of Communicative Action. Volume One: Reason and the Rationalization of Society* (Boston: Beacon Press, 1984), pp. 43-74. For a number of reasons, religious world views would seem to fall into the category of the premodern.

5. The whole work is devoted to a historical investigation into the forms of the relationship of knowledge to interests of one kind or another, but for a summary see the appendix, pp. 301-17.

6. In *Communication and the Evolution of Society,* pp. 1-68.

7. See J. L. Austin, *How to Do Things with Words* (Cambridge: Harvard University Press, 1962), and J. Searle, "A Taxonomy of Illocutionary Acts," in *Expression and Meaning* (Cambridge: Cambridge University Press, 1976), and *Speech Acts: An Essay in the Philosophy of Language* (London: Cambridge University Press, 1969).

8. On the notion of the ideal speech situation, see Habermas, "Towards a Theory of Communicative Competence," *Inquiry* 13 (1970): 360-75; John B. Thompson, "Universal Pragmatics," in *Habermas: Critical Debates*, ed. John B. Thompson and David Held (Cambridge, Mass.: M.I.T. Press, 1982), pp. 116-33, esp. pp. 128-31; and Thomas McCarthy, *The Critical Theory of Jürgen Habermas* (Cambridge, Mass.: M.I.T. Press, 1978), esp. pp. 307-10.

9. McCarthy, *Critical Theory*, p. 306.

10. "Towards a Theory of Communicative Competence," 368.

11. *Reason and Rationalization*, p. 3.

12. See *RR*, p. 23 for a diagrammatic presentation of these distinctions.

13. *Plurality and Ambiguity: Hermeneutics, Religion, Hope* (San Francisco: Harper & Row, 1987), p. 19.

14. Fred Dallmayr discusses the variety of understandings of conversation as a philosophical model in "Conversation, Discourse and Politics," in his collection of essays, *Polis and Praxis: Exercises in Contemporary Political Theory* (Cambridge, Mass.: M.I.T. Press, 1984), pp. 192-223.

15. "Wahrheitstheorien," in *Wirklichkeit und Reflexion: Festschrift für Walter Schulz* (Pfüllingen: Neske, 1973), p. 219, quoted here in McCarthy's translation in *The Critical Theory of Jürgen Habermas*, p. 299.

16. For a related attempt to locate ethics in communication, see Karl-Otto Apel, *Towards a Transformation of Philosophy* (London: Routledge & Kegan Paul, 1980), esp. pp. 225-300.

17. Seyla Benhabib, *Critique, Norm and Utopia* (New York: Columbia University Press, 1986).

18. *Moralbewusstsein und kommunikatives Handeln* (Frankfurt-am-Main: Suhrkamp, 1983), p. 105. The translation is Benhabib's.

19. Benhabib, *Critique*, p. 311.

20. Ibid., p. 313.

21. Ibid., p. 312.

22. Ibid., p. 315.

23. Lawrence Kohlberg, *Collected Papers on Moral Development and Moral Education* (Cambridge, Mass.: Moral Education and Research Foundation, 1973).

24. *Lifeworld and System: A Critique of Functionalist Reason* (Boston: Beacon Press, 1988).

25. Boston: Beacon Press, 1973.

26. *LS*, pp. 123-24.

27. Ibid., p. 124
28. Ibid., p. 124.
29. Ibid., p. 125.
30. Ibid., p. 136.
31. Ibid., p. 142.
32. Ibid., p. 144.
33. Ibid., p. 145.
34. Ibid., p. 150.
35. *Critical Debates*, p. 251.
36. Benhabib, *Critique*, p. 312.
37. Ibid., p. 313.
38. Ibid., p. 312.
39. Ibid., p. 313.
40. Ibid., pp. 314-15.
41. Ibid., p. 315.
42. *LC*, p. 112.
43. Ibid., p. 113.
44. See for example, *Strukturprobleme des kapitalistischen Staates* (Frankfurt: Suhrkamp, 1977).
45. *Critical Debates*, p. 138. The actual wording here is that of Stephen Lukes.
46. *LC*, p. 117.
47. *LS*, p. 182.
48. Ibid., p. 182.
49. Ibid., p. 184.
50. Ibid., p. 183.
51. Ibid., p. 384.
52. Ibid., p. 385.
53. Ibid., p. 386.
54. Ibid., p. 392.
55. Ibid., p. 393.
56. Ibid., pp. 394-95.

3. THE VALUE OF CRITICAL THEORY FOR CATHOLIC THEOLOGY

1. Three collections of documents of CST are currently available in English. The earliest is Joseph Gremillion's *The Gospel of Peace and Justice: Catholic Social Teaching Since Pope John* (Maryknoll, N.Y.: Orbis Books, 1976). This includes a lengthy and enthusiastic "Overview and Prospectus" and many documents, both papal and episcopal, from the years 1961–75. The second is *Renewing the Earth* (Garden City, N.Y.: Image, 1977). The most recent compilation is *Proclaiming Justice and*

Peace, ed. Michael Walsh and Brian Davies (Mystic, Conn.: Twenty-Third Publications, 1985). There is no comprehensive collection, but throughout this text I shall as far as possible use the Gremillion collection.

2. The list of documents is a litany of Latin phrases familiar to literate Catholics but a strange catalog to others. It begins with Leo XIII's *Rerum Novarum* (1891), followed by Pius XI's *Quadragesimo Anno* (1931). With John XXIII the pace quickens: *Mater et Magistra* (1961) was followed rapidly by *Pacem in Terris* (1963). The bishops of the Second Vatican Council produced their statement on the "church in the modern world" entitled *Gaudium et Spes* in 1965, and Pope Paul VI added *Populorum Progressio* two years later. The same pope's *Octagesimo Adveniens* appeared in 1971. In the intervening years the bishops of Latin America, meeting in Medellin, Colombia, prepared several documents, which, though they do not strictly speaking carry the same authority as papal teaching, need to be considered for their profound influence on the praxis of the church. John Paul II has produced two major letters on social issues, *Laborem Exercens* (1981) and *Sollicitudo Rei Socialis* (1987).

3. The following comments summarize a much fuller discussion in "The Politics of Catholic Social Teaching," *Cross Currents* 35 (Winter 1985–86): 393-407.

4. Maryknoll, N.Y.: Orbis Books.

5. Walsh and Davies, *Justice and Peace,* pp. 271-311.

6. *The Priority of Labor* (Ramsey, N.J.: Paulist Press, 1981). This commentary also incorporates the text of John Paul's encyclical letter.

7. Ibid., p. 81.

8. *Freedom with Justice* (New York: Harper & Row, 1984).

9. Dorr, *Option for the Poor,* p. 140.

10. Novak, *Freedom with Justice,* p. 135.

11. Ibid., p. 156.

12. *The Monthly Review* 34 (July-August 1982): 1-42.

13. See Paul Lakeland, "Distinguishing the Scribes: The Composition of Vatican Documents," *The Month* 7 (June 1974): 595-99.

14. "The Popes and Politics: Shifting Patterns in 'Catholic Social Doctrine.'" *Daedalus* 111 (Winter 1982): 85-98. This article is reprinted in a most useful new collection, *Readings in Moral Theology No. 5: Official Catholic Social Teaching,* ed. Charles E. Curran and Richard A. McCormick, S. J. (New York: Paulist Press, 1986), pp. 264-84. Hebblethwaite's article should discourage the use of the term "Catholic Social Teaching," since it suggests a rather monolithic and universalist approach to social teaching. However, for purposes of ease of reference I have retained the term.

15. *Octagesimo Adveniens,* par. 3. See Gremillion, *Peace and Justice,* p. 487.

16. Hebblethwaite, "Popes and Politics," p. 96.

17. *Church, Charism, and Power: Liberation Theology and the Institutional Church* (New York: Crossroad, 1985).
18. Ibid., p. 39.
19. Ibid., p. 55.
20. The notion of the church and the world in a dialogue from which both can learn is treated in some detail by Juan Luis Segundo in *The Community Called Church* (Maryknoll, N.Y.: Orbis Books, 1973), particularly in ch. 5.
21. Boff, *Church, Charism, and Power,* pp. 138-43.
22. I am not arguing here that the resources of the Catholic tradition require such a relativization of the historical to the suprahistorical, but that because the world in the Catholic tradition is not an autonomous "kingdom" this is one possible direction for the tradition to take, and in fact the one that the institution has always favored. Another equally plausible direction, one taken by Catholic political theology and theology of liberation, at least in the hands of a Juan Luis Segundo, is the relativization of the language of church and revelation to the absolute demands of a salvation that must be worked out in historical terms. On this see Segundo's much-discussed article, "Capitalism-Socialism: A Theological Crux," in *Liberation South, Liberation North,* ed. Michael Novak (Washington, D.C.: American Enterprise Institute, 1981), pp. 7-23.
23. Par. 6.5 (Walsh and Davies, *Justice and Peace,* p. 281).
24. Chicago: University of Chicago Press, 1958.
25. Par. 4.1 (Walsh and Davies, *Justice and Peace,* p. 278).
26. *RR,* p. 50.
27. For the text of the letter, see *Origins* 17, n. 38 (1988): 641-60. See also Paul Lakeland, "Development and Catholic Social Teaching: Pope John Paul's New Encyclical," *The Month* 21 (June 1988): 706-10.
28. See *Origins* 17 (March 3, 1988): 648, par. 21.
29. Ibid., 651, par. 30.
30. Ibid.
31. See Robert J. Schreiter, *Constructing Local Theologies* (Maryknoll, N.Y.: Orbis Books, 1985).
32. See, above all, *In Memory of Her,* by Elizabeth Schussler Fiorenza (New York: Crossroad, 1983).
33. See Michael J. Himes and Kenneth R. Himes, "The Myth of Self-Interest," *Commonweal* 125 (September 23, 1988): 493-98.
34. Matthew Lamb, *Solidarity with Victims: Toward a Theology of Social Transformation* (New York: Crossroad, 1982), pp. 61-99.
35. Ibid., p. 68.
36. Ibid., p. 73.
37. Ibid., p. 75.
38. Ibid., p. 76.
39. Ibid., p. 82.

40. Ibid., p. 87.
41. Ibid., p. 84.
42. *The Structure of Scientific Revolutions* (Chicago: University of Chicago Press, 1970).
43. *All That Is Solid Melts into Air: The Experience of Modernity* (New York: Simon & Schuster, 1982).
44. Metz, *Theology of the World* (New York: Seabury Press, 1973).
45. Jürgen Habermas, *The Philosophical Discourse of Modernity* (Cambridge, Mass.: M.I.T., 1987).
46. For a useful article distinguishing between various accounts of postmodernity, see Michael W. Messmer, "Making Sense Of/With Postmodernism," *Soundings* 68 (Fall 1985): 404-27.

4. THE CHURCH: COMMUNITY OF COMMUNICATIVE ACTION

1. Edward Farley, *Ecclesial Reflection: An Anatomy of Theological Method* (Philadelphia: Fortress Press, 1982).
2. On a theology of praxis, see Dorothee Soelle, *Political Theology* (Philadelphia: Fortress Press, 1978).
3. *RR*, pp. 273-337.
4. Ibid., fig. 16, p. 329.
5. Ibid., p. 333.
6. *The Future of Roman Catholic Theology: Vatican II—Catalyst for Change* (Philadelphia: Fortress Press, 1970), p. 117.
7. The literature of commentary on the Second Vatican Council is enormous. For the documents themselves, see *Vatican Council II: The Conciliar and Post Conciliar Documents*, ed. Austin Flannery (Collegeville, Minn.: Liturgical Press, 1975). Anyone seriously interested in the debates that led to the documents and how the final texts were arrived at must consult the *Commentary on the Documents of Vatican II*, ed. Herbert Vorgrimler, 6 vols. (New York: Herder & Herder, 1967).
8. Quoted in Dulles, *Models of the Church*, pp. 41-42.
9. Ibid., p. 43.
10. I am drawing extensively in the following pages from the excellent "History of the Constitution" by Gerard Philips found in *Commentary on the Documents of Vatican II*, vol. 1, pp. 105-37.
11. Many of the works already noted perform this task. See esp. Segundo, *The Community Called Church*, and Dulles, *Models of the Church*.
12. This was most clearly the case in the final report of the 1985 extraordinary Synod of Bishops in Rome. See Joseph A. Komonchak, "The Synod of 1985 and the Notion of the Church," in *Chicago Studies* 26 (November 1987): 330-45. Other more extensive discussions of that

synod are *Synod 1985—An Evaluation,* ed. G. Alberigo and J. Provost (Edinburgh: T. & T. Clark, 1986), and *Synod Extraordinary: The Inside Story of the Rome Synod, November-December 1985,* by Peter Hebblethwaite (Garden City, N.Y.: Doubleday, 1986).

13. Komonchak, "Synod of 1985," p. 335.

14. George A. Lindbeck, *The Future of Roman Catholic Theology: Vatican II—Catalyst for Change* (Philadelphia: Fortress Press, 1970), p. 34.

15. Ibid., p. 35.

16. Ibid., pp. 37-38.

17. On this see Segundo, *The Community Called Church,* pp. 98-136.

18. Indeed, this is a particular emphasis of the Catholic tradition in social ethics. Since the time of the Second Vatican Council, and particularly in the last encyclical letter of John XXIII, *Pacem in Terris,* the official social teaching of the Catholic church has greatly expanded the idea of rights beyond the personal, individual rights to "life, liberty, and the pursuit of happiness," to very specific "economic rights" like the right to employment, health care, and disability benefits. See David Hollenbach, *Claims in Conflict* (New York: Paulist Press, 1979).

19. *Lumen Gentium* 20, quoted in Flannery, *Vatican Council II,* p. 371.

20. See Dulles, *Models of the Church,* pp. 39-66.

21. The two principal recent letters of the U.S. National Conference of Catholic Bishops should be noted here: *The Challenge of Peace: God's Promise and Our Response* (Washington, D.C.: U.S. Catholic Conference, 1983) and *The Third Draft: Economic Justice for All: Catholic Social Teaching and the U.S. Economy,* in *Origins* 16 (June 5, 1986). For a study of the implications of this line of teaching, see Dennis P. McCann, *New Experiment in Democracy: The Challenge for American Catholicism* (Kansas City, Mo.: Sheed & Ward, 1987).

22. See for example Alvaro Barreiro, *Basic Ecclesial Communities: The Evangelization of the Poor* (Maryknoll, N.Y.: Orbis Books, 1982); Leonardo Boff, *Ecclesiogenesis: The Base Communities Re-invent the Church* (Maryknoll, N.Y.: Orbis Books, 1986); Thomas G. Bruneau, *The Church in Brazil: The Politics of Religion* (Austin: University of Texas Press, 1982); and Harvey G. Cox, *Religion in the Secular City: Towards a Postmodern Theology* (New York: Simon & Schuster, 1984).

23. See Gremillion, *Peace and Justice,* pp. 445-76, for the texts of some of the Medellin documents.

24. "Poverty of the Church," par. 4, in Gremillion, *Peace and Justice,* pp. 472-73.

25. See Thomas Bruneau, "The Catholic Church and Development in Latin America: The Role of the Basic Christian Communities," *World Development* 8 (1980): 535-44.

26. Perhaps the best place to go to get a sense of the humble scale of these momentous happenings is to a recent article in the *New Yorker.* See

Jane Kramer, "Letter from the Elysian Fields," *The New Yorker* (March 2, 1987), pp. 40-75.

27. Leonardo Boff, *Ecclesiogenesis: The Base Communities Reinvent the Church* (Maryknoll, N.Y.: Orbis Books, 1986), p. 2.

28. Ibid., pp. 8-9.

29. Ibid., pp. 5-6.

30. *The Emergent Church: The Future of Christianity in a Post-Bourgeois World* (London: SCM Press, 1981).

31. Ibid. See esp. "Toward the Second Reformation," pp. 48-66.

32. Ibid., p. 83.

33. See Sharon D. Welch, *Communities of Resistance and Solidarity: A Feminist Theology of Liberation* (Maryknoll, N.Y.: Orbis Books, 1985).

34. See for example the dyspeptic anti-feminism of Allan Bloom, in *The Closing of the American Mind* (New York: Simon & Schuster, 1987).

35. This capacity of the gospel not to be victimized by the prejudices of its own time is one example of what Metz calls "productive non-contemporaneity." See "Productive Non-contemporaneity" in *"Observations on the Spiritual Situation of the Age"* (Cambridge, Mass.: M.I.T. Press, 1984), pp. 169-77. Of course, it requires a certain capacity for discernment not to move from the sexism of the age into a less durable but equally deceptive fad. Though there is possibly a lunatic fringe to the feminist movement, if so, it is a much narrower fringe and considerably farther removed from the center of feminism than most feminism-watchers would like to believe. That feminism is not simply a fad is apparent in a number of factors: the clarity and acuteness of feminist historical scholarship; the humanizing influence of feminist social analysis; the justice of the attention that feminism has brought to the social situation of women and children in particular, and all the socially deprived in general; the wealth of insight that feminist scholars bring to the analysis of classic texts of patriarchy and large philosophical movements; and, perhaps above all, the development of alternatives to the patriarchal discourse of power.

36. *Women-Church: Theology and Practice of Feminist Liturgical Communities* (San Francisco: Harper & Row, 1985).

37. Ibid., p. 3.

38. *LS*, p. 393.

39. Ruether, *Women-Church*, p. 59.

40. Ibid., p. 75.

41. Ibid., p. 87.

42. Ibid., p. 32.

43. Ibid., p. 33.

44. See Nancy Fraser, "What's Critical About Critical Theory? The Case of Habermas and Gender," in *Feminism as Critique*, ed. Seyla Benhabib and Drucilla Cornell (Minneapolis: University of Minnesota Press, 1987), pp. 31-56. This particular volume is an excellent example

of the way in which feminist thought produces insights that would otherwise not have been available.

5. TRADITION, THEOLOGY, AND DISCOURSE

1. *Lumen Gentium* 20, quoted in Flannery, *Vatican Council II*, p. 371.
2. The most interesting recent work on this issue has been undertaken by John E. Thiel, in articles in *Theological Studies* and *The Heythrop Journal* discussed in preceding chapters. I am obviously deeply indebted in my remarks at this point to his pioneering work on the role of the theologian. He, however, does not raise the question of the peculiar status of the lay theologian.
3. *Lumen Gentium* 31, quoted in Flannery, *Vatican Council II*, p. 388.
4. Ibid., 32, p. 389.
5. Ibid., 33, p. 390.
6. Ibid., 36, p. 393.
7. Ibid., 37, p. 395.
8. *Apostolicam Actuositatem*, quoted in Flannery, *Vatican Council II*, pp. 766-98.
9. Ibid., 6, p. 773.
10. Ibid., 29, p. 793.
11. *Ecclesial Reflection: An Anatomy of Theological Method* (Philadelphia: Fortress Press, 1982).
12. Ibid., p. 35.
13. Ibid., p. 97.
14. Ibid., p. 105.
15. Ibid., p. 112.
16. Ibid., p. 113.
17. Ibid., pp. 112-13.
18. "Theological Responsibility: Beyond the Classical Paradigm," *Theological Studies* 47 (December 1986): 573-98.
19. Ibid., p. 575.
20. Ibid., pp. 578-79.
21. Ibid., p. 580.
22. Ibid., p. 595.
23. Ibid., p. 596.
24. "The Ecclesiastical Magisterium and Theology," by Otto Semelroth and Karl Lehmann, in *Readings in Moral Theology No. 3: The Magisterium and Morality*, ed. Charles E. Curran and Richard A. McCormick (New York: Paulist Press, 1982), pp. 151-70. The theses of which this document is composed were drafted by the authors at the request of, and were approved by, the members of the International Theological

Commission at a plenary session in the fall of 1975. The twelve theses are followed in the text by a brief commentary from the same authors.
25. Words of Pope Paul VI, "Address to the International Congress on the Theology of Vatican II," *Acta Apostolica Sedis* 58 (October 1, 1966): 890.
26. Semelroth and Lehmann, "Ecclesiastical Magisterium," p. 155.
27. Ibid., p. 156.
28. Ibid., p. 166.
29. *Reason and the Rationalization of Society (RR)*, pp. 286-328.
30. Ibid., p. 287.
31. Ibid., p. 293.
32. Ibid., p. 298.
33. Ibid., p. 307.
34. Ibid., p. 328.
35. "Wahrheitstheorien," in *Wirklichkeit und Reflexion: Walter Schulz zum 60. Geburtstag* (Pfüllingen: Neske, 1973), p. 219. I have utilized Thomas McCarthy's translation of this passage in *The Critical Theory of Jürgen Habermas*, p. 299.
36. See, for example, a decree of the Congregation for the Doctrine of the Faith, "Mysterium Ecclesiae," *Acta Apostolica Sedis* 65 (July 31, 1973): 396-408.
37. *Finite and Infinite Games: A Vision of Life as Play and Possibility* (New York: Free Press, 1986).
38. *Lumen Gentium* 25, quoted in Flannery, *Vatican Council II*, p. 379.
39. Ibid., p. 380.

6. THE ETHICAL DISCOURSE OF THE CHURCH

1. In Flannery, *Vatican Council II*, pp. 903-1001.
2. *Origins* 16 (November 27, 1986), pp. 409-55. A most useful selection of essays from a variety of viewpoints on the bishops' letter is *The Catholic Challenge to the American Economy: Reflections on the U.S. Bishops' Pastoral Letter on Catholic Social Teaching and the U.S. Economy*, ed. Thomas M. Gannon, S.J. (New York: Macmillan, 1987).
3. *Economic Justice*, para. 27, p. 415.
4. Para. 135, p. 426.
5. *Origins* 16 (November 13, 1986): 377-82.
6. *Death by Bread Alone* (Philadelphia: Fortress Press, 1978), p. 18.
7. In Gremillion, *Peace and Justice*, pp. 484-512.
8. *Economic Justice*, para. 70, p. 419.
9. In Gremillion, *Peace and Justice*, pp. 471-76.
10. Though Vatican documents utilize the slightly different phrase, "love of preference for the poor." See for example the quite fascinating exchange between Cardinal Ratzinger, Prefect of the Congregation for the Doctrine of the Faith, and Don Pedro Casaldaliga, progressive

Brazilian bishop, during the latter's investigation by the former, in Casaldaliga's "La Piedra, Asis y la espiga de mais: Cronica y carta de mi viaje a Roma," *Amenecer* 57 (July-September 1988): 24-27.
11. *LC,* pp. 102-17.
12. Ibid., p. 105.
13. Ibid., p. 107.
14. Ibid., p. 108.
15. Ibid., p. 110.
16. "A Reply to My Critics," in *Habermas: Critical Debates,* p. 251.
17. *Moralbewusstsein,* p. 105. The translation is Benhabib's.
18. For an interesting discussion of Habermas's ethical project in this context, see Charles Davis, "Reason, Tradition, Community: The Search for Ethical Foundations," in *Foundations of Ethics,* ed. Leroy S. Rouner (Notre Dame: University of Notre Dame Press, 1983), pp. 37-56.
19. *LS,* p. 182, fig. 27.

7. CATHOLICISM AND POSTMODERNITY

1. "Justice in the World," Synod of Bishops Second General Assembly, November 30, 1971, in Gremillion, *Peace and Justice,* p. 514.
2. *The Anti-Aesthetic: Essays on Postmodern Culture,* ed. Hal Foster (Port Townsend, Wash.: Bay Press, 1983), p. xii.
3. In one of the more helpful attempts to explicate postmodernism, Michael Messmer provides a highly useful set of distinctions. Some commentators, he explains, "emphasize postmodernism as an *aesthetic* phenomenon which emerges in relation to, perhaps especially in reaction against, modernism." A second group see postmodernism as resistance to a totalizing form of knowledge, and this category he designates *epistemic* postmodernism. Still another direction is taken in *socio-cultural* explications, which focus on the political character of art. However, as Messmer himself points out, there is no rigid separation between these categories. See Michael W. Messmer, "Making Sense Of/With Postmodernism," *Soundings* 68 (Fall 1985): 404-26.
4. See "Neoconservative Culture Criticism in the United States and West Germany: An Intellectual Movement in Two Political Cultures," in *Habermas and Modernity,* ed. Richard J. Bernstein (Cambridge, Mass.: M.I.T. Press, 1985), pp. 78-94, and "Modernity—An Incomplete Project," in Foster, ed., *The Anti-Aesthetic,* pp. 3-15.
5. In "Postmodernism and Consumer Society," in *The Anti-Aesthetic,* p. 125.
6. *The Post-Modern Aura: The Act of Fiction in an Age of Inflation* (Evanston, Ill.: Northwestern University Press, 1985).

7. *The Return to Cosmology: Postmodern Science and the Theology of Nature* (Berkeley: University of California Press, 1982), p. 254.

8. "Productive Noncontemporaneity," in *Observations on "The Spiritual Situation of the Age"* (Cambridge, Mass.: M.I.T. Press, 1984), pp. 169-77.

9. See *Religion in the Secular City: Toward a Postmodern Theology* (New York: Simon & Schuster, 1984).

10. *The Nature of Doctrine: Religion and Theology in a Postliberal Age* (Philadelphia: Westminster, 1984).

11. Esp. *The Catholic Moment: The Paradox of the Church in the Postmodern World* (San Francisco: Harper & Row, 1987).

12. *Erring: A Postmodern A/theology* (Chicago: University of Chicago Press, 1987).

13. *What Is Living, What Is Dead in Christianity Today? Breaking the Liberal-Conservative Deadlock* (San Francisco: Harper & Row, 1986).

14. *PDM*, p. 40.

15. Ibid., p. 42.

16. Ibid., p. 56.

17. Ibid., p. 59.

18. Ibid., pp. 96-97.

19. Ibid., p. 74.

20. Ibid., p. 323.

21. "Modernity—An Incomplete Project," in Foster, ed., *The Anti-Aesthetic;* originally published as "Modernity Versus Postmodernity" in *New German Critique* 22 (Winter 1981).

22. Foster, ed., *The Anti-Aesthetic*, pp. 6-7.

23. *The Cultural Contradictions of Capitalism* (New York: Harper & Row, 1977).

24. Foster, ed., *The Anti-Aesthetic*, p. 9.

25. Ibid., p. 8.

26. Ibid., p. 13.

27. See Franz-Theo Gottwald, "Religion oder Diskurs? Zur Kritik des Habermasschen Religionsverständnisses" *Zeitschrift für Religions und Geistesgeschichte* 37 (1985): 193-202; Hans-Joachim Höhn, *Kirche und kommunikatives Handlung* (Frankfurt: Josef Knecht, 1985); Ingo Mörth, "La sociologie de la religion comme Théorie Critique," *Social Compass* 27 (1980): 27-50; Helmut Peukert, *Science, Action, and Fundamental Theology: Towards a Theology of Communicative Action* (Cambridge, Mass.: M.I.T. Press, 1984); and Thomas G. Walsh, "Religion and Communicative Action," *Thought* 62 (March 1987): 111-25.

28. See *RR*, pp. 43-74.

29. *LC*, p. 121.

30. Helmut Peukert, *Science, Action, and Fundamental Theology: Towards a Theology of Communicative Action* (Cambridge, Mass.: M.I.T. Press, 1984).

31. Ibid., p. 2.

32. Ibid., p. 11.

33. Ibid., p. 12.
34. Ibid., p. 13.
35. Ibid., p. 14.
36. Ibid., p. 202.
37. As for example in the "Instruction on Certain Aspects of the Theology of Liberation," sect. IX, par. 3, *The National Catholic Reporter* (September 21, 1984): 13.
38. Peukert, *Science, Action, and Fundamental Theology*, p. 207.
39. See Lenhardt, "Anamnestic Solidarity: The Proletariat and Its *Manes*," *Telos* 25 (1975): 133-55.
40. Peukert, *Science, Action, and Fundamental Theology*, p. 209.
41. Ibid., p. 211.
42. Ibid., p. 235.
43. Ibid., p. 241.
44. In *Liberation South: Liberation North*, ed. Michael Novak (Washington, D.C.: American Enterprise Institute, 1981), pp. 7-23.
45. For an excellent recent work on ministry see *Ministry: Leadership in the Community of Jesus Christ*, by Edward Schillebeeckx (New York: Crossroad, 1986). See also Leonardo Boff's *Ecclesiogenesis: The Base Communities Re-invent the Church* (Maryknoll, N.Y.: Orbis Books, 1986), particularly ch. 6, *"Quaestio Disputata* 11: The Lay Coordinator and the Celebration of the Lord's Supper," pp. 61-75.
46. See Penny Lenoux, "The Pope and Medellin: Casting Out the People's Church," *Nation* 247 (27 August-3 September, 1988): 161-69.
47. *The Emergent Church*, p. 89.
48. *Death by Bread Alone*, p. 14.
49. Metz, *The Emergent Church*, p. 90.
50. Ibid., p. 91.
51. Ibid., p. 90.
52. Cambridge: Cambridge University Press, 1980.
53. *What Is Living, What Is Dead in Christianity Today? Breaking the Liberal-Conservative Deadlock* (San Francisco: Harper & Row, 1986).
54. Ibid., p. 2.
55. "Symposium on Religion and Politics," *Telos* 16 (Winter 1983–84): 115-57.
56. Ibid., p. 129.
57. Ibid., p. 130.
58. "On Social Identity," *Telos* 19 (Spring 1974), p. 99, quoted in Davis, *Theology and Political Society*, p. 165.
59. Davis, *Theology and Political Society*, p. 171.
60. Ibid., p. 173.
61. Ibid., p. 178.
62. Ibid., p. 174.

BIBLIOGRAPHY

Alberigo, G., and J. Provost, eds. *Synod 1985—An Evaluation*. Edinburgh: T. & T. Clark, 1986.

Alexander, Jeffrey C. "Review Essay: Habermas's New Critical Theory: Its Promise and Problems." *American Journal of Sociology* 91 (September 1985): 400-424.

Austin, J. L. *How to Do Things with Words*. Cambridge: Cambridge University Press, 1962.

Avineri, Shlomo. *Hegel's Theory of the Modern State*. Cambridge: Cambridge University Press, 1972.

————. *The Social and Political Thought of Karl Marx*. Cambridge: Cambridge University Press, 1968.

Barreiro, Alvaro. *Basic Ecclesial Communities: The Evangelization of the Poor*. Maryknoll, N.Y.: Orbis Books, 1982.

Baum, Gregory. *The Priority of Labor*. Ramsey, N.J.: Paulist Press, 1981.

Bell, Daniel. *The Cultural Contradictions of Capitalism*. New York: Harper & Row, 1977.

Bellah, Robert, et al. *Habits of the Heart: Individualism and Commitment in American Life*. Berkeley: University of California Press, 1985.

Benhabib, Seyla. *Critique, Norm and Utopia: A Study of the Foundations of Critical Theory*. New York: Columbia University Press, 1986.

Berman, Marshall. *All That Is Solid Melts into Air: The Experience of Modernity*. New York: Simon & Schuster, 1982.

Bernstein, Richard J. *Beyond Objectivism and Relativism: Science, Hermeneutics, and Praxis*. Philadelphia: University of Pennsylvania Press, 1983.

Bernstein, Richard J., ed. *Habermas and Modernity*. Cambridge, Mass.: M.I.T. Press, 1985.

Bloom, Allan. *The Closing of the American Mind*. New York: Simon & Schuster, 1987.

Boff, Leonardo. *Church, Charism and Power: Liberation Theology and the Institutional Church*. New York: Crossroad Publishing Co., 1985.

261

Bibliography

————. *Ecclesiogenesis: The Base Communities Re-Invent the Church*. Maryknoll, N.Y.: Orbis Books, 1986.

Braudel, Fernand. *Civilization and Capitalism, 15th–18th Century, Vol. Two: The Wheels of Commerce*. New York: Harper & Row, 1982.

Bruneau, Thomas G. "The Catholic Church and Development in Latin America: The Role of the Basic Christian Communities." *World Development* 8 (1980): 535-44.

————. *The Church in Brazil: The Politics of Religion*. Austin: University of Texas Press, 1982.

Buck-Morse, Susan. *The Origin of Negative Dialectics*. New York: Free Press, 1977.

Carse, James P. *Finite and Infinite Games: A Vision of Life as Play and Possibility*. New York: Free Press, 1986.

Connerton, Paul. *The Tragedy of Enlightenment: An Essay on the Frankfurt School*. Cambridge: Cambridge University Press, 1980.

Cox, Harvey G. *Religion in the Secular City: Towards a Postmodern Theology*. New York: Simon & Schuster, 1984.

Curran, Charles. *Directions in Catholic Social Ethics*. Notre Dame, Ind.: University of Notre Dame Press, 1985.

Curran, Charles, and Richard A. McCormick, eds. *Readings in Catholic Moral Theology No. 5: Official Catholic Social Teaching*. New York: Paulist Press, 1986.

Dallmayr, Fred R. *Polis and Praxis: Exercises in Contemporary Political Theory*. Cambridge: M.I.T. Press, 1984.

Davis, Charles. "Reason, Tradition, Community: The Search for Ethical Foundations." In *Foundations of Ethics*, pp. 37-56. Ed. Leroy S. Rouner. Notre Dame, Ind.: University of Notre Dame Press, 1983.

————. *Theology and Political Society*. Cambridge: Cambridge University Press, 1980.

————. *What Is Living, What Is Dead in Christianity Today? Breaking the Liberal-Conservative Deadlock*. San Francisco: Harper & Row, 1987.

Dickey, Laurence. *Hegel: Religion, Economics, and the Politics of Spirit, 1770–1807*. Cambridge: Cambridge University Press, 1987.

Dulles, Avery. *Models of the Church*. Garden City, N.Y.: Doubleday, 1974.

Dupre, Louis. *Marx's Social Critique of Culture*. New Haven, Conn.: Yale University Press, 1983.

Farley, Edward. *Ecclesial Reflection: An Anatomy of Theological Method*. Philadelphia: Fortress Press, 1982.

Fiorenza, Elizabeth Schussler. *In Memory of Her: A Feminist Reconstruction of Christian Origins*. New York: Crossroad Publishing Co., 1983.

Foster, Hal, ed. *The Anti-Aesthetic: Essays on Postmodern Culture*. Port Townsend, Wash.: Bay Press, 1983.

Geuss, Raymond. *The Idea of a Critical Theory: Habermas and the Frankfurt School*. New York: Cambridge University Press, 1981.

Glebe-Moller, Jens. *A Political Dogmatic*. Philadelphia: Fortress Press, 1987.

Gottlieb, Roger S. "The Contemporary Critical Theory of Jürgen Habermas." *Ethics* 91 (January 1981): 280-95.

Gottwald, Franz-Theo. "Religion oder Diskurs? Zur Kritik des Habermasschen Religionsverständnisses." *Zeitschrift für Religions und Geistesgeschichte* 37 (1985): 193-202.

Bibliography

Gremillion, Joseph, ed. *The Gospel of Peace and Justice: Catholic Social Teaching Since Pope John.* Maryknoll, N.Y.: Orbis Books, 1976.

Habermas, Jürgen. *Communication and the Evolution of Society.* Boston: Beacon Press, 1979.

———. *Legitimation Crisis.* Boston: Beacon Press, 1975.

———. *Knowledge and Human Interests.* Boston: Beacon Press, 1971.

———. *Moralbewusstsein und kommunikatives Handeln.* Frankfurt: Suhrkamp, 1979.

———. *The Philosophical Discourse of Modernity: Twelve Lectures.* Studies in Contemporary German Social Thought. Cambridge: M.I.T. Press, 1987.

———. *Philosophical-Political Profiles.* Studies in Contemporary German Social Thought. Cambridge: M.I.T. Press, 1983.

———. *Strukturwandel der Offentlichkeit.* Frankfurt: Suhrkamp, 1974.

———. *The Theory of Communicative Action. Volume One: Reason and the Rationalization of Society. Volume Two: Lifeworld and System.* Boston: Beacon Press, 1984, 1988.

———. *Zur Rekonstruktion des historischen Materialismus.* Frankfurt: Suhrkamp, 1976.

Habermas, Jürgen, ed. *Observations on "The Spiritual Situation of the Age": Contemporary German Perspectives.* Studies in Contemporary German Social Thought. Cambridge: M.I.T. Press, 1985.

Hassan, Ihab. *The Dismemberment of Orpheus: Towards a Postmodern Literature.* New York: Oxford University Press, 1971.

———. *Paracriticisms: Seven Speculations of the Times.* Urbana, Ill.: University of Illinois, 1975.

Hawthorn, Geoffrey. *Enlightenment and Despair: A History of Social Theory.* 2nd ed. Cambridge: Cambridge University Press, 1987.

Hebblethwaite, Peter. *Synod Extraordinary: The Inside Story of the Rome Synod, November-December 1985.* Garden City, N.Y.: Doubleday, 1986.

———. "The Popes and Politics: Shifting Patterns in 'Catholic Social Doctrine.' " *Daedalus* 111 (Winter 1982): 85-98.

Himes, Michael J., and Kenneth R. Himes. "The Myth of Self-Interest." *Commonweal* 125 (September 23, 1988): 493-98.

Höhn, Hans-Joachim. *Kirche und kommunikatives Handeln.* Frankfurt: Joseph Knecht, 1985.

Holland, Joe, and Peter Henriot. *Social Analysis: Linking Faith with Justice.* Marynoll, N.Y.: Orbis Books, 1983.

Horkheimer, Max. *Critical Theory: Selected Essays.* New York: Herder & Herder, 1972.

———. *Critique of Instrumental Reason.* New York: Seabury Press, 1974.

———. *Eclipse of Reason.* New York: Seabury Press, 1974.

Horkheimer, Max, and Theodor Adorno. *Dialectic of Enlightenment.* New York: Herder & Herder, 1972.

Jay, Martin. *The Dialectical Imagination: A History of the Frankfurt School and the Institute of Social Research, 1923-1950.* Boston: Little, Brown & Co., 1973.

Kelly, George Armstrong. *Hegel's Retreat from Eleusis: Studies in Political Thought.* Princeton: Princeton University Press, 1978.

Kilcourse, George, ed. *The Linguistic Turn and Contemporary Theology.* Current Issues in Theology 2. Atlanta, Ga.: Mercer University Press for the Catholic Theological Society of America, 1987.

Bibliography

Kohlberg, Lawrence. *Collected Papers on Moral Development and Moral Education.* Cambridge, Mass.: Moral Education and Research Foundation, 1973.

Komonchak, Joseph. "The Synod of 1985 and the Notion of the Church." *Chicago Studies* 26 (November 1987): 330-45.

Kramer, Jane. "Letter from the Elysian Fields." *New Yorker* (March 2, 1987): 40-75.

Kuhn, Thomas. *The Structure of Scientific Revolutions.* Chicago: University of Chicago Press, 1970.

Lakeland, Paul. "Development and Catholic Social Teaching: Pope John Paul's New Encyclical." *The Month* 21 (June 1988): 706-10.

———. "Distinguishing the Scribes: The Composition of Vatican Documents." *The Month* 7 (June 1974): 595-99.

Lamb, Matthew L. *Solidarity with Victims: Toward a Theology of Social Transformation.* New York: Crossroad Publishing Co., 1982.

Lane, Dermot A. *Foundations for a Social Theology: Praxis, Process, and Salvation.* New York: Paulist Press, 1984.

Lenhardt, Christian. "Anamnestic Solidarity: The Proletariat and Its *Manes.*" *Telos* 25 (1975): 133-55.

Lernoux, Penny. "The Pope and Medellin: Casting Out the People's Church." *The Nation* 247 (27 August-3 September, 1988): 161-69.

Lindbeck, George. *The Future of Roman Catholic Theology: Vatican II, Catalyst for Change.* Philadelphia: Fortress Press, 1970.

———. *The Nature of Doctrine: Religion and Theology in a Postliberal Age.* Philadelphia: Westminster Press, 1984.

McCann, Dennis P., *New Experiment in Democracy: The Challenge for American Catholicism.* Kansas City, Mo.: Sheed & Ward, 1987.

McCann, Dennis P., and Charles R. Strain. *Polity and Praxis: A Program for American Practical Theology.* Minneapolis: Winston Press, 1985.

McCarthy, Thomas. *The Critical Theory of Jürgen Habermas.* Cambridge: M.I.T. Press, 1978.

Marcuse, Herbert. *Negations: Essays in Critical Theory.* Boston: Beacon Press, 1968.

Martin, David. *A General Theory of Secularization.* New York: Harper & Row, 1978.

Messmer, Michael W. "Making Sense of/with Postmodernism." *Soundings* 68 (fall 1985): 404-26.

Metz, Johann Baptist. *The Emergent Church: The Future of Christianity in a Post-Bourgeois World.* London: SCM Press, 1981.

———. *Faith in History and Society: Toward a Practical Fundamental Theology.* New York: Seabury Press, 1980.

———. *Theology of the World.* New York: Seabury Press, 1973.

Molnar, Thomas. *Politics and the State: The Catholic View.* Chicago: Franciscan Herald Press, 1980.

Mörth, Ingo. "La sociologie de la religion comme Theorie Critique." *Social Compass* 27 (1980): 27-50.

Novak, Michael. *Freedom with Justice.* New York: Harper & Row, 1984.

Novak, Michael, ed. *Liberation South: Liberation North.* Washington, D.C.: American Enterprise Institute, 1981.

O'Neil, John, ed. *On Critical Theory.* New York: Seabury Press, 1976.

Pelczynski, Z. A., ed. *The State and Civil Society: Studies in Hegel's Political Philosophy.* Cambridge: Cambridge University Press, 1984.

Bibliography

Pettit, Philip. "Habermas on Truth and Justice." In *Marx and Marxisms*, pp. 207-28. Royal Institute of Philosophy Lecture Series: 14. Ed. G. H. R. Parkinson. Cambridge: Cambridge University Press, 1982.
Peukert, Helmut. *Science, Action, and Fundamental Theology: Toward a Theology of Communicative Action. Studies in Contemporary German Social Thought.* Cambridge: M.I.T. Press, 1984.
Roderick, Rick. *Habermas and the Foundations of Critical Theory.* London: Macmillan, 1986.
Ruether, Rosemary Radford. *Women-Church: Theology and Practice of Feminist Liturgical Communities.* San Francisco: Harper & Row, 1985.

Schillebeeckx, Edward. *Ministry: Leadership in the Community of Jesus Christ.* New York: Crossroad Publishing Co., 1986.
Schreiter, Robert J. *Constructing Local Theologies.* Maryknoll, N.Y.: Orbis Books, 1985.
Searle, J. *Expression and Meaning.* Cambridge: Cambridge University Press, 1976.
———. *Speech Acts: An Essay in the Philosophy of Language.* London: Cambridge University Press, 1969.
Segundo, Juan Luis. *The Community Called Church.* Maryknoll, N.Y.: Orbis Books, 1973.
Siebert, Rudolf. "Communication Without Domination." In *Communication in the Church*, pp. 81-94. Ed. Gregory Baum and Andrew Greeley. New York: Seabury Press, 1978.
Skinner, Quentin, ed. *The Return of Grand Theory in the Human Sciences.* Cambridge: Cambridge University Press, 1985.
Smith, Steven B. "Hegel's Idea of a Critical Theory." *Political Theory* 15 (February 1987): 99-126.
Soelle, Dorothee. *Death by Bread Alone.* Philadelphia: Fortress Press, 1978.
Stern, Laurent. "Hermeneutics and Intellectual History." *Journal of the History of Ideas* 46 (April 1985): 287-96.

Taylor, Charles. *Hegel and Modern Society.* Cambridge: Cambridge University Press, 1979.
Taylor, Mark C. *Erring: A Postmodern A/Theology.* Chicago: University of Chicago Press, 1987.
Theissen, Gerd. *A Critical Faith: A Case for Religion.* Philadelphia: Fortress Press, 1979.
Thiel, John E. "J. S. Drey on Doctrinal Development: The Context of Theological Encyclopedia." *Heythrop Journal* 27 (1986): 290-305.
———. "Orthodoxy and Heterodoxy in Schleiermacher's Theological Encyclopedia: Doctrinal Development and Theological Creativity." *Heythrop Journal* 25 (1984): 142-57.
———. "Theological Responsibility: Beyond the Classical Paradigm." *Theological Studies* 47 (December 1986): 573-98.
Thompson, John B., and David Held, eds. *Habermas: Critical Debates.* Cambridge: M.I.T. Press, 1982.
Toews, J. M. *Hegelianism: The Path Toward Dialectical Humanism, 1805–1841.* Cambridge: Cambridge University Press, 1980.
Toulmin, Stephen D. *The Return to Cosmology: Postmodern Science and the Theology of Nature.* Berkeley: University of California Press, 1982.

Tracy, David. *Plurality and Ambiguity: Hermeneutics, Religion, Hope*. San Francisco: Harper & Row, 1987.

Walsh, Michael, and Brian Davies, eds. *Proclaiming Justice and Peace*. Mystic, Conn.: Twenty-Third Publications, 1985.

Walsh, Thomas G. "Religion and Communicative Action." *Thought* 62 (March 1987): 111-25.

Welch, Sharon D. *Communities of Resistance and Solidarity: A Feminist Theology of Liberation*. Maryknoll, N.Y.: Orbis Books, 1985.

Wolff, Philippe. *The Cultural Awakening*. New York: Pantheon Books, 1968.

INDEX

267